Moving to Majorca

Moving to Majorca

Provence on Wheels With Unforgettable Characters

Robert F. Burgess

Writers Club Press
San Jose New York Lincoln Shanghai

Moving to Majorca
Provence on Wheels With Unforgettable Characters

Published by Writers Club Press
an imprint of iUniverse.com, Inc.

For information address:
iUniverse.com, Inc.
620 North 48th Street
Suite 201
Lincoln, NE 68504-3467
www.iuniverse.com

Cover design by Robert F. Burgess

ISBN:0-595-09058-3

Printed in the United States of America

With Love To Julie Who Made This
Such a Memorable Adventure

Contents

1

Taking Off

It was October. The ice and snow of winter came early to Switzerland that year but we beat it by a day. We were aboard one of Switzerland's fast electric trains speeding south toward warmer Italy as winter came in from the north the night before. "Just seeing it gives me the shivers," said Julie, looking out the coach's steamed windows as the countryside swept by. Outside it looked as though Mother Nature had laid a ruler across the countryside and chalked a white line. Everything above it was coated with ice and snow; everything below it was free of the icy touch and glowed with the golden hues of fall. Where lush green forests marched down the mountainside the day before, the trees were now bent and bowed beneath a mantle of snow.

But below that icy line everything was brightly clean and sharply etched. Jagged amber fields of weeds, stalks and grasses still glistening with early morning frost swept pass. Colors blurred. Rustic brown or white chalets broke the scene, their shutters painted in gay reds, greens and yellows, windows open wide to the crisp October air, white goose-down comforters flung over balcony rails, stabbing flashes of red geranium-filled window boxes. Then more golden fall pastures, these fast-moving linear kaleidoscopic views always topped by that white frosting of a layered cake. We were spared that frosty topping only because this valley of the Jura was warmed by the Lake of Neuchâtel that lay large and gray as a slate plateau out the opposite windows of the train. Even in deepest winter the lake would not freeze but its wind-blown waves would appear to be snowdrifts scudding across its wrinkled dark surface. Long before that, thankfully, we would be well into sunny Italy.

Having recently come from Florida where we live, sun and warmth we understood. Julie and I were newlyweds. I hoped to show her a little of Europe from a perspective seldom chosen by American tourists. We wanted to ride a motor scooter across Italy and France to Spain. If we were careful we could travel economically independent for three months. What we didn't foresee then was that this relatively short trip would prove so enjoyable that it would stretch into a three-and-a-half-year long sojourn abroad.

Julie had never been to Europe before. I knew it would be a great way to see it. I had been abroad long ago, thanks to the generosity of the U.S. Army. Years later I went back to see what had changed and to study foreign languages at universities abroad. To beat the traffic congestion I got where I wanted to go quickly on an Italian Lambretta motor scooter. Everyone from bank presidents to students used them for fast, inner-city transportation. They still do.

Anyway, long before we married I told Julie that riding one of those zippy new Italian models from northern Italy down to the blue Mediterranean and across 700 miles of balmy riviera beaches to Sunny Spain would be an unforgettable adventure. We would see that magnificent country up close and personal, savoring new customs and food, meeting people one-on-one, and best of all having the time of our lives doing it. She liked the idea. Shortly after we married the adventure began late in September.

Wanting to savor every phase of the trip we caught a slow boat from New York to Le Harvre, France. No rush then but there were places we wanted to go before winter moved into northern Europe. Arriving in Paris at night aboard the Paris/Le Havre boat train we opted not to go to a hotel. We were too excited to sleep. Instead we spent the rest of the night walking and sightseeing the "City of Lights" until time to catch our early morning train for Switzerland.

Tired but still exhilarated, we napped on the super-fast rail connection to our next destination. A swift train change in Genova and we went directly to the small lakeside town of Neuchâtel, Switzerland, arriving as planned for the start of its October *Féte de Vendange*. This weeklong festival celebrates the gathering of the area's grapes and the beginning of the first stages of making the famous Neuchâtel white wine for which this alpine area is renown. Neuchâtel is the Swiss town where I had last attended university. Marvelous food, parades, fountains that spew "green wine" (grape juice), confetti deep streets, and much imbibing and sharing of spirits marks this annual event. Certainly nothing about all that had changed. The *Féte* would be a perfect send-off for our riviera adventure. Old Swiss friends made us so welcome that it was hard to leave.

With winter coming on sooner than expected in this alpine region we needed little urging. Speeding southward through the Alps, we were glad to leave the snow and ice behind. The following day found us in the lowlands of northern Italy, enjoying views of Lake Garda and the beautiful lake region on our way to Milano, our next stop. It was there that we would go to the Lambretta company and purchase a scooter. I had written in advance. They were expecting us.

When we reached Milano the weather was not as sunny and warm as we had hoped. Apparently, someone in northern Italy had left the back-door open. The city was cold, gray, and gloomy. Nothing was freezing yet, but winter was definitely still blowing its misty breath down our backs. It made us more anxious than ever to finish our business there so we could get further south to where the weather was warm. Just the word "rivieras" made us recall movie scenes of that magnificent Mediterranean coast with its palm trees, cliff-hanging white villas, boat-packed harbors, sunny beaches and sunbathing tourists.

We found a small, inexpensive hotel over a good restaurant on the south side of town. Largely working class Italians patronized the restaurant. It was always crowded, and understandably so. The food was excellent, and inexpensive. Baskets of fresh baked bread were served steaming from the domed red brick ovens in back. Along with them came sumptuous antipastos of fresh greens, sliced sweet red-skinned onions, hot and cold beans garnished with anchovies and parsley, sprinkled with garlic flavored olive oil, and wine vinegar. Heaping bowls of steaming *Spaghetti ala Milanese* with its pool of dark, rich tomato and meat sauce often followed these. After that if you had room, you were served the main courses of the meal.

We barely made it through the preliminary *antipastas*, enjoying them with a pitcher of deep red tongue-tingling Chianti so strong it always left a taste of iron in our mouth. Or as the Italians were proud to tell us, one needed the flavor of Chianti to clean the palette and sharpen the taste buds so that one could get on with the joy of more tasty treats from the kitchen.

After a walk we might drop into another working class restaurant or Trattoria for a coffee. You knew the place had character if there were no tablecloths on the tables and your waitress always figured your bill on the corner of the table with a piece of chalk. From this you might guess that these were not the caliber of restaurants catering to tourists' tastes. In fact, we never saw tourists in those restaurants. Too bad because they missed a treat.

One place we especially liked we dubbed "The Pirate's Den." By day the tables were crowded with working class Italians. Mostly men in rumpled drab brown or black jackets and trousers often wearing short-brimmed caps pulled low on their brows. Usually a smoldering cigarette butt stuck to a corner of their lips so substantially that they could talk, drink, eat or play dominos without dislodging it.

The Pirate's Den always had atmosphere, most of it layered in clouds of blue cigarette smoke writhing overhead. If the men were not eating, they usually drank small, steaming black cups of Espresso coffee, then played cards or dominoes. Others sometimes played a game called "*Uno, Due, Tre*, or "One, Two, Three."

The game seemed to be a national pastime. At first we wondered why men often stood in tight knots on street corners shouting over and over "*Uno, Due, Tre!*" Then one opponent slapped the other's wrist and everyone laughed.

Only when we were able to look down on a gaming group from our hotel window did we realize what was going on. For those who have never seen it, it's a game called "Paper, Scissors and Rock." Best part is that two or more can play it anywhere using nothing more than their hands. Here's the Italian version:

Small groups of men stand facing each other, holding their hands in front of them, one hand a fist, the other palm up. Then they loudly shout in unison three times: "*Uno, Due, Tre!*"

Each time they say a number, they strike the palm of one hand with the fist of the other. On the third strike, at the utterance of the shouted word "*Tre*", their fisted hand opens and does one of four things. It either lays one finger, two fingers, a flat hand, or a fist on their opened palm.

Seeing what everyone has done immediately brings a burst of laughter. Then one man reaches out and with his first two fingers proceeds to slap them down smartly on the wrists of all the other wincing men in the group.

The idea is that on the third time you strike your palm you either smack it with your fist again, or open your clenched fist and show either one, two or three fingers or more. One finger symbolizes a "stick," two are scissors, three or more are "paper" and a fist is a "rock." To win, your gesture has to be superior to the others, for example: fist (rock) breaks stick (one finger), and scissors (two fingers), but paper (flat hand), covers rock, and thereby wins, unless someone has thrown "scissors" (two fingers), which of course cuts paper. "Stick" on the other hand can break "scissors" or "paper" but of course can be broken by "rock." May sound complicated but you learn quickly. The winner gets to smack all losers on their wrists.

We found the Lambretta factory on the opposite side of Milano from our hotel or from practically everything else in that metropolitan city. Since I had alerted them earlier to our plans, they appeared ready for us when we arrived at their front office with our correspondence in hand.

After a flurry of secretarial activity, we were greeted warmly by *Signori* Fazio, a large, friendly man in a three-piece dark blue suit wearing a bright red artificial carnation in his lapel.

"*Buon giorno, buon giorno!*" Good-day, good-day, he effused, arms outstretched, round cheeks glowing like winesaps on a winter's bough. "Welcome to Milano. What can it be our pleasure to do for you today?"

I again explained in English that I had written the company a letter and showed him our correspondence. I started to explain what we intended to do with their scooter but halfway through my speech I realized that *Signori* Fazio's cheerful welcome had exhausted most of his knowledge of English. So I backed up and began again, much slower this time, using my limited knowledge of Italian to explain the situation. If I missed a word here or there I tossed in the word in English or French. Since *Signori* Fazio smiled constantly and nodded frequently, I had no real indication of how much of this he understood.

But he was still smiling when I finished.

"*Bene, bene,*" good, good, he said "We have for you a very nice *motoretta. No problema, Signori Boorgus.* But first there is the…ah…how you say *cartas, documenti*…? "

"Oh, yes. The papers, the documents…." I paused. "Which *documenti* are we talking about? Our passports?

"No, no, no. *Passaporti non,* no." He wagged his pudgy forefinger. The *documenti PERMESSO!*

"Ahhhh, the permission documents…the *permits?*"

"*Si, si, si, esattomenti,*" yes, exactly, beamed our company contact. Then, seeing the surprise on my face he fanned his hands, pooched his lips reassuringly and murmured, *"No, no, no fa niente."* Nothing at all, meaning I guessed that they were nothing to trouble ourselves about, a mere trifle.

"Good," I smiled. "Just a few permits," I assured my wife. "Nothing to it."

What *Signori* Fazio failed to tell us was that the permits he mentioned so casually had to be acquired at numerous different government agencies scattered around Milano. Along with the permits for the scooter were those enabling us to travel internationally with it. Since the Lambretta factory was at one end of the city and all the other agencies were more or less downtown, we went back and forth from one to the other for the next few days. We had to get everything properly signed, stamped with an official seal, then paid for according to whatever different fees were required. At one point I was asked whether or not I was a licensed exporter, and if not, perhaps I required an exporter's license. To complicate matters, the clerk spoke no English whatsoever.

When I appeared at the tiny portico under his agency's sign, he opened the narrow window and peered out his grill at me with cold, beady eyes. In tight black vest and high-pocketed pants, a green plastic eye-shade pulled low over a furrowed brow he looked like a lean, mean riverboat gambler. After explaining my mission to him in pigeon Italian, he asked, "Where do you intend sending the scooter?"

"Not sending. Driving." I pantomimed the activity.

"To which country?"

I shrugged. "Who knows? France for sure, then Spain…Probably others….I didn't want to get limited to one country. I wanted us free to go anywhere with it, if possible.

"And then you bring the scooter back to Italy?"

Again I shrugged. "Maybe *si*, maybe no." I smiled. Where we might end up could be a long way from Italy. I certainly didn't want to have to come all the way back to Milano on the scooter if I could avoid it.

The official squinted at me suspiciously from under his green visor.

"You need an exporter's license to do that," he finally said in Italian.

"No, no, no. You don't understand," I said. "I don't wish to go into the export business. I am a tourist. I just want to drive the motor scooter out of the country."

"Which makes you an exporter," insisted the clerk, getting a bit miffed at my ignorance.

"Is there no other way?" I asked.

"Only if you bring the *motoretta* back to Italy when you are through with it.

I stared at him. "But it is *my motoretta*. I pay much Lira for it. For all I know, I may end up in Timbuktu." The green eye-shaded clerk glared at me

"Then the *motoretta* is for *ESP-POR-TA-ZI-ONE* He shouted triumphantly. "And for that you need a license!" His fist smacked his counter emphatically.

"All right," I said meekly. "How much is that?"

When he told me I asked him to repeat it. I was sure I heard wrong. In fact the more we talked the more wrong it all became. Finally, I just nodded weakly, thanked him, and stepped back as he slammed down his little cubical window. Settling back down on the stool behind his desk the clerk still glared at me from under his green shade. When I saw his lips moving I knew he was still talking to me. I was glad I couldn't hear.

Back to the Lambretta Company we went.

Signori Fazio listened to our laments with a pained expression on his face. A moment later he had his secretary phone someone with whom he spoke animatedly, gesturing expansively before the telephone as if he were in full view of the person on the other end of the line.

When finished, he was all smiles again. He assured us that now everything was taken care of. We would only have to visit one more agency for our international driver's license, and then we could be on our way. There had been a misunderstanding. It was all cleared up now and that very afternoon we could take delivery of our *motoretta* with no further delay.

True to his word, our bright, shiny red and gray Lambretta motor scooter was wheeled into the showroom for our approval.

The machine looked great but it had only one seat. That certainly wasn't large enough for two.

When I called this to *Signori* Fazio's attention, his eyebrows arched, he held up a commanding hand, then disappeared momentarily into his office. Shortly he reappeared brandishing what looked like a bicycle seat.

"For *La Signora*," he waved the shiny black pillion seat. "Our gift to you for your *pazienza*."

Ah yes, our patience. We smiled and thanked him for the gift. I asked if he could perhaps have a mechanic attach it for us and make sure the scooter was fully prepared for a long distance trip. I also thought it might be a good idea to have them put on a plastic windshield accessory to keep the bugs out of my face.

Moments later the final trappings were on, including a luggage rack over the spare wheel. I tentatively pushed on the gift pillion seat where Julie would ride to make sure it was secure. Nothing wobbled or rattled. At *Signori* Fazio's orders our license plate had also been installed which suggested that we were now fully permitted to scooter out of the country.

One small matter remained. I had not driven a motor scooter for years. Would I still remember how to do it, at least well enough to drive out into the streets where we would instantly be at the mercy of Milano's kamikaze drivers?

"Maybe I'd better try it, first," I suggested.

"*Si, si!*" *Signori* Fazio gestured toward the courtyard.

We pushed the machine outdoors. Two of the mechanics held the scooter while I climbed aboard, forgetting to kick the starter pedal with my foot before getting on. One of the mechanics obligingly kicked it for me. The scooter's engine roared to life with its characteristic fast-popping noise like a car's muffler burbling underwater. We all smiled at one another.

One of the grinning mechanics held out his hand, closed his fingers and twisted it at the wrist indicating I was to squeeze the clutch lever to shift into first gear. Then, with the other hand he signaled how I was to give it gas. The left handle-grip lever was the clutch, the right one the front wheel brake. Twisting the right handle-grip gave it gas. The heel of my right foot could tread a pedal that put on a rear wheel brake. It was all very basic. You just had to remember which was which, and when to use it.

I shifted into first, tentatively released the clutch lever and lurched across the small courtyard, turning just in time to avoid hitting the opposite wall. I got the feeling that this new scooter had all the controls mounted in reverse from my old scooter. Nothing seemed too familiar except the hand and foot brakes. Applied together they tried to throw me over the handlebars.

My wife stood to one side of our test-driving area with a dubious look on her face. I got the impression that not only was she beginning to doubt my skill in driving the scooter across Europe, but there was some question in her mind as to whether I could even drive it properly out of the show-room courtyard. Especially with her clinging tightly to the newly mounted gift pillion seat.

Signori Fazio must have gotten the same impression because he quickly offered to have the motor scooter delivered by truck to our hotel on the other side of town for our convenience.

I thanked him in profound relief. I had no great urge to tangle with Milano's madcap traffic any sooner than absolutely necessary.

As we left the factory's show-room, *Signori* Fazio, three of his secretaries and four mechanics followed us outdoors to shake our hands, bid us goodbye, and to wish us good luck on our trip. It was a touching send-off.

2

South to Genova

The next morning I wheeled our new scooter out of the hotel hallway, set it up on its stand, and loaded it for our trip. We would head south to Genova, then follow the Mediterranean coast southwestward across the Italian and French Rivieras to Spain. "Sunny Spain." It had to be warm there. After all, it was just across the Straits from Africa. It never occurred to us that Spain lies in the same latitudes as the northern United States which often suffer severe winters.

Since the scooter was too small for all of our luggage, what we couldn't carry we had shipped on to Spain. The train baggage agent told us we would have no problem getting it out of Italy and across France without us. But Spanish authorities insisted that we personally see it through customs when it entered Spain.

From talking to Italian customs officials and checking our road maps, we decided that we would ship our baggage to intersect our route at a French customs station on the Mediterranean called Port Bou. We never considered what would happen to our things if we were delayed and didn't reach Port Bou about the time our luggage did.

On the scooter's luggage rack behind Julie's gift pillion seat we stacked a small suitcase, a Singer Sewing Machine box converted into a camera equipment case, a camera tripod, a rolled blanket, and a plastic zippered case carrying our book of road maps across Europe. Everything was held on with elastic shock cords. It was a hefty load.

The morning of our departure, Milano traffic surged through a gray sea of exhaust fumes and fog. Moreover, it was cold. Julie wore leg-snug black slacks, a short tan fur-collared overcoat with sweaters underneath. Since billed caps could blow off in the wind, we carried black French berets, mainly to keep the rain off our heads until we found shelter. We carried no other raingear. Who ever heard of it raining on the rivieras?

For this foggy morning, Julie snugged down a silk scarf over her head because she could tuck it in around the collar of the coat to protect her ears. I wore khaki pants and a Navy blue fleece-lined nylon windbreaker over a black turtleneck sweater. We both had on warm leather gloves. Our large plastic windshield would deflect most of the cold wind.

I rolled the tail-heavy scooter into the gutter, kicked the starter lever and the Lambretta instantly sputtered into its muffled fast-popping purr. Since the stack of luggage blocked Julie's easy access to her seat, I held the bike while she got into position on her pillion seat. Then I climbed on in front of her. Her hands locked on the handgrip between our seats. Her feet rested on narrow decks on each side of the scooter.

Shifting the scooter into first gear, I asked. "All ready?"

"As ready as ever, I guess."

I gradually released the clutch handle and with a more raucous popping of our mechanical steed, we lunged forward and wobbled uncertainly out into the brisk-flowing stream of Milano's bumper-to-bumper morning traffic.

Somehow we found a slot and fitted ourselves in behind a truck carrying a mountain of caged chickens, the wildly squawking cargo littering everything in its wake with feathers, straw and other assorted by-products. Behind us a loudly clattering streetcar seemed to have its bell stuck permanently in the on position. The tram's rattlings and bangings associated with various electrical snaps, pops and crackles from its overhead electrical line were unnerving. I didn't have to look back to see how close it was. My rear view mirror glimpse of it careening along on its clanging collision course was as much as I cared to see.

All the weight on the rear of the scooter made the front end so light I wondered when it would lift off the payment to perform an unintentional "wheelie". If it did, I knew the ravenous traffic would have its way with us instantly. Those bleary-eyed Monday morning drivers looked as though they would love to have us for breakfast. Their snuffling fiats, chugging trucks, clattering trams, honking sedans, swarmed around us like hungry sharks. You couldn't have pried my fingers off the handgrips. Nor could you have pried Julie's arms from around my waist where they were now tightly locked.

My eyes locked just as tightly on the jiggling rusty bumper of the squawking chicken truck belching exhaust in our faces a scooter's length ahead. I meant to keep that distance. At least the shambling truck provided some measure of protection from ahead. Made no difference that we were being pelted by chicken feathers and worse. This was a fight for survival!

The dangers in front, behind and on both sides of us, were nothing compared to the dangers underneath us. I tried not think about that. But from past bad experiences I knew about dew-dampened cobblestones under a scooter's wheels and how quickly they could cause an upset while whatever juggernaut was to your rear finished you off. And if slick cobblestones were not bad enough, tram tracks, those treacherous ribbons of shiny steel, were just as disastrous to a two-wheeler. Once wet they were slick as ice. You were fine if you went over them one wheel at a time, but get two wheels on them at the same time and you could spin off into instant oblivion.

All circumstances considered we did some serious motor scootering until traffic began to thin out. But it wasn't until we reached the outskirts of Milano before we relaxed and breathed more easily. The first break we got we pulled off the road for a much needed unwinding. Then we laughed and congratulated ourselves. Hey! We survived! Everything's downhill now. No sweat!

After that, we started to enjoy the experience. Soon, only an occasional truck and ourselves were heading south on International Highway N135 for Genova. After that it was roughly 700 miles more before we would rendezvous with our shipped baggage on the Spanish border at Port Bou.

Despite our sweaters and coats, it was cold.

"How nice it's going to be to get to the rivieras and warmer weather," I called over my shoulder.

"Oooo, yes," Julie called back over the noise of the wind. "I can hardly wait." On the open highway, the wind's constant chill went straight through our coats and sweaters. About once an hour we would locate some roadside restaurant to pull in and warm up. Everyone greeted us with broad smiles and sympathetic comments about our need to travel by *motoretta* in such uncomfortable weather.

As we sipped steaming mugs of *cafe latte,* often with hot crusty rolls just out of the oven with wood embers embedded in the bottom crusts, Italians along the way tried to guess our nationality.

Usually they asked first if we were French. The next guess was German. After that they started in on the Scandinavians. Usually before that point we told them we were Americans. This fact invariably caused raised eyebrows and a slow shaking of the head, as the speaker pondered this incongruity.

Some told us we were the first Americans they ever saw traveling by *motoretta.* Most *Americanos* went by train, or by bus in groups, they observed. Or sometimes in a big, beautiful *automobile Americano.* The last was always followed by the words: *"molto caro!"* (pronounced "MOOOL-toh KAAAH-row,)* at the same time the speaker rubbed his thumb and forefinger together, meaning, "Veeery expeeensive."

Just the idea of Americans traveling by motor scooter across Europe in the winter was more than most people could comprehend. Realizing it was true always drew interesting responses. Some people stared blankly. Others grinned foolishly. Many praised our bravery, obviously pleased to find Americans traveling in so lowly a fashion. Others murmured words of sympathy for my wife, shook their head at me, and wondered perhaps if we had lost our minds. Especially when everyone knew that all Americans were rich and always traveled first class. Americans choosing to ride a motor scooter was simply incomprehensible to them.

Our frequent warm-up stops refreshed us for the highway ahead. Slowly but surely the towns of Binasco, Pavia, Casteggio and Voghera rolled by effortlessly. But after that the highway began climbing through brown-grassed foothills that soon turned more mountainous north of Genova.

Dropping back into the higher-pitched whine of second gear, we passed large, lumbering trucks wheezing and laboring up the steeper grades. Most saluted our passing with a blast of their air horns. Where did these mountains come from? I didn't notice them on the map.

That afternoon we took a by-pass skirting the bustling port of Genova. Once we crested the high terrain, everything now was steeply downhill. With a muted roar we swept down the coastal cliffs to sea level, warmed if only emotionally by our first sight of the seething blue Mediterranean heaving huge foam-flecked waves onto the rocky coast. With the crashing sea to our left, we followed Highway 1 along the coast southwestward toward San Remo and the Italian Riviera.

3

Italian Ups and Downs

Despite an occasional glimmer of sun burning through the heavy gray overcast, it was still cold. Where oh where were those sun-baked balmy beaches of the tour-guide rivieras?

Our road soon became a serpentine up and down ride between fishing villages and summer resorts. We snaked steeply upward, crossed over the brink, then snaked steeply downward, all over rocky vertical cliffs lush with hanging vegetation and villas. The really only flat areas with the beaches were on the brief down-to-sea-level parts of the road. There the view was right out of the travel brochures, minus the sunshine. Over-turned fishing boats and drying nets decorated the rocky beaches. Each dip down from the heights revealed yet another charming fishing village, one after another, each one seemingly determined to out-charm its neighbors.

Everything along the coast was terraced and stacked across the clifftops, or crowded into the valleys. The highway rose and fell in measured cadence. All the high points were palm trees and cliff-hanging villas. All the low points were picture perfect classic marinas. A pleasant mixture of pastel buildings, gaily painted boats, bleached brown fishing nets, faded restaurant verandas, deserted outdoor cafes, their wrought iron chairs turned upside down on tables. Torn paper posters that once announced some gala occasion, were now faded and flapping in the wind. Everything suggested the kind of activities vacationers surely enjoyed in great numbers during the warmer days of summer.

Now, however, in the realty of approaching winter, the vacationers were long gone, their absence marked by the abundance of hotel and pension signs offering lodging to the occasional wayfarer.

Toward evening, when we reached the seaside town of Savona, our impression was that the entire city was devoted to ceramics and the work of local artists. The place looked more tropical than most. We had begun to see more palm trees which suggested that perhaps at long last we were reaching balmier latitudes.

But it was just an illusion. The weather remained uncomfortably cold. When we finally stopped for the night at a clean, nicely painted boarding house named Pensione Savona, we discovered that none of the hotels or other over-night establishments in the area had turned on their heat yet. As best we could understand it this was the law. No matter how cold it got before some pre- appointed date in mid-winter, establishments were forbidden to turn on their heat. When I asked about some kind of warmth for our room, it was as though I had blasphemed.

"Too soon, too soon!" cried our aproned, landlady, *Signora* Bellalucca of the tightly curled henna-dyed rust colored hair and full, very serious face. She was a short, rotund lady wearing an apron gaily decorated with flowers and the occasional tomato stain. Apparently our arrival caught her in the midst of cooking the evening meal. For that reason she clutched a sauce-stained wooden spoon in the same hand as the pen with which she was signing us into her ledger. Simultaneously she tried to answer my question as to the availability of room heat.

"*Pìu tarde! Pìu tarde!*" Much later!" She shouted wagging the spoon at me for added emphasis. "When winter comes!"

I turned to Julie, collar buttoned up to her chin, hands buried in her coat pockets. "No heat until winter," I murmured."

"Doubt I'll last that long," murmured my wife.

The landlady scowled at her. "You cold?" she asked in Italian.

"Excuse me?" said Julie.

"*FREDDO…FREDDO!*" she repeated loudly, as if volume would break the language barrier.

"She's asking if you're cold," I said quickly.

Julie nodded uncertainly.

"Poor baby," said the *Signora*, reaching over the counter to touch her cheek. "But no fear. I make you warm."

Julie glanced at me for a translation. So did the *Signora*.

"She will make you warm," I translated.

Si, si!" Julie's benefactress smiled broadly. "*No problema. Sta notte su matrimonio fa CALIENTE!*" *Signora* Bellalucca punctuated each word with her spoon as if she were adroitly punching holes in the crust of an apple pie.

Julie nodded and smiled.

"Thank you very much." I said, as our landlady swiftly excused herself and swished back to her kitchen.

We carried our things to an upstairs bedroom. "What was that all about?" Julie inquired.

"Maybe I misunderstood, but I think it was something about heating up our matrimony."

"Ummmm," was all my wife said.

Our room was huge. A large dark mahogany armoire dominated one end of it. A large and extremely regal double bed occupied the other end. One wall had floor-to-ceiling windows facing the sea. Their white curtains stood out crisply as if freshly starched. A bouquet of artificial lily-of-the-valley blossoms and faded blue violets filled a small brass vase on a white doily atop a massive brown dresser standing against the wall opposite the windows. Two tasseled pink-shaded lamps sat on a pair of night tables on either side of the bed. And *what* a bed it was!

Awesome. It had to have been a master woodcarver's *piece de resistance:* a great big double bed with magnificently carved corner posts six feet tall representing what looked like intertwined celestial clouds topped by a pair of mischievously smirking cherubs. The headboard alone was a masterful depiction of paradise. This colossal work of art dominated the entire room.

Its size even dominated that of the bathroom down the hall. Small as it was, it was to be shared with the other guests. As we cautiously explored it, we found the usual facilities not much different that others accept that the inside of the toilet bowl was a ceramic work of art depicting a scene of lavender flowers intertwined with more cherubs. There seemed to be a fixation with this celestial theme. But in a toilet bowl?

A lavatory and bathtub occupied the rest of the tiny bathroom. What looked like a small steam engine was attached to the wall at one end of the bathtub. Eyeing it, we wondered what was involved in getting enough hot water to take a bath.

It was apparently some kind of water-heating contraption that fed the footed porcelain white tub. This marvel of shiny chrome with gas burner, gleaming water tank and assorted worn brass knobs and handles was linked to the plaster-cracked wall by an equally complex series of jointed and ingeniously bracketed water pipes. A small carefully lettered sign hung from one of the knobs by a brass chain. It had just one word printed on it by someone with an unsteady black paintbrush. In Italian it said: "Ask." The word was crookedly underlined.

I told Julie what it said.

"It must have read our minds," she said, staring at the water-heater dubiously. "It looks dangerous."

She pointed to a slotted box bolted to one side of the heater. "What do you suppose that's for?"

I looked it over. "It seems to be some kind of place to put coins, like those banks kids used to have where you put the coins in a slot on the top but you had to know the three letter combination to unlock the door in front." This box, however, had no combination lock. A key could be used on its side for probably the same purpose.

As we were to learn later, this ingenious device was yet another way to conserve energy. It was a pay water-heater. When you dropped a certain denomination of Italian coin in the slot, and turned a knob you got gas enough to heat the water in the little tank for one very fast bath.

Once we learned the secret of the contraption, we had to try it. We ended up spending four coins and taking double bathes each. Not having been really warm since leaving Florida, just soaking in the luxury of all that hot water was more than worth it.

The pension's small dining room was as immaculately clean and orderly as our bedroom. Five tables occupied the room, but there were only two other couples being served. Both were elderly. As we entered the room and seated ourselves, everyone greeted us and we wished each other good appetite. After that things got underway.

Under the watchful eye and beaming countenance of our landlady, dinner was served elegantly to each table by an efficient pair of uniformed waiters. A nice antipasto salad was followed by a small platter of spaghetti, *(salsa ala Savona)*. Once this was finished, along came veal scaloppini with small braised potatoes and English peas on the side. Fresh homemade bread and pitchers of dark red house wine complimented the meal. Everything was topped off finally with a small dessert of sliced fruit and goat cheese. For the finale, the *Signora* served demitasses of steaming Expresso.

Since we were famished, it was a gastronomical feast. We toasted the *Signora* and her staff so many times that she insisted that everyone partake of another pitcher of wine, compliments of Pensione Savona. It was a delightful evening, even if we were a little limber-legged as we finally climbed the stairs to our room.

The pink tasseled little night lamps had been lit beside our bed, and the heavy covers were turned down between the massive columns of cherubs. Other than those warm touches the big high-ceiling bedroom was as cold as an icebox. The tall windows rattled in their frames from a brisk wind blowing off the churning Mediterranean, and a shutter hinge squealed from time to time. We hurried into our pajamas and jumped under the covers.

Almost as quickly we jumped out again, our feet shocked by their contact with something foreign in the foot of our bed.

"What is it?" My wife pointed nervously at the two bulges at the foot of our bed covers. We slowly turned back the blankets. There lay two, full, tightly corked wine bottles wrapped in towels.

I reached down and unrolled a bottle. "It was filled with hot water!"

For a moment we stared at them, then almost shouted together, "hot water bottles!" Literally.

"That's what our landlady meant by heating up our marriage." We both stifled laughter until it occurred to me what the *Signora* had really said about warming up "our marriage" after we had checked in. Suddenly, the big bed with its cherubs made sense. It was not our matrimony she was heating up, it was her "*matrimonio*." Double beds such as ours were called matrimonial beds or "*matrimonios*," in Italy. Suddenly it all made sense.

By now we were both shivering more from suppressed mirth than from the cold. Then, eagerly we leaped back into that big celestial work of art, pulled the covers to our chins and luxuriated in the marvelous warmth that suffused the foot of our bed, thanks to our ingenious landlady.

Her thoughtful kindness we would never forget.

4

Rollercoasting the Rivieras

After breakfast the next morning, we were about to leave when *Signora* Bellalucca hurried out of her kitchen to tell us good-bye. We stood at the door, bags and baggage in hand, bundled in our overcoat, jacket and sweaters. *La Signora* inspected us. From her expression she was not happy with what she saw. I gathered she thought there was serious room for improvement. The first to come under attack was my wife

Scowling, our landlady grasped the front of Julie's coat and pulled it forward.

"*Guarda! Guarda!* Look! Look! You have no feeling for your wife!"

Open mouthed we stared at her.

Being a short, square woman, she had to reach up to do it, but to our surprise, she pulled Julie's coat forward with one hand and ran her other hand down inside it.

"See there! *NIENTE!* Nothing! Wait. Stay where you are!"

The *Signora* rushed back to her kitchen, while we stared after her.

Eyes wide, Julie turned to me.

"Don't even ask," I said. "She just yelled that you didn't have anything there."

Julie, who is amply endowed in that area, looked too stunned to speak.

The *Signora's* shuffling slippers brought her rushing back into the room clutching several newspapers. These she swiftly folded and began stuffing down the inside of Julie's coat.

"For the cold! For the cold!" she repeated loudly in Italian. They keep you *CALDO*. Warm! Warm!" She shouted the word over and over in Italian, again trying to break the language barrier.

I grinned. "She's insulating you for the cold," I told Julie.

"Oh! *Grazia*! Thank you," my wife managed to say.

The bright-eyed determined little woman turned to me and shook her head. She chastised me for making my wife face the cold so poorly dressed. She said I was no better. Brusquely, and a bit roughly, I thought, she stuffed layer upon layer of newspapers down the front of my jacket.

Finally, with us properly prepared to meet the weather, she pushed us out the door. We thanked her again for her kindness.

"*Niente!*" it was nothing at all, she said, waving us off. As we went down the steps toward our waiting scooter, we crinkled and rustled like walking packages.

Back we went at high speed along the up and down coastal highway. Sharp morning mists heavy with the scent of the sea, stung our faces. It was a fresh, good feeling. The *Signora's* newspaper insulation cut the chill amazingly well.

"Who would have thought it," Julie said at my shoulder. "When she shoved her hand inside of my coat I thought she had lost her mind."

"Me too, " I laughed. At least her newspaper is keeping us nice and warm."

If we thought we had seen up and down highways before Savona, they were nothing compared to those that came after Savona. Here indeed was what our rest stop citizens laughing referred to as "roller coaster country." The Lambretta wailed in high-pitched discontent from valley to summit, from tunnel to tunnel across the entire Italian Riviera. Our ears resented it but our eyes were lavishly rewarded. Despite the solid overcast, the views were stunning. We could only imagine this rugged beauty bathed in riviera sunshine. In the summer it probably looked like a bustling beach resort in the States. But now, off-season it looked like any other beach resort caught in the cold grip of winter: empty.

Despite the diversities of our roadway, we were making good time, averaging about 100 miles a day. The foggy, threatening weather since Milano finally broke down into a cold drizzle that afternoon when we reached Ventimiglia near the Italian-Monaco border. After looking over this attractive little coastal town, we found an inexpensive hotel for the night.

The next morning it was still gloomy and cold, but only on the Italian Riviera. As we crossed over into the tiny French principality of Monaco, things miraculously cleared up. As we wheeled up in front of the famous Casino de Monte Carlo, the sun began shining in all its riviera glory. Here, finally was the picture we had seen in the travel brochures! Our spirits soared like kites.

We parked the scooter at the curb. I was unpacking the camera for photographs when a burly doorman in a stunning gold and blue uniform approached.

"*On ne peut pas arrêtez ici!*" One can't stop here, he said. The gold braided man pointed at our scooter.

"But we go to the casino," I told him in my impeccable French.

"Good, good. But you cannot stop here!" He turned and pointed toward the next block which was as empty as the one where we were. "Go there," he said. "Stop there but not here."

"*Pourquoi pas* ici?" Why not here, my curiosity compelled me to ask.

"Because," said the doorman, tugging on his earlobe, "your machine makes too much noise. You disturb our clients."

"Ah haaaaah," I nodded broadly, "I understand." I smiled and held my finger to my lips.

"*Oui! oui! C'est ça!*" Smiling too now he clamped his forefinger to his lips. "Shhhhhhhh!"

Very quietly we eased the scooter off its stand and began pushing it toward the next empty block. The beaming doorman, resplendent in his uniform, snapped to attention and saluted us.

We parked the Lambretta a block away, locked it, and walked back to take some pictures of the casino and the famous harbor it overlooked. The doorman saluted us once again as we passed through the doors of the splendid structure for a quick look inside.

The casino's interior was pure elegance. Shimmering brocades and gold gilt. But no one was there. Not a soul. Not even a cleaning lady. The place was so empty it echoed. Even the gaming rooms were deserted. The doorman had the whole elegant empty place, including the two empty blocks of boulevard in front, to himself.

"Probably just the way he likes it," observed Julie.

As we passed him on the way out he again snapped to attention, smiled officiously and touched his forefinger smartly to the brim of his gold-braided cap.

"*Merci*," we both said, walking quietly toward our motor scooter in the next block. From our view the world famous gambling casino at Monte Carlo left much to be desired.

Back on the main road, we were again awed by the verticalness of it all. "It's like fairy tale country with the houses perched all the way down the sides of the mountains to the sea," Julie observed.

She was right. And everything was on such a surprising small scale. Monaco is so tiny that just as you get use to it, you are leaving it. It was the first serious sunshine we had seen in weeks. The skies had cleared, turned blue and the sun beamed down on us when we entered the country. It was still shining brightly when we left. But the minute we left Monaco to continue down the famous French Riviera, we were again immersed in the chilly overcast weather that had plagued us the entire trip. At least now it had a French flavor.

5

Like Ships That Pass in the Night

We rolled across the Cote d'Azure: Nice, Antibes, Juan-le-Pins, Cannes, continually impressed by the amazing way people had managed to pack so many structures into such a small piece of multi-terraced seaside property. Pastel villas clung precariously to the tiered terrain like colored candy dots sprinkled lavishly over a child's sugar frosted birthday cake.

As we passed through the famous resort city of Cannes, we looked so avidly at the now bleak empty beach that we took a wrong turn and ended up on N–98, a coastal secondary road to Frejus.

It was an easy mistake, one we wouldn't have intentionally made, but one that proved far more interesting than had we stayed on the main highway.

This side-road meandering along the edge of the Mediterranean was a scenic smorgasbord. In its 22 miles we saw not one living soul. What we did see, however, were great pine forests, jagged brown cliffs, soaring seagulls, and a crystal blue sea.

Where were the mile high stacks of villas, the tunnels, the railroads, the interlacing narrow paths and roads? Why not the slightest congestion so typical of all the rivieras? Was this coast too far from the commercial scene, a coast too unspoiled to live on? Whatever the reason, it was delightful.

At Frejus we left the coast and headed inland to avoid a big chunk of southern France that held the commercial ports of Toulon and

Marseille. Again, we stayed to a secondary route to avoid heavy traffic, this time taking N–7 and hoping that once we reached the flat expanse of the Rhone Valley we could recoup mileage lost through recurrent bouts with fog, mists and see-saw roads. So, westward we went behind the coastal Maure Mountain range picking up Brignoles on the road to Aix-en-Provence.

The mists thickened into icy rain. This time heavy. We stopped and dug out our berets. Little help but they kept our heads from immediate soaking. My windscreen had picked up enough vehicular sludge that raindrops slithered around it like frantic amoebas. To see, I squinted over the top of it. Aviator's goggles or a diver's facemask would have been a blessing. But we looked strange enough as it was. We had to get out of the downpour before we had an accident.

A dimly-lit roadside inn appeared out of the rain at Aix-en-Provence. As we pulled in, another bundled up couple in berets parked their baggage-burdened Vespa and hurried inside. I glanced enviously at the well-lashed waterproof raincoat protecting their things.

Unloading the luggage rack and hauling all our belongings inside like Gypsies was one of the less agreeable necessities of our venture. The suitcase and Singer Sewing Machine case always made innkeepers suspect I was trying to sell them something.

"*Bon jour!*" We nodded to the other couple as we sat down at a table close to a huge, red-glowing coal stove that filled the room with warmth.

The other couple looked as bedraggled as ourselves. Julie slipped off her soggy scarf and beret and was trying to do things with her hair.

"Did you travel far on your scooter?" the man called to me in French.

"From Italy," I said.

"*Nous aussi!* We too," he smiled. They had removed their berets and were wringing them out. "From where? he asked.

"Milano," I said. "*Et vous?*"

"Sicily"

"*Trés loin!* A long ways."

"*Oui, oui.* But we came from Paris."

"*Ah, alors, trés, trés* loin!" I raised my eyebrows at this. Paris was far indeed considering they had first gone down to the southern boot of Italy."

"It's very cold for us here," the man said in French. "We live in southern California."

"*What!*" I said in English. "You're Americans?"

"Yes. And you too?

We all laughed. "Then why the heck are we speaking French?"

This brought more laughter. The four of us quickly introduced ourselves and they joined us at our table. They were Bill and Nancy Forsyth from Palo Alto, California. Both had come to study art in Paris. They lived there through the fall until it got too cold for them. Then they decided to leave.

"We thought it would be fun to head south as far as we could go and find someplace warm for the winter," grinned Bill. "But Sicily wasn't it."

"You can't get much further south than that," I said.

"Oh it was warm enough," said Nancy with a slight English accent. "The trouble was the people didn't like us being there."

Bill shook his head. "Really strange," he said. "It's such a man's world down there that women are nothing. If you see a couple walking along the road, the man always leads and the woman walks behind him"

"That was the real bitch of it," said Nancy. "When I walked beside Bill the street urchins threw stones at us."

"*They what?*" Julie asked.

"True. Oh very true. They dislike us being an equal with our men," she insisted. "Threw stones. Can you imagine that?"

"She's right," said Bill. "We got on the Vespa and got out there as fast as we could. Sicily might be warm but that's about all it has going for it. They're still barbarians."

"Where to now?" I asked, hoping that they might be interested in joining us on a trip to Spain.

"Back to Paris, I guess. At least they keep the cafés warm in the winter. We can eat, sip coffee and stay warm during the day even if the weather is miserable. Might even do some sketches there. The French understand things like that."

Our waitress brought four large steaming bowls of *café au lait* and the bread we had ordered.

We tore off chunks of the crusty slant-sliced slabs, daubed them with Dijon mustard and ate ravenously. After that we indulged in a course of French onion soup in heavy crockery bowls with thick Gruyere cheese melted through it. Even if we hadn't been half frozen and famished, it still was the finest French Onion soup we had ever tasted. While we shared it with our friends along with a mild white wine of the region, I asked Bill and Nancy if they would be interested in going to Spain.

"No," said Bill. "I understand it's just as cold there. They say this has been one of the earliest and coldest winters Europe has had. I doubt the Spanish cafés have heat yet. With restrictions that prevent them turning on the heat in the hotels until a certain time of year, it's really bad. An early cold snap and everyone freezes. I bet the luxury class hotels don't have that problem. Money talks. Frankly, we can hardly wait to get back to Paris and those warm cafés. If we make it through the winter, we'll probably enroll at an art school in the spring."

We spent the evening with our fellow travelers, enjoyed supper at the little restaurant, shared a couple extra carafes of house wine with them, then following the proprietor's directions, we motored down the road a ways to find an inexpensive hotel.

The next morning we bid each other good-bye and good luck, then the Vespa and the Lambretta went in opposite directions. The Forsyths headed northward up the Rhone Valley on heavily trafficked highway A7 toward Paris while we split off on secondary road 113 westward across the broad expanses of the Buche-Du-Rhone country toward Arles. The weather was brisk and as usual, overcast. At least the rain had stopped.

6

Fighting the Mistral and Tramontana

What bothered us more than anything now, was the wind. Not only was it cold, but it was strong. I didn't envy our friends having to fight their way through the teeth of it all the way up the valley to Paris. It was bad enough taking it on our flank as we were doing. Somewhere northwest of Marseille, at one of our rest stops, someone asked us how we tolerated the wind on our motor scooter.

"I said we wished it were behind us."

The pinch-faced man with nicotine-stained fingers broke into a toothless laugh at that thought.

"If you take the mistral behind you here, it'll sail you to sea," he laughed.

As we left I told Julie, "No wonder its been pushing us all over the place. We're getting the mistral."

"How bad can that get?"

At its worse it can hit hurricane speeds of over one hundred miles an hour. But usually it's just a strong blow. I told her it was much the same in other parts of Europe where at this time of year when high-speed winds sweep down out of the cold mountains through the valleys to the warmer Mediterranean. Same occurs in north Italy. In Trieste on the northern Adriatic it's called the bora. It blows out of the Italian/Austrian Alps and down into the Adriatic with such force it sometimes pushes vehicles off icy roads and topples pedestrians. Ropes sometimes have to be strung around the streets so pedestrians can pull themselves along.

"I wonder what kind of wind they've got in Spain?" Julie said.

We didn't know then about something Spaniards call the tramontana but we would soon find out. First, however, we got to taste some of France's mistral.

Everything had been fine as long as buffering houses and trees on both sides of the road flanked us. But then the route branched and we started along N–572 across the wide open valley floor toward Arles. It was a lonely road unprotected on all sides. In fact, the only thing between us and the mistral was a spaced row of tall skinny leafless trees.

Suddenly, the cold wind that annually buffets Marseille with gusts that sometimes reach 120-miles-an-hour began to blow at us. It came from the north down the full sweep of the valley, striking us solidly on our right flank. We zigzagged from one side of that road to the other until I learned how to steer against the blast. As long as I steered against it this straightened out our course all right until something impeded the wind's force. A tree or a line of spaced trees was all it took to upset us. When a tree to our right blocked the blast for even a split second, the effect was like leaning against a brick wall and having it suddenly jerked away from you. With a row of trees it repeated itself.

Upwind spaced rows of trees made it virtually impossible to steer a straight course. As soon as I compensated for the wind by steering right to go straight ahead, the abrupt stopping of the wind by a tree, sent us careening to the right. As soon as I corrected and got us straight again, the wind's blast blew us to the left, forcing me to quickly compensate back to the right. All this pushing and compensating sent us swerving wildly from one side of the road to the other. It was unavoidable. Thankfully, we were out there alone. No other traffic appeared. It had better sense.

By the time we reached Arles in the late afternoon, we were worn out from being buffeted back and forth by the Mistral. What a welcome surprise to find that ancient Arles had solved this wind problem. The whole town was completely walled in. They may have done it for other reasons, but what better way to keep wintry drafts out of town?

Arles came through the ravages of time a bit bruised but little changed. Buildings inside the wall looked as though they had never been renovated since Julius Caesar's time. Cobblestone streets were so narrow you could almost stretch out your arms and touch old stone buildings crammed along both sides. Certainly two vehicles could never pass each other on avenues no wider than a chariot. The street we followed led straight to a Roman amphitheater. The city that once entertained plebeians of the past with battles between Roman gladiators and wild animals, entertains today's plebeians with battles between matadors and bulls. How little we change.

Shortly, we got lost in a maze of streets so narrow a donkey cart could—and did—cause a hopeless traffic jam. Arles may be the only city in the world that prefers to expand *inside* its city limits rather than beyond them. Eventually, we found our way to a small hotel. Though the Mistral howled loudly all night long over our ancient, tiled roof, not even a cold draft disturbed us.

Next morning we were on the road early. Leaving the walled city to revel in it's past we swung southward on N–113 with the Mistral whooping up a fine tail wind behind us. For once it was great to have the gale going with us rather than against us.

Though they were many miles apart, the cities of Montpellier, Sete, and Baziers, fell behind like magic. Taking route N–9 we continued to Narbonne, spent the night, and the next day went on to Perpignan.

There, it was time to leave the main road and detour onto secondary road N–114 which the map showed angling in a fairly straight, skinny gray line toward the coast and the French custom station at Cerbére.

Across the border from it was Port Bou, Spain where we would enter that country with all of our reclaimed baggage.

Regarding that route, what should have tipped me off about the real condition of that "fairly straight" gray line on our road map were those oh so subtle smudges off to the side of our route. Had I looked more closely at those and read the fine print, I would have seen such things as "Col De La Perche" 5,211 feet high, and "Pic Du Caniou," 9,190 feet high. Mountain peaks flanked our "almost straight" gray map line. Thanks to our ignorance we were heading into high mountain country about as innocent as it was possible to get.

After a few miles of this "almost straight line" map road that was actually crooked as a corkscrew, I realized that even harried map-makers take poetic license. When the pavement ran out, we were left with a broken rock road that grew narrower the higher we climbed. It reached a point where two cars would have had trouble passing. Not a pleasant thought since no guardrails existed. From all appearances the clever road crew had simply widened the original mountain goat trail.

And the wind was against us again, stronger than ever. With the Lambretta whining in second and sometimes first gears, we climbed that rocky goat trail weaving from side to side on that narrow rocky trail, buffeted now on all sides by cold gusts of wind.

From our high cliff-side vantage point, we saw far below us a small freighter struggling to make way against slathering gray seas of mountainous waves, their foam-lathered crests washing over the vessel's decks from stem to stern. If the ship wasn't in distress, it looked as though it should be.

The higher we climbed on this cliff-side road, the stronger the wind blew. Finally, the rocky road widened. We weaved toward the small stone French custom station perched perilously atop the mountain peak at Cerbére.

The place looked deserted. The station gate was down. When you enter a country most custom stations are beehives of activity, but relatively quiet when you are exiting one. An officer meets your vehicle, checks your papers, and waves you on your way.

But not today at Cerbére. There, no one came out. Two grim faces peered out at us through a soot-stained steamed window. If we planned to pass that border gate, it was apparently up to us to initiate formalities.

I sympathized with the border guards. No one in his right mind wanted to stick his head out of this godforsaken mountaintop outpost in a gale if he didn't have too. I could almost hear them:

"Hey, Pierre, there's two crazies on a motor scooter outside wanting to cross!"

"*Mon Dieu*, hide yourself, maybe they'll go away!"

"Naw, they're parking it."

"Scooter idiots! They're crazy. You go, I went last time."

"That was *last week*. This is *this* week. Hey, one of them is a *femme!*"

"Huh? Let me see!"

"*Fait attention, embecile!* Now they're both coming in!"

Julie and I set the scooter on its stand and started for the custom's house. Halfway there, we heard a crash behind us.

The wind had blown the scooter over.

I hurried back and righted it, pointing it into the wind. The faces were at the window again. We hurried inside.

Two uniformed officials sprang to the counter to assist us. A coal stove squatting in a corner had heated the place so hot our eyes watered.

"*Monsieur, Madame*, you wish to depart France?" one of them asked. The other grinned broadly, directing it mostly at my wife.

I agreed that we did, and handed him our passports. "The mistral blows hard," I said.

"*Pas le mistral,*" the smiling one said. "Here we have the *tramontana*. The Spanish wind. Very bad." He wrinkled his nose.

The first official handed our papers back to us. He too looked more benevolently upon us now that the formalities were over.

He tried his English. "You…cold…on scooter?" He looked at my wife and hugged his shoulders. She smiled and nodded.

"*On besoin un peu de cognac,*" he grinned.

I agreed, one certainly did need a little brandy.

Suddenly, something crashed outside. The Frenchmen ran to their window. The wind had picked up our scooter, shoved it across the road and dropped it wrong-side-up on the edge of the cliff.

The Frenchmen stared at the scooter, then stared at us and shrugged as only Frenchmen can shrug.

By then I was racing out the door to get it before the wind did any more damage.

I managed to get the Lambretta back on its feet and squared away our baggage while Julie kept a firm hand on the machine. Then we carefully cranked her up, climbed aboard and wobbled through the now open gate.

As we careened off down the rocky trail to Spain with the tramontana howling in our ears, the two border guards watched us out of sight from another steamed and sooty office window. Our presence at their isolated customs station probably gave them something to talk about for a week.

7

Rendezvous at Port Bou

We corkscrewed downhill now to the border station town of Port Bou. Spanish customs was at the railroad station where I would reclaim our luggage and accompany it on its official entry into Spain. After that we could do whatever we wanted with it, which would be to send it right back into the baggage car that would haul it to our next main stop: Barcelona.

To save Julie having to do customs, I made sure she was comfortable at a warm Port Bou restaurant. I left her enjoying a large cup of *café leche* and *coissants*, the last we would have of those marvelous French pastries until we returned to France.

Spanish customs had two dirty-smocked baggage handlers bring out our two locked suitcases and place them on the luggage counter. Beside them rested our scooter suitcase and Singer Sewing Machine box. The two brown-uniformed officials stared hard at our small collection, as if sheer concentration alone would reveal which locked bag contained the contraband.

Behind them, looking as cheerful as totem poles, stood two gray-uniformed *Guardia Civil* frontier policemen with shiny black leather holsters, belts and Napoleon-type hats. Each had a carbine slung over his shoulder. The whole entourage looked as though it hadn't entertained a happy thought in the last ten years.

Finally making up his mind, one of the thoughtful customs officers, a fellow with quick, beady eyes and a pencil-thin mustache, stepped forward and tapped a bony finger on the black sewing machine box.

I knew it! That box always got more attention than we did. It was the kind of well-made, leather-covered, chrome-latched and locked case that just naturally attracts attention. Especially from sneak thieves and suspicious customs agents.

I unlocked it. Pencil-thin leaned forward and looked into its depths. With a flutter of fingers he indicated I was to unload its contents.

Out came the rolls of film, the Rolleiflex, the 35mm camera, and all the accessories.

Again the agent looked into the box and touched its inner walls. Satisfying himself that it was truly empty, he picked up and examined each of the cameras closely.

His beady eyes nailed mine. "No for sale in *España*."

"Oh, is that true?" I said.

He stared at me unblinking. His bony finger tapped loudly on the Rolleiflex camera. More loudly this time he emphatically said, "YOU…NO…SALE…*ESPAÑA!*"

"Oh, no, no. All my cameras. No sale. Never…ever!" I hastily assured him.

"Good." And to make sure I didn't, he carefully noted the serial numbers of both cameras in my passport with the pointed suggestion that I have the same *maquinas fotograficas* or photographic machines with me when I left Spain.

Next, I was asked to unlock and open all the other bags for inspection. With each, the two customs officials pushed and prodded, lifted and looked, moving methodically from bag to bag.

As he was going through the frilly things in my wife's suitcase, pencil-thin's fingers suddenly closed on an unfamiliar packaged object. Had he at last found contraband? His lips pursed, his eyes narrowed. He whipped it into view.

"*Que es esto?*" he demanded. "What is this?"

I stared at the paper-wrapped Tampax held so jauntily between his fingers like a cigar. I stammered. I mumbled. Even if I'd known the word I couldn't have explained what it was to the man.

He waited. I flushed. He waited some more.

Finally, the best I could do was blurt out in French that it was something for the Madam.

Apparently he got the idea because he quickly buried it under a nightgown and slammed the suitcase shut. I heaved a sigh of relief.

Everything after that was downhill. Even the papers for the motor scooter were acceptable. All we had to do was remember not to sell it in Spain or we could surely expect dire consequences. It had to go back to Italy to be sold. After the Tampax incident I was agreeable to anything.

After that, I zippered everything, pad-locked the works and shipped the bags to Barcelona.

Moments later, I rejoined my wife at the restaurant. She asked how it had gone. As I told her, her eyes began to tear up, the corners of her mouth twitched, she appeared to be holding her breath.

Frankly, I failed to see any humor in it.

Back again astride our steed we took what our map indicated as "an important secondary road" to Frejus. Again, I should have guessed from the map's squiggly line what we were getting into. Maps don't show those kinds of things unless the road just misses tying itself into knots.

As we corkscrewed up, down and sideways through those coastal Pyrenees, we began to lose daylight. Things were looking especially less than bright as the narrow, meandering rocky road seemed to go nowhere with any habitation in sight. As the miles rolled away I wondered what would happen if we got caught in the dark on this lonely, cold, mountain road to nowhere. Or worse, what if we finally ran out of gas? We had not seen another vehicle, or any sign of life at all.

Finally, late in the afternoon, we approached a town. As we entered it, we thought how strangely vacant were all the buildings along the outskirts of the place. But soon we were going through the heart of the town and still not a living soul appeared. Everyone was gone. The entire place was a ghost town!

Moreover, some distance down the road, we encountered another empty village. All the buildings were intact and seemed as if they had recently been occupied. Still, no sign of life appeared. Not even a stray cat or barking dog. It was as though everyone had moved out. But why?

It reminded us of the coast we had seen when we missed our turn at Cannes in France and wandered along a deserted coastal road frequented only by seagulls. This road was almost the same, but here we lacked any view of the sea. Nothing but brown rocks and brown stone buildings. As if it were a place time forgot. The drab, brown dusty ghost towns on this Spanish coast sent shivers through us, and it wasn't all from the cold.

With relief, just as it grew dark, we picked up the main road and our overnight destination at Figueras.

Once back on the main route with other vehicles the next morning, we felt better about things. The weather even seemed a bit warmer now the more southward we went, but still the sun remained hidden.

When we finally reached Barcelona, it was time to take a break from our scooter travel and see some of this large city. We moved into a hotel and enjoyed sightseeing Barcelona. After a few days of doing the tourist thing we checked our options.

We had covered our first 700 miles. Either we could continue down the Costa Brava where every 85 miles more would put us into another more southern latitude of warmth, or we could break the trip right there, catch a boat for the Balearic Islands 132 miles out into the Mediterranean halfway between Spain and Africa, and see what

Frederic Chopin and George Sand found so intriguing about the island of Majorca.

When I asked Julie what she wanted to do, she never hesitated. Her choice was Majorca.

The next morning, with our full compliment of retrieved baggage piled in a taxi accompanied by Julie, we made our way to the waterfront. Somehow we got all our gear, ourselves and the Lambretta aboard the Balearic Islands bound ferry boat without losing anything.

Next stop halfway to Africa and the sun-kissed shores of Majorca!

8

Our Island in the Sun

It was an overnight boat trip. At 8 o'clock the next morning, no balmy beaches met our eager eyes when we saw where we had sent ourselves. In the early morning mists, our ferry eased past the large sharp-shouldered rock island. We looked but saw no golden beaches. The island looked like a tired brown dinosaur, its back high in the air, its long neck and legs angling down in steep grades to disappear into the sea.

Our ferry worked its way around this recumbent stone shape to enter a large southern bay. Crowding the shoreline quays sat a line of squat gray, fishing trawlers from whose booms draped arcs of heavy brown nets. Other nets spread wide across the stone quays like thick-meshed spider webs dotted with fishermen mending them over their laps. Behind the port beneath a galaxy of spires stood a magnificent cathedral. Just as carefully as our boat had entered this harbor, it eased up to a large concrete pier. With squeals and squawks from tall timber pilings, we docked at the busy port of Palma de Mallorca.

Quickly we claimed our Lambretta and got our gear ashore. At the end of the boat pier we hailed a taxi. It was a vintage black French Citröen. Unaccountably in Spain, all the taxis seemed to be French Citröens, always old and always black. The seats were leather, severely cracked and faded from wear. The outside of this one looked well kept. Just a bit of age on it, like its owner, the walrus mustached fellow who whipped off his small black beret, bowed low, and smiling broadly, opened the door for my wife. Our courteous driver volunteered that his name was Luis Vicenti, pronounced Vee-CHEN-tee, and that he was a Basque from northern Spain, presently residing in Mallorca for no other reason than to be of service to us.

When he realized that I would be riding the scooter, our luggage was swiftly stowed half in front with Mr. Vicenti, half in the back seat with Julie. As we started up with a sputter and a roar, I followed the exhaust-belching vehicle up the stone quay and a few blocks along a tree-lined boulevard to where we had requested going: the American Express Company.

Señor Vicinte appeared overwhelmed when I gave him somewhat more than an average tip with our fare. For a moment he held the dirty, wrinkled bills and coins in the palm of his creased hand and stared at them. Then again he whipped off his cap, bowed, and scurried with surprising alacrity around his taxi to snatch open the door of the American Express for us.

"Gracias, gracias, Señor!" he said, pressing a wrinkled and dirty card into my hand with his name and telephone number on it. "At your service always," he pledged with another deep bow.

Wherever in the world one happens to be, the good old American Express Company is the travelers home companion, the expatriate's primary resource for currency, information, compassion, and most welcome of all: mail from home.

The amiable clerk behind her grilled window, provided us with some of everything they had to offer: a pile of accumulated mail, local currency in exchange for our travelers checks, local maps and lists of available hotels, restaurants and gift shops, real estate agents; booklets describing Majorca's (or as the Spanish spell it, Mallorca, pronouncing it mah-YOR-ca) various religious, historical and inspirational sights worth seeing, religious fiestas, and dates of important bull fights.

Our selection of a hotel from this literature was based mostly on its location only a couple streets away. We could balance our luggage on the scooter and walk it that far.

Our hotel faced a narrow walkway barely large enough for motor scooters and two-way pedestrians. It reminded us of Arls. A sign over the narrow passageway told us we were there. It read: Hotel Montenegro. A large, imposing wooden door with massive hinges and a huge keyhole, marked its entrance. We opened it into a dim office lobby. A woman in a flowered shawl sprang to attention behind a desk as we entered.

She was a thin, striking woman, jet black hair piled atop her head and held in place with Mother-of-Pearl decorated tortoise-shell combs, black eyes flashing behind long-lashed black-mascara-edged eyelids. Complimenting this was a sharply angular face with thin, heavily reddened lips. Her shallow cheeks were lightly rouged.

"*Buenas dias!*" she smiled, her voice raspy and almost hoarse. "How may we serve you?"

In broken Italian and French, I explained that we would like a room for several nights.

Using hand gestures and speaking Mallorcain, a language that mixes French, Italian and Spanish words into an island patois of its own, she communicated with us.

She introduced herself as the proprietress, *Señorita* Silvestre. She would be happy to accommodate us with a room, and if we wished, the hotel also served meals on the European Plan. A breakfast of coffee, bread and marmalade in the morning; a full course dinner served late according to custom. We would be expected to pay in advance.

"I asked if the hotel's rooms were heated."

"No, no," said the *Señorita*, wagging her forefinger in the approved international negative gesture. "Not until winter."

I didn't dare ask when winter began.

Our room was large, with ceilings high overhead, so high that they got lost in the gloom of the low amperage glow from a table lamp sitting between two calico red coverlet covered single beds. The usual giant mahogany armoire buttressing one end of the room swallowed our baggage without a whimper. Two large windows should have let in lots of light, but they faced high-walled buildings across the narrow walkway that effectively blocked out any stray sunlight. As for a bathroom, shared facilities were down the drafty hall. Our motor scooter sat safely locked outside the hotel.

Once we settled in to our room, we set off on foot to see some of Palma. A couple blocks away was the tree-lined wide boulevard that looked like the main street in town. It was called the Borne, (Bor-nay). Pedestrians walked the widest central part of it while vehicles kept to the narrow streets along its sides. One group supposedly watched out for the other. Pedestrians observed the same rules of the road as the vehicles. The right lane of the boulevard was for the northbound strollers and the left lane was for the southbound foot traffic. Faster walkers could pass when they saw openings and were willing to risk spurts of speed up the center of the concourse.

People were the main attractions of this thoroughfare. Most were wrapped in warm overcoats against the early chill of winter. One woman in particular wore a long black coat almost reaching the ground. She was a tall, seemingly large woman from the back. And it was from the back that she first caught our attention.

"What *is* that woman doing?" Julie asked. She nodded toward the statuesque woman who sauntered along slowly some distance ahead of us, her hands buried deep in her pockets.

"What do you mean what's she doing? She's just strolling along like everyone else," I said.

"But watch her. Every time a man comes up in front of her, she flips open her coat!"

I perked up, eyes now more alert.

The woman in black looked perfectly innocent to me. She did seem to be weaving a bit, however. Not like someone who had too much to drink. More like a man, for example, seeing an attractive girl coming toward him some distance ahead in a crowd of pedestrians might begin to slant his course to bring himself closer to the quarry so that when she passed, he got a good eyeful.

That was the kind of sidewalk weaving this woman was doing, each time seeming to target some man coming toward her, then casually angling over to pass close to him.

"Now watch what she does when that fellow in the tan raincoat meets her," said Julie.

The woman never seemed to look directly at her oncoming target until the last moment, just before they were to pass. Then she did a strange thing. One of her hands in her pockets moved sideways, flipping open the front half of her coat.

The man glanced at her, almost imperceptibly shook his head, and passed on by.

"Wow! A female flasher!"

"Wait! Don't walk so fast!" My wife grabbed my arm and held me back.

"We've got to look at this from all angles," I said.

"Uh-huh. I know. But you better do it from back here."

We followed the woman at a safe distance. There was no doubt but that she was a professional. A clever one at that. Her modus operandi was covert, but always the same. She cruised slowly up the boulevard, looking fully over-coated one minute, then the next, with a flick of her arm, surreptitiously showing her wares to any man who looked. And look they did. From my perspective most of the men she flashed went bug-eyed.

Suddenly Julie stopped in her tracks. "Now this is too much," she said.

"What?" For an instant I had lost the lady in the crowd ahead.

"She just flashed a woman!"

"She what?"

"I swear."

"Oh, no way. You must be mistaking."

"Nope. It was that woman with the toy poodle and the bag of groceries coming toward us."

I glanced at the woman as she passed. She was a middle aged bleached blond built like the bag of groceries she carried.

"No way," I insisted.

"She did too," Julie insisted. "She flashed the woman just like she flashed the men."

I had to admit that that was pretty bad.

"Oh, oh! "

"What's wrong now?"

Julie ducked her head. "Don't look now but she's turned around. *She's walking back toward us!*"

I averted my eyes. "Is her coat open or closed?" I asked hopefully.

"Closed, Dummy."

Momentarily, my first impulse was to turn around too, as Julie was doing, and flee while the fleeing was good. But something told me to stay my ground, something stronger than fear of embarrassment. Some basic instinct prompted me to act as though we had seen nothing.

"Just keep walking," I said under my breath, taking hold of my wife's hand and trying to act nonchalant about it.

"But she's coming right toward us!"

That's okay," she's keeping her coat closed. She probably knows we're married."

Suddenly the woman was directly in front of us, a stunning, smiling brunette in a huge bulky black overcoat.

At close range, still smiling at us, she abruptly threw back both her arms and whipped open that big black coat as wide as she could possibly open it.

The sight stopped us dead in our tracks!

Our eyes bugged as the woman brazenly showed us everything she had, all of it displayed in small neat rows of pockets sewn from top to bottom on the inside of her great coat.

"Cigars, cigarettes, chewing gum, fountain pens, lighters…" the woman crooned in a low, throaty voice.

"Uh…no thank you."

Without even getting out of step, the woman snapped shut the front of her overcoat and continued walking past us as though nothing had happened.

In silence we turned and watched as she continued down the Borne, flashing her wares at anyone who looked.

Boy, what a letdown.

Later, when we stopped to rest at a sidewalk cafe, I casually pointed out the woman in black to our waiter.

"*Que passa?*" What's going on with the woman?" I inquired.

The alert waiter's eyes darted swiftly to the passing people. "Which woman?" he asked.

"*Alto…vestiti negri.* Tall…black clothes," I said.

About then the woman did her flashing thing for a little old lady in a black shawl.

"Oh, that's just Eudora," said the waiter, obviously disappointed that he hadn't seen something scandalous.

"But what is this?" I mimicked throwing open the front of my jacket.

He leaned down close to my ear. "She…sell…*contrabando!*" He stood up straight in his black pants, white shirt with a black-bowtie waiter's uniform and rolled his eyes heavenward while fanning his hand under his chin. Another powerful international gesture meaning, My oh my! "Veeery prohibited here in Mallorca," he whispered. "Police no like smuggling."

"Ah-hahhh," I said, understanding.

"Always take care…" The man touched his cheek under his eye and pulled it slightly downward. "*Policia* look!"

His meaning was clear. I thanked him for enlightening us.

We soon learned that the smuggling of small luxury items such as foreign cigarettes, pens, lighters, soap etc. and the almost overt sale of these items on the street was a way of life for the Mallorcains. After all, they had practiced it for generations. Why not continue? In good times or bad, it was just business."

Such was the reasoning of the average Mallorcain. Frontier police guarding the island's shores saw what they wanted to see. Payoffs were not unheard of. Smuggling was a tradition on Majorca. It was that simple.

9

Forted Up by the Bubbly

Another tradition common throughout Spain, we were to discover, was the late dinner hour. People met in the bars to chat, sip watered red wine, and munch on appetizers late in the afternoon. No one got serious about eating until closer to 9 p.m. After that, the whole affair might be continued until midnight, depending on the company and the conversation.

At the appropriate late hour, we appeared in Montenegro's warm dining room for the main meal of the day. It was a clean, well-lighted place with a half dozen tables, each one large enough for four diners. Tablecloths decorated with colorful, gay floral designs were on each table. A centerpiece ceramic container of bright-hued artificial flowers added a homey touch to the tables. Most of the artwork on the walls was faded but nicely framed prints of Saints and the Virgin Mother. Near them were hung several signed black and white photographs of flamenco dancers. It was a cheerful looking room. Best of all, since it was beside the kitchen, it was the warmest room in the hotel.

"Hi there! Are you guys English or American?" A cheery voice inquired as we started to sit down at a table.

It was a couple two tables down, two rather rotund folks wearing layered sweaters. Both the man and wife beamed at us.

"We're Americans," I said.

"Great. Come share our table with us, we can all chat together."

She was blond, hair pulled back in a bun. He was shorter, smiling under thick eyebrows and a beard that was just starting to shadow his chin.

"By all means, do join us," said the man, getting up and pulling out the chairs.

Pleased to see someone from home, we joined them and introduced ourselves. They said they were Harper and Binky Preeg from Missoula, Montana. At least she was, the wife swiftly explained. Harper was from San Francisco. He played the flute, she the cello. They both met six months ago at a music conservatory in Italy, fell madly in love and got married. They were honeymooning on Majorca.

When we explained our situation, Binky thought we were the bravest people she had ever met.

"Imagine, Harper. Scooting across Europe on a Lambretta!"

Binky's pale blue eyes flashed, her plump cheeks flushed.

Harper paused pensively, his bushy eyebrows arched over his shaded brown eyes. "Sorry," he said slowly. "I can't." He grinned broadly. "But then, I'm quite a sissy."

"Hell he is," said Binky. "He married me, didn't he?" She walloped Julie on the back.

I asked if they had brought their musical instruments with them. Binky said Harper had his and she planned to rent a cello, just to keep her hand in.

"We play duets together," volunteered Harper.

That's nice," said Julie. We both smiled. I couldn't remember ever hearing just a cello and flute together before, but they probably made great music.

"Do you play by any chance?" Harper inquired.

Julie shot me a reproachful glance but I accidentally let it slip that we were both ex-clarinet players.

"What do you mean, 'ex'"? asked Harper.

"Use-to-be," I hastened to explain. "High school band and such. We both retired our clarinets ages ago."

"Too bad," said Binky. "I'm sure we could find some somewhere. Have a heck of a fine quartet you know."

"Yes." I was sure two clarinets and a flute accompanied by a cello would make for some entertaining sounds.

While we talked, other of the Montenegro guests had come into the dining room and seated themselves. Most looked European.

The main course, served by a young girl in an appropriate waitress uniform, was a white filet of fish broiled in olive oil and touched up with a sprig of parsley. It tasted mellow-flavored and good. Both Harper and Binky praised it heartily. When we had almost finished, I caught the waitress' eye and inquired what kind of fish it was.

Laughingly she told me, but none of us understood. And each time she repeated the name, she giggled. It sounded like the name of an island off the California coast. When I still didn't get the connection, she made a claw of her fingers and grabbed my shoulder. "*Tiburon...tiburon,*" she giggled and again grabbed my shoulder.

"Better look that one up." Binky produced a small dictionary from a huge cloth handbag stashed on her lap. She flipped through the pages. Her eyes lit up. "Hey, here it is...'shark!'"

Harper cleared his throat. "Thank you Binky." He pushed his half-eaten helping aside. Our waitress tried to keep a straight face but her eyes danced mischievously.

After dinner we were joined by a fellow I had noticed earlier sitting with three older men. After his dinner companions left, he brought over his half filled carafe of red wine and asked politely if we minded him joining us.

The Preegs swiftly introduced Englishman Peter Dorset, a tall, rangy fellow with curly light brown hair down to his shirt collar. Nice even features, a bit too handsome maybe, but good eyes. Dark brown ones that looked straight at you when he talked. He said he had lived in Majorca a year, worked at the British Airlines office by day, did primitive oil paintings by night. He wore tweeds that looked practical for the cool weather. The ends of his fingers were stained dark. Paint stains, I guessed.

"What kind of primitive painting do you do?" Julie asked him.

Nothing fancy. Very basic stuff. What the tourists like."

"He had a show last year in Madrid. Even *Time Magazine* wrote him up!" said Binky.

"Umm, great. Is some of your work here on the island?"

"Sure. Here and there."

"When you go into the Yacht Club Bar down on the Pasao Maritimo, look left," said Binky. "It's a big painting of black trees on a blood red landscape. You can't miss it."

"I always wished I could paint?" said Julie. "It must take a lot of patience."

"No. Really bloody little." Our primitive artist took a long swig of his wine. "It helps if you get a little stoked on *vino*," he grinned. "Brings out my inspiration."

"How?" I asked, curious about what inspired primitive artists.

"Well, I paint better. Makes things go faster. I get ideas, then try to get them down fast before the inspiration leaves. Like if I'm really feeling it, I line up about six canvases, see. Then I dip my hands in the paint and just go down the row. I can do all the pieces in about twenty minutes."

"Twenty minutes?" Harper asked.

"Yeah, about that."

"But that's little over three minutes a painting!"

Dorset shrugged. "That's about all it takes to catch the inspiration and slap it down on canvas." A theory Michelangelo would have found interesting.

"And he sells them for $500 to $600 apiece!" Binky added with gusto.

Dorset shrugged. "Whatever the market can stand." He smiled. "They make a quid here and there. Tourists love original art, you know."

We looked with new respect on our British friend. Anyone who could produce that kind of thing and sell it for serious money unquestionably had talent. Primitive or otherwise.

When we exhausted the wine. Binky instructed Harper to go get champagne. She felt the need to fortify herself and us for the rigors of our frigid rooms. Do bring back some bubbly, she instructed. "Several bottles."

I joined Harper to carry the goods. I was curious whether the Preegs had champagne stocks in their room or whether he had an outside source.

Harper's source was a bodega around the corner from the hotel. You wouldn't have guessed its existence but for a sign over its door. No tourist concession this. No sidewalk-to-eaves display windows like wine shops on the Borne. No show of imported beverages, jam-packed between elaborately and artistically filled glass containers of multi-colored olives layered in complex designs with other pickled goodies. No indeed. This bodega was for the locals. Any serious drinker sober enough to stumble across the establishment's heavy hewn, darkly stained olive wood threshold was welcome.

"*Buenas noche!*" Goodnight, was the intended greeting that came quickly after the jangling of the bell over the door as we stepped in, but that was not how it sounded. The words from inside the shop were run together and expelled violently the way one might expel a watermelon seed if one were striving for a world record: "Bohnohtch!".

Harper responded by expelling the same explosive "Bohnohtch!" greeting back at him. I was learning Mallorcain.

A bare 25-watt bulb suspended from the ceiling cast a faint yellow glow over the jumble of barrels, vats, and assorted loose unlabeled bottles surrounding the heavily scared old wood counter of this ancient wine cellar.

From out of the shadows, his head wreathed in clouds of blue smoke, appeared the owner and proprietor. Harper introduced us. He was *Señor* Segovia. We shook hands. The bodega owner looked at me out of the corner of his eye. He wore fingerless knit gloves, a deeply stained dark leather apron and a heavy brown knit stocking cap with holes in it through which thrust wispy gray hair like pieces of straw. The wine-keeper's well-creased face was the color of his smoked goat-skin wine bags hanging on a cob-webby beam behind his counter. His features crinkled into a wreath of smiles at our presence. The smoky halo hovering over his head came from a French *Gauloise Bleu* glued to the extreme corner of his cracked lips. Even in a cellar rich with the fumes of ancient fermentations, its breathtakingly pungent aroma was unmistakable.

"You desire?" *Señor* Segovia's voice trailed off, leaving room for us to fill in the blank.

"Champagne!"

"But of course." The leathery wine-keeper kissed his fingertips without disturbing the half-smoked Gauloise. "How many?"

"Six should do it, shouldn't it?" Harper asked me.

"Adequately," I said.

Harper conveyed the number to Mister Segovia who reached behind him and withdrew bottle after gold-foil-capped bottle from an apparently well-stocked big wood crate. In the dimly lit shop I saw the heavy green bottles of bubbly lying in rows of straw one-atop-another. I wondered what all this extravagance was about to cost us.

Señor Segovia sat each bottle gently on the counter and just as carefully wrapped each in a sheet of newspaper. When all six were ready, he produced a stub of a pencil from out of the folds of his stocking cap and quickly figured our bill on a scrap of paper.

As I reached for my wallet, Harper stopped me. "My treat tonight. Most of this will go back to the room with us anyway. Binky likes to sip it off and on to keep her warm. Our room is an iceberg."

At my insistence, Harper let me split the cost with him. With the comment that I shouldn't worry about it. It would be my turn to do the champagne tomorrow night.

We paid our bill with a little tip thrown in, a little something as the Europeans call it, "for a drink." *Señor* Segovia, rushed around from behind his counter to unlatch the door and see us out. Again he blew out the explosive "Bohnohch!" at us and again we in turn blew it back at him. As I squeezed past the grinning wine-keeper in the doorway I noted that the *Gauloise* had finally sizzled out at the corner of his lips, undoubtedly not to be displaced until he got ready for another one.

In the street I asked Harper if he was sure the bill was correct. He agreed it was.

"But how could it be?" I asked. "We just paid hardly anything for a bottle of champagne!"

Harper's eyebrows twitched at me over his armful of bottles. "It's hell, ain't it?" He hastened to explain as we walked back. "It's not the real stuff. Spain makes its own bubbly. Some of it may even go to tourists as the real thing. Probably smuggled in from the mainland. Who knows. At that price Segovia probably even makes his own."

The after dinner champagne ritual became a nightly custom with our new friends at the Montenegro. *Señor* Segovia's faux champagne was just as full of tingly air bubbles and fruity flavor as any we had ever tasted. It's name may have been bogus but we found this Spanish product delightful. It served its purpose beautifully. After several glasses, everything warmed up with the kind of warmth the government thankfully had yet to regulate. We toasted all faux champagne makers.

Despite the wine, however, our big room at the Montenegro stayed so cold when we went to bed that our only alternative was to put on all our sweaters and overcoats, climb under the covers, and dream of warmer times.

What a heck of a deal and we're almost in Africa, I thought just before slipping into a faux champagne induced slumber bundled up like a mummy.

10

Off the Beaten Path

We soon learned why Palma's off-the-main-boulevard thoroughfares were built so narrow. These passages were made not for vehicular traffic but for walkers. No formal plan determined their course. No north and south streets with east and west avenues. As spontaneous as rabbit runs, they rambled all over the place, providing meandering routes through the labyrinthine canyons between the continuous buildings. People who lived along these passageways carried on a way of life different from anywhere else in Palma.

The corridors were used long before the invention of the combustion engine, which explained why they were made just wide enough for people to pass. Ponderous loads moved along them on burro-drawn two-wheeled carts. When traffic got heavy, people stepped into doorways to let it pass. A steady stream of food, fuel and mountains of firewood made its way along these narrow passages in this manner, pulled by direct descendants of Mallorcain pack animals that performed the same service centuries ago.

Between the burro-drawn traffic walked women in black shawls carrying net-bags of groceries, others dressed as domestics adroitly balanced overflowing laundry baskets atop their heads. Among them were white-aproned bakers balancing baskets of bread, white-jacketed waiters delivering trays of fancy cakes to someone's party, and of course, the inevitably curious tourists.

The latter came in all shapes and sizes, in ones, twos, and in crowds. Nationalities were guessed from the clothes they wore. Everyone penetrated these narrow back streets tentatively, cautiously, some led swiftly by tour guides, while others strolled more slowly, savoring the sights. Most, however, let their curiosity bring them. They were the slow walkers, the cautious curious who poked their handbags, umbrellas, cameras, or husbands ahead of them to break trail. Bravely they followed these mysterious, winding, climbing, well-trod trails into the unknown as gamely as Stanley stalking Livingston in darkest Africa. One way or another, everyone usually found their way out of the maze by nightfall. For those who lingered after dark, ancient street lamps once flickering the blue and gold of gas flames, now glowed low-voltage electric light. The only casualties of these narrow back streets were the occasional sailors on liberty who discovered how many bodegas could be found there.

The aromas permeating these thoroughfares were as intriguing as their inhabitants. Restaurants pumped out fragrances ranging from burnt coffee grounds and spilled garbage, to fresh-baked bread and saffron-scented *Paella Mallorcain*, the popular herb-yellowed rice with succulent vegetables and marine creatures cooked ensemble. A delight to the senses. But along with these more pleasant scents were also mingled aromas of donkey carts, spilled wine gone stale and the usual ancient aromas of ageless back streets.

These off-the-main street narrow vehicle-free thoroughfares were the people's streets, busy walkways used for all purposes. People stood on their stoops and chatted, leaned over the alleyway balconies and chatted, or just loitered in groups and chatted. Underfoot the children played. Some sat on the stone stoops and watched as others played tag among the pedestrians and donkey carts. Archways often opened into small plazas where busily chatting women crowded around gushing fountains to wash laundry; or the arches led into tranquil Spanish gardens backed by sumptuous apartments facing other streets. Finding such startling green lushness among these crowded sandstone buildings was like discovering an oasis in a desert. In one of them, four little girls played hopscotch on the hexagonal squares of its sidewalk with a piece of petrified bread while just feet away people argued, babies bawled, donkeys brayed, radios blared, kids kicked tin cans against stone walls, and an army of pedestrians marched past. Through it all, the hopscotchers missed not a hop.

After visiting some of the usual tourist sights in Palma, we began looking into such places as the fish market and the flea market. The local fish market in the northeast sector of the city suggested it might be another olfactory adventure.

But we were wrong. No small corner operation this, it was a city block-sized warehouse filled with fish and fish vendors permeated with as clean an aroma as possible to imagine in a warehouse full of fish. The reason, I suspect, is because the place was bright, cool, and spotlessly clean. If one's nose felt left out, however, not so one's eyes. The place was a visual feast.

Every marine creature that ever crept or crawled, slithered or squirmed, sat perfectly still, or swam through the sea, was there. From sea creatures tinier than your pinky, to those whose mouths were big enough to engulf your head, they all had found their way to this remarkable market. Nothing got left out. Moreover, many of them were displayed quite artistically.

Fish of every description lay nicely placed in neat rows on concrete counters. Behind them white-aproned fish mongers, always within arm's reach of a shiny chrome scales, fussed and primped over their charges. They stacked and arranged, placed in rows of different sized fish in ranks of their own size. All the flat flounders and rays were artistically arranged in groupings resembling flower petals. Boxes were propped on edge to show fresh land snails slithering around. A wood crate of normal sized shrimp might have a dozen of its largest arranged artfully along the rim of the crate to tempt customers. Beside them might be a tray of shrimp whose members were 8-inches long. Four of them would make a meal for two people. Large bluefin tuna lay like shiny sharp-nosed blue torpedoes beside one that had been sliced in two to show its succulent cross-section. Lobsters, crabs and worm-like crustaceans defying description shared equal billing. African lobster tails wider than a man's splayed fingers were displayed beside brethren smaller than a freshwater crayfish. Wood tubs of slithering eels rubbed shoulders with stacks of squid and octopuses so fresh they had to occasionally be restrained from squirming off the counter. A slab-sided flounder looking odd enough by itself with two eyes on one side of its head, sat among an army of glassy-eyed flounder all arranged in neat step-like ranks so that all eyes aimed front and center at the passing parade of customers. Small sharks got hardly any fancy display, whereas something as exotic looking as a deep-sea hag fish with its long eel-like body and devilishly long curved fangs, was arranged more for shock appeal than something to appeal to the taste buds.

So many fish were on display there was no room to spare. With such crowded counters vendors had to be careful not to hit their heads on competitors' scales. Each pile of fish contained a small stick sign with the number of pesetas charged for a kilo of whatever it was. Vendors could weigh, clean and filet a purchase almost as quickly as it takes to tell about it. Never any lost motions. From what was being sold, we wondered what was left in the sea yet to sell. Not a fish was overlooked, not even the nursery stock. What a magnificent harvest! What rich waters these must be. Some vendors displayed rows of brightly colored fish no larger than one's little finger. When I inquired how you prepared such a dainty morsel to eat, one word answered my question: "Soup!"

"You like *la sopa pescado?*" someone asked at my shoulder.

I turned, surprised to see our taxi driver, Vicenti. Had it not been for his mustache, I might not have recognized him. He was out of uniform, dressed in the long white apron and peaked white cap many of the men wore behind the fish counters.

We greeted him warmly, and inquired what he was doing disguised as a fish vendor. He informed us that despite appearances, he was a man of many talents. Moreover, his brother-in-law was the captain of one of the large commercial fishing boats in the harbor. Vicenti helped sell his fish when the catch was good.

"You like fish?" Vicenti pointed at the especially malevolent looking hag fish and made motions with his hands.

"*Si, si,*" I said. "*Muy bien.*Very good."

Vicenti grinned and kept pumping his two fists back and forth, repeating the question.

"I think he's asking if you like to fish," said Julie. "If you like to *go* fishing.?

"*Si, si!*" Vicenti grinned so broadly we saw two gold bicuspids we failed to notice on our first meeting.

"Yes, I like fishing," and I pumped my fists the way Vicenti did.

"Truly?" Vicenti asked. "Okay. Then I fix for you," he beamed.

As we verbally wrestled around with what it was our taxi driver was fixing for us, it finally became apparent that he wanted to set up a fishing trip. He would speak to his brother-in-law about the possibility of taking us on a fishing trip aboard his relative's boat so we could see exactly how it was all done.

"Good," I said. "That would be very kind of you." I told him where we were staying. He said he would leave word there in a couple days.

With a doffing of his hat and his less formal chauffeur bow, the wiry little man bid us adios and hurried off to take up his fish vendoring duties.

"I think you better count me out on that one," said Julie.

"But you like fishing."

"Sure but not for any of those things we saw. I'll do mine from shore with a cane pole. You go. They'll never miss me. Besides, I think there's some superstition about women on fishing boats, anyway. Maybe Harper will go with you."

"Well, we'll see. It might not even come off," I said.

11

Recycling the Past

That afternoon we found Majorca's flea market. It was buried far back behind the more touristy part of Palma. It was not there every day, just on Sundays. You had to know how to find it. A small travel guide to the island published by one of its expatriates led as there. It was a marvelous place.

It occupied an entire tree-lined street. Here was recycling at its best. Anything ever made, no matter what its condition, was displayed there. It was as though the entire contents of a junkyard was separated piece by piece and lovingly laid out on display by itself on the tiled walk side-by-side with a million other pieces of old, oddities of the past. No matter how old, broken or abused, it was all for sale. Yours for the bargaining. Used and abused automobile parts were displayed with equal vigor along with the mechanical entrails of motorcycles, bicycles, scooters, and baby strollers.

It took a discerning eye to know which was what. And if in doubt, a quick question to the vendor who sat behind or amongst his offerings, always got an answer. It might not always answer your question but you got an answer.

After the "general items" came specialty items. An elderly woman sat on a wooden kitchen chair in black kerchief, heavy black overcoat and black felt slippers. Her specialty was chains. Her display laid around her on the sidewalk. Most were heavy-duty work chains of every description. Some with strange looking links and peculiar attachments vague-ly resembling manacles, might have come straight out of a castle dun-geon. They were all there, not in piles of links but stretched out decora-tively like metal snakes so by-passers could see exactly what they were buying. Beside them were pipes, pulleys, and mysteriously bent and shaped rods of all sizes.

Next to the iron merchant and the chain woman was the bottle man. Like the fish in the market, the bottles were carefully arranged by size in ranks and files by the hundreds. They ranged from the smallest vial and discarded aspirin bottle to the grandest mega-gallon wine jug, some of the latter still in their wrapped rope outer containers shaped for carry-ing and sitting. Others devoid of these wrappings showed their inner beauty of bubbled and flawed green or clear glass fraught with the imperfections of the hasty local bottle blowers.

One of the latter—a big green one—caught Julie's eye at once and the dickering over price began. No one had any idea what we were going to do with a 20-gallon long-necked green wine jug, but the treasure was too fine to pass up. In a moment of weakness, we surrendered the pese-tas for the prize and it was ours to lug along over my shoulder. The widely grinning bottle vendor was happy to find someone willing to accept his third offered price. My wife was equally pleased to obtain such a natural work of art. I figured if it didn't fit on the motor scoot-er, we could ship the treasure home.

Unfortunately, before we escaped with the one fine example of Mallorcain glass blowing at its worse, we spotted an even larger hand-blown clear glass wine jug rippling with imperfectly swirled, bubbled and hair-line cracked glass too strikingly crude to resist. Julie hardly even bargained for that one. It was amazing how easily it was done. In mere minutes we acquired two large items of extremely imperfect crys-tal that would never fit on our motor scooter, but which perhaps could hold a year's supply of wine for us.

Beside the bottle merchant was the tin smith sitting amid a galaxy of newly fashioned tin funnels, pans, big and little pitchers, cups, mugs and cans so bright you had to shade your eyes to look directly at him. Again, there was nothing haphazard about the way he displayed his wares. With what must have taken infinite patience, everything was arranged by its size, shape and kind.

After the tin smith came the wood-worker's wares, then the leather worker, the man selling old ceramic tiles, the electrician who was trying to sell everything from broken switches and mountains of discarded wire, to old burned out light bulbs of every size imaginable. We wondered who might want those.

Spaced between the vendors were individuals selling trays of toys, food, and assorted patent medicines. One enterprising sidewalk salesman had testimonials printed on cards clipped all over his coat and display tray while he gestured and talked about the miracles of the pills he was selling. What attracted bystanders more than the signs and his loud hawking was the long sharp knife apparently driven through the man's gesticulating left forearm just above the wrist.

That got attention. Nobody seemed to care that the red-daubed rag wrapped around his arm where the blade of the knife protruded on both sides might hide some ploy. Passersby were already engrossed in the man's spiel. The trick knife had done its trick.

Somewhere along the way we acquired another objet d'art to accompany the two big wine jugs I carried over my shoulders. Neither of us knew what it was, but it would have been a fine conversation starter at any party. Especially when hung on a wall. My wife, however, had visions of it holding a potted plant. In either event, from among all of the other far more practical brush-bottomed brooms, wicker racks, new and used wicker and rope baskets of all conceivable kinds, this one alone caught our eye as being the most provocative of all.

"What is it?" asked Julie.

"A basket?"

"I know that, but what's it for?"

"Beats me. Its got such a rounded bottom it would never set up straight as long and narrow as it is."

"Might make a nice planter in a windowsill though."

"What windowsill? Our room is still dark at 11 o'clock in the morning. A plant would die."

"Well, *hopefully*, we're not going to stay at the Monetenegro all of our lives."

"And with Christmas coming it could make a great gift for someone…."

My wife looked at me to see if I was smiling.

"Just one thing bothers me," I said. "It's that leather glove or something stitched onto the end of it"

"There's the man, ask him what it is."

The basket-and-broom merchant wearing large sunglasses and an over-sized black beret pulled so low to his ears it made his head look like a big mushroom, saw the object of our attention, snatched it up and homed in on us with a large smile.

"You desire?" he asked.

"No, no." I said. "But what is it?"

"*Una cesta*. A basket," he said.

I told him I could see that. But what kind of basket? For what? For fish?"

The man stared at me for the blink of an eye, then said. "Oh, *Si, si!* Very good for fish." He held the basket out to us. "You take. Put in big fish." He swished his hand back and forth inside the long basket, showing us how nicely the fish would fit there.

"No, that can't be right," said Julie. "It's too long and slender for a serving tray. Especially with that leather glove sewed on the end of it, for crying out loud. What's that for?"

"Maybe it's something used for catching fish."

I glanced at the smiling vendor and made a scoop with my hand. "For catch fish?" I made a scooping up motion in the air.

"*Si, si!*" A chorus of voices answered around us. Our discussion had attracted a small crowd.

"*MUY bien!*" said a woman at my elbow in a rabbit-fur-collared coat and kerchief who carried a couple canaries in a tiny homemade cage. "Good basket. Very strong." She too made the scooping motion with her free arm.

I nodded politely and smiled at the helpful lady. But out of the corner of my mouth I said to my wife, "Beats me. They somehow use it for scooping up fish, I guess."

"That's all right, get it anyway. It looks like its scooping days are over. We'll make a planter out of it."

"Excuse me," said a voice in Spanish over my shoulder. "Do you know the *cesta*?"

"No," I admitted. "We don't know this basket at all."

"But you play?"

"What?"

"*Pelota.* Ball. *Juego de palota.* Play ball?" The distinguished black-over-coated gentleman in the moustache and goatee swished his arm vigorously through the air.

As he did, the crowd broke out with a spontaneous "*Olé!*"

"Ah, baseball. Homerun!" I said expectantly.

Some of the crowd with me answered yes indeed, bazebawl. But my goateed friend shook his head no. "No bazebawl," he said.

"Permit me." Swiftly reaching inside his coat he produced a card and handed it to me

It said: FRONTON BALEAR, under which was an address. In the corner it read: Manager, José Maximilian.

"We shook hands. We smiled at each other and I introduced my wife. I still had no idea what the man managed. Thankfully, by then the people around us were losing interest and going about their business. Meanwhile, without haggling over the price, my wife purchased the basket-like object that had started all the conversation in the first place.

"I'm sorry, " I told our new acquaintance, "But what is a '*fronton*'?"

"Ahhhh....ball...court....You know jai-alai?" And again he swished his arm through the air. He pointed at the basket. To throw ball. Play jai-alai."

As it slowly began to make sense, so did the glove attached to one end of the long claw-like basket. It was this long curved wicker basket that extended a person's arm by a good two feet so that jai-alai players could catch and throw the ball.

"Yes, yes. I think we understand now," I told the fronton manager. "Jai-alai. No baseball." We laughed.

Señor Maximilian tapped our purchase. "You...come...*fronton*," he told me in his halting English. "I teach you Spanish ballgame."

"Thank you," I said. "I might do that."

Still smiling, the *fronton* manager touched his finger to his brow and hurried on his way.

"That was kind of him," said Julie.

"It surely was."

"Does that mean I don't get to use my purchase as a planter?"

"Maybe. We better wait and see how the jai-alai lessons go first."

When we finally reached the flea market's used books, perusing them was easier than I thought. Nothing was written in English. Except one thick hardcover book in its original paper dust jacket. The volumn looked as though no one had bothered to read it. It was Ernest Hemingway's *Death In the Afternoon*.

"Guess I better get it," I told Julie. "If we're going to learn anything about bullfighting, we'd better get started."

"I hope you don't meet a manager who wants to teach you *that*!" she said

12

Fisherfolks

Later that afternoon, after hauling our purchases back to the Montenegro in a taxi, Julie and I drove the Lambretta a short ways down the coast where we had seen people fishing off the rocks with long cane-poles.

Parking the Lambretta beside the highway we carefully began climbing toward the anglers. As we approached they welcomed us with broad smiles and vigorous hand-waving, obviously pleased to see *exstranjeros* risking life and limb to climb out through rugged rocks without fishing gear just to watch the action.

When we arrived they all greeted us as though we were family. They were having a wonderful time. Several families were there, ranging from the smallest child to the eldest *patron*. The latter vigorously kept up a constant litany of encouragement to everyone concerned. They had packed picnic lunches in wicker baskets which they kindly offered us, along with swigs from their wine bottles. Thanking them for their generosity we declined.

The steep rocks were so rough and convoluted that each angler clung to whatever projection afforded itself, fishing straight down the rocky precipice into any number of rock pockets and coves directly below. With the waves crashing in and out and the anglers clinging to their perches like determined limpets, it seemed like a rather precarious sport but they were all as adroit in getting around these rocks as mountain goats. It was obviously not their first time there.

Along with a long cane pole, each angler carried a small container of bread dough. From his perch in the rocks he made dough-balls the size of marbles and began pitching them into the water.

After about eight such dough-balls, he then baited his fishhook with a similar sized piece of bacon fat. This he tossed out in the center of the area he had been baiting with dough balls. About the time the bacon bait dropped down into the crystal clear water, one of the rock fish that had been feeding on the bread, took the look-alike fat ball and discovered his mistake too late.

The fish caught was usually about three inches long. Everyone cheered the catcher and the catch was swiftly dropped into a small pail. Back went the angler to pitching dough balls, and then the false one. It was great fun and the competition between families ran high. Whenever anyone caught a fish that was six inches long, it was cause for celebration. Everyone shouted excitedly and hurried over to inspect the catch, passing it around so that everyone saw it, then the *bota*, the leather bag of wine with its tiny horn mouthpiece for squirting the wine into one's mouth made its rounds. Everyone squirted themselves a healthy victory drink of *vino tinto* before returning to the hunt, eager for the next big catch.

It was an interesting way of fishing. Nobody seemed to be catching anything but very small fish, but size seemed less important than the fact that everyone was enjoying themselves.

When I asked one of the fishermen if they ever caught larger fish, he smiled at me from under his tilted beret and shook his head.

"Where are all the big fish?" I asked.

He shrugged. "All gone," he said. He pointed at the rocks below him, intertwined his gnarled fingers and said the nets had taken them all. Through gestures and sputtered words I managed to get the meaning. "They hang their nets right here on the rocks they trawl so close," I understood him to say. He pointed toward one of the trawlers that was even then moving out of the harbor with its big nets swaying in the wind.

I nodded that I understood.

The man shot me a "that's the way it goes" look and shrugged. I suspected that if these rock fishermen couldn't afford the expensive big fish we saw in the market, at least they had the makings for a fine fish soup.

A couple days later, Vicenti caught us coming out of the American Express. He was back in the taxi business again chauffeuring tourists in his old Citröen.

"*Muy buenos amigos mio!*" he greeted us enthusiastically. "I have good news from my brother-in-law, the captain."

Vicenti told us that he had explained to his brother-in-law that two *Norteamericanos, muy simpatico*, were interested in seeing how the fishermen caught fish on Mallorca. He said we would be "honored guests" aboard if we didn't mind fishing on an overnight trip to *Isola Cabrera*, "Goat Island" twenty-nine miles away. All we needed was a "*permiso*" from the harbormaster and to meet the fishing boat *Esperanza* moored along the quay before she sailed two days from then. His brother-in-law's name was Captain Quintana.

I thanked Vicenti for the trouble he had gone to, apologized for my wife not going, but said I had a friend who might enjoy it. I promised to get the proper documents from the harbor official, and to find the boat in advance.

"*Bueno. No problema,*" our taxi driving friend assured us, grinning broadly. "*Hasta la vista!*" With a wave, and a blast of blue Citröen vapors, Vicenti roared off to the waterfront to meet the incoming boat from Barcelona.

Harper was almost beside himself with enthusiasm when I asked if he wanted to go with me on the *Esperanza* fishing trip.

"What a super idea!" he said. "Give Binky a break from having to be with me all the time."

While we were gone, Julie and Binky planned to look into some of the real-estate offices we had seen showing pictures of island villas for rent. It might be the solution to having heat: a fireplace of our own! Not to mention a real house to live in! We had talked over the idea earlier but had not seriously looked into it. With Julie and Binky working up renewed enthusiasm for the quest, Harper and I felt less guilty about getting out of the way and going fishing. Let the experts do the house-hunting.

The day before we were to leave, Harper and I went down to the waterfront and eyed the more sturdy looking crafts moored in picturesque confusion to the stone wharf. The boats came in all sizes and shapes, like so many things on this island.

The long piers and branching quays of the Club Nautico handled the fancy, super-expensive power yachts and sailing vessels of the affluent. There they sat one after another, resplendent in their immaculate brilliance, resting like magnificent white swans in their orderly little ponds.

Closer ashore, however, crookedly moored amongst a forest of masts along the sea-wall of the Paseo Maritimos were the work boats, some of the small ones garishly painted in violent reds, yellows, and oranges. Their half-furled sails, drooping rigging, dangling nets, teetered baskets, jumbled oars and general disarray was in striking contrast to the slick, clean, orderly, shipshape demeanor of their next-door neighbors at the yacht club whose spotless white yachts stood out in striking contrast to this motley fleet.

No sportily dressed yachtsmen here, these were working fishermen. The men wore heavy rubber boots, thick canvas trousers, wool shirts, sweaters and jackets that warmed them at sea every day of their lives. Disorder came naturally. All that mattered to them was that everything worked. To a man, they invariably protected their heads with heavy black berets. And almost to a man, each usually kept a cigarette smoldering in the corner of his lips. Often a brand of black tobacco believed conducive to general good health because the smoke was strong enough to pucker nostrils. A single deeply inhaled drag on one of these cigarettes could curl toenails, proof positive that black tobacco was good for anything.

All the fishing vessels along this area were moored with their bows pointing into the stone quay. Some of the smaller ones were double-ended with pointed bow and stern, their gunwales lined with spaced iron thole pins where the men manned the oars when winds were unfavorable. Others had crudely built engine boxes amidships and square sterns where several large-globe, metal smoke-stack-ventilated kerosene lamps hung out over the water on braced supports. These were lights for the nighttime squid fishermen.

As the cobbled quay turned back toward the sea, there were moored the big 200 and 300 ton fishing barks, their single heavy masts mounted just aft their deck house, their decks crowded with the massive iron winches and coiled cables of the trawler fleet. Heavy brown nets often draped from masthead to stern, drying in the sun. Others had spread their damaged nets on the quay where wizened old men sat laboriously mending the huge trawls.

Harper and I looked over the fleet but failed to find the *Esperanza*. So we searched for the official who was to issue our permission to go fishing.

Our first stop was the Mariners' Union. They pointed us in the direction of the Port Authority's office. In due course we were presented to the Commandant of the Port, gold braid and all. He was a portly gentleman with a deeply tanned face, gray eyes, and cropped black hair streaked with gray. Once he understood who we were, the harbor official greeted us with a smile that was more bemusement than protocol. He asked curiously why we tourists wanted to waste our time aboard one of the dirty fishing boats. We weren't going into the smuggling business were we? His smile widened.

Harper who seemed to have a fairly good command of the language explained that we had seen the impressive display of fish in the market and now as curious tourists we were more than ever interested in seeing exactly how these fish were caught.

Apparently pleased by our curiosity, the beaming *Commandante di Puerto* gave us the registration number of the *Esperanza* and told us in which part of the wharf she would be found. He suggested we check in advance with the captain, and that our *permiso*, officially signed and stamped would be in the hands of our captain in time to sail the following night. As we were about to leave he shook our hands, wished us good luck fishing and sent on our way to find the vessel whose name in English meant "Hope."

13

Aboard the Good Ship *Esperanza*

We finally found the fishing trawler *Esperanza* tucked in between two other giant trawlers at the far end of the wharf. She looked no different than the rest, just a big, gray, massive fishing boat with a rough hewn telephone post of a mast thrust up behind the small four-port wheelhouse whose only festive touch was to be painted guacamole green from its middle to the deck.

The vessel's trawl net draped like an elongated brown cocoon from masthead to stern. Three men aft busily shoveled crushed ice into the hold. A man in a black beret and heavy-knit yellowed turtleneck sweater stood at the wheelhouse door studying a chart. A 12-foot-long plank reached from the wharf to the vessel's starboard bow where it was tied to a bow bitt. Below the gangplank was the bark's name painted in squared black letters. Well down her hull between her green-painted scupper line and her red-painted water line printed in tall black block letters and numerals was the vessel's registration number.

We walked up to the bow of the trawler and called to the man at the wheelhouse. We asked if Captain Quintana was aboard.

"*Soy Quintana,* " he said. He lay the chart in the wheelhouse and strode up to the bow. "*Que queras?*" he asked.

As best I could I explained that I was *Señor* Vicenti's friend who wanted to see the fishing.

The captain squinted at us for a moment, then said, "Ahhhh, *si. El Norteamericano con la barba!*" Grinning, he stroked his chin and nodded at my beard. Then he glanced around. "But where is your wife?"

I explained that my friend Harper had come in her place.

"*Bueno.* I understand," he said. Fishing is not for women."

He led us aft to meet the two men shoveling ice. Both were heavy-set with creased faces the color of oiled leather. One was named Ramon, the other Gustavo. When we shook hands, theirs were rough with calluses, their grip hard as iron.

Both grinned and in gutteral voices mumbled, "*Mucho gusto.*"

Then the captain took us below deck. We followed him down through the hatch and steep steps leading to the forecastle just forward the foot of the mast. It was the crew's quarters in the forepeak of the vessel.

With no room to stand up, you stayed bent over. Angled along the port and starboard bulkheads were wooden sleeping racks, one above the other where six men could sleep three to a side. The racks were spaced so closely together that you either got into them on your stomach or on your back. And there you stayed. The racks were too close together to allow room to turn over. Each had a sideboard and thin stained mattress to cushion the bare boards on its bottom.

From the battered, smoked pots and pans hanging on nails from the large wooden foot of the stubby mast this area was used for cooking. But there was no sign of anything to cook on.

Captain Quintana pointed out the racks we would occupy, then led us out of the hold. He peered at each of us closely, as if wondering if we had any second thoughts yet about going fishing Mallorcain style.

But that wasn't what was really on his mind. He pointed at each of us, then he rubbed his stomach, rolled his eyes and acted out the classic symptoms of a good case of sea sickness. Then he again pointed at each of us and asked if we got sick like that.

Naturally Harper and I assured him that that was never any problem with us.

No, no." Harper wagged his finger at the thought.

Quintana frowned. *"Seguro?"* You're sure?

"No problema," smiled Harper confidently.

"Bueno!" Good. Until tonight at eleven, he said. We all shook hands again and Harper and I made our way ashore.

Walking back to the Borne, Harper wondered aloud where they cooked and what kind of food they ate on the *Esperanza*.

Considering the size of our sleeping quarters, I wondered where they planned to put Julie if she had come along.

Late that night, but well before the appointed hour we went aboard the *Esperanza*. The crew was already aboard and working. We tried to keep out of the way. Our crew acknowledged us with a grin and a nod but the men kept working, clearing the decks, tying off or coiling long loose lines, securing the vessel for the sea.

When everything was ready, the bow hawser was dragged aboard, along with the gangplank. Lines were tossed back that had moored us to adjacent boats at the wharf and the engineer cranked up the *Esperanza's* noisy engine.

In short order we were on our way out into the harbor with the colored lights of hotels and restaurants along the waterfront reflected in rainbows across the black mirrored harbor waters. Then with a roll and a groan from the old ships' timbers, we were out of the port and moving steadily toward the broad dark seas ahead. A chill breeze cut across the deck.

Working methodically in the glow of a deck light, the crew lowered the big trawl net, shackled it to its cables and eased it overboard.

Once the big pouch went down and spread open, the steel cables running over the large steel stern rollers strummed taut. The *Esperanza* slowed considerably under the increased strain. From the engine room the clattering of her machinery took on a more labored pitch.

Only the trawler's running lights and a half moon illuminated our presence on that black sea. As soon as the net was out, the crew vanished down the forecastle hatch as swiftly as rabbits popping into their burrow. In the faint glow of our wake all I saw was the dark figure of Captain Quintana with his heavy coat collar turned up, his beret pulled down to his ears. He was bent forward, his hands on the greased trawl cables, pushing first on one, then the other.

"Looks like it's just us and him," said Harper. "The crew disappeared so fast I thought they had abandoned ship."

"Guess that's all the excitement there is for the night." I said.

"Unless you want to race me to our stateroom," Harper replied.

14

Passage to Cabrera

"*Señor! Hola! Señor!*" Someone nudged my leg. I opened my eyes. I smelled smoke. A figure crouched beside me, outlined in a faint red glow. He jabbed me again.

"*Que pasa?* What's going on?" I asked.

The shape backed off. I painfully squeezed sideways out of my rack.

A patch of gray filtered down from the narrow hatch overhead. Beneath it the man who had awakened me squatted near a bucket of glowing charcoal in front of the mast foot. He stirred what smelled like strong coffee in a paint pail. I shivered in the chill of the Mediterranean dawn. Shoving the coarse blanket back into the rack, I checked to make sure I hadn't crushed my camera in the night. It was all right. I rubbed the welts its strap left on my neck and fumbled for my shoes on the rough wood deck below. Except for them, I was dressed.

The man in the shadows squeezed a ropy mixture of condensed milk and sugar out of a toothpaste tube into the pungent concoction in the paint pail. He sloshed it around a couple times, then poured some into a tin cup and held it out to me grinning.

"*Gracias.*" I gratefully took the steaming cup, wrapping my hands around it for warmth.

"If that's coffee," came a groggy voice from Harper's rack, "tell 'em no sugar."

"You tell I em," I said, shuddering as the syrupy liquid scorched a trail into the pit of my stomach. "He's already doctored the pot. I took two more healthy gulps, more for the warmth it offered than for the taste. Flavor-wise it tasted like ground up cigar butts.

I got up, bent over to keep from hitting the overhead. The deck was not level, it and the whole place was tilted and turning. My camera hung like an iron halter around my neck. I grabbed for a handhold and tried to go up the foot-worn ladder.

The cook caught my leg and pulled me back. He shooed away some cockroaches on the yellowed mast foot and plucked off another tin cup. Pouring it half full he handed it to me, motioning toward Harper's still recumbent form.

"Here's your morning wake-up, Harper." I reached it across to him. "It'll cure anything you're ever likely to catch."

"Thanks, buddy." Harper's hand crawled out from under his blanket and collected the offering. Half extracting himself from his slot, he took a sip.

With a quick swallow he gulped and wheezed. "Whowee!"

The cook chuckled. He pointed a knobby finger at my cup. I shrugged and held it out for more of his brew. Charcoal smoke was thick under the overhead. You didn't crouch there long. Thanking my benefactor with more than tears of gratitude in my eyes, I stepped up the first ladder rung, sat my cup topside, then climbed through the hatch into fresh air.

Everything was moving up and down and sideways in the flat gray world around us. The sea heaved and frothed, rigging rattled and banged, while the crew moved back and forth over the slippery wet deck that tilted first one way, then another. The motion didn't bother them in the least. They moved as easily as if the boat were moored in port.

The howling wind and throbbing diesel cleared away my last drowsy vestiges of sleep. Taking a big gulp of coffee, I looked around.

Somewhere ahead of us was the fog-bound island of Cabrera. Behind us a night's passage away lay the cliffs of Mallorca. On the high-pitched stern of the trawler, the stocky figure of Captain Quintana, now wearing a heavy sheep-skin vest, stood out against the eastern sky. Apparently, he had stayed there all night, his big hands pushing on the greasy trawl cables.

On the deck in front of him sat the trawler's compass in a black box. I'm sure he knew our course by heart.

The men never spoke. No one gave any orders. Everyone seemed to know what to do. The engineer stuck his long, bony face out of the engine room and wiped his sweaty brow with a dirty rag. His shapeless beret looked as though he used it regularly for cleaning his engine's pistons. He watched the captain. Then I noticed that even though the crew was busy, they all watched him, as if expecting a signal.

A signal for what? I wondered. What would he be signaling for in the middle of the Mediterranean with it not fully daylight yet?

Then, I knew why they had awakened me. The captain wanted me to see what was about to happen.

Quintana looked at the engineer and raised his clenched fist. The engineer ducked back into the engine room. The *Esperanza's* diesel slowed to a low-pitched growl. The crewmen in the stern moved aft and a couple stood by the big winch.

With another signal from Quintana, a small steam engine started, the machinery clanked into noisy action, lines were given a turn around drums, and the main cables began screeching in.

The *Esperanza* squatted on her haunches as her cables ground dripping and grating over the steel drums, slowly dragging up the heavy bottom-trawling fibrous brown net bag that had entrapped fish all night long.

It was a tedious process but the men knew what had to be done. Harper joined me with his steaming cup of coffee. The cook came topside to lend a hand. He was a gentle-faced man with large, big-knuckled hands. Tufts of white hair stuck out from under his cap, and his dark seamy face was made larger by a two-day growth of white beard. Being the eldest aboard, the others addressed him respectfully as "*Tío*" (Uncle), or "Pap."

Dawn came more rapidly now, brightening the gray sky.

"Did the captain get any sleep last night?" asked Harper.

"I don't know. When I came up he was where we left him still pushing on those cables."

"Damn!" said Harper. "It was colder than hell last night too."

Soon the huge mesh pouch of the trawl net was alongside. The men worked the equipment swiftly, unshackling some of the tackle, and re-shackling others. Chains rattled, the winch changed pitch. Blocks and tackle now were rigged to the mast boom and the lifting, hauling of the big pouch began in earnest.

The mast groaned, blocks squealed. The trawler canted heavily to starboard as the ponderous load rose slowly up out of the sea.

For a moment it hung alongside, swinging ponderously with the roll of the boat, dripping steadily from all quarters. Then as the crew assisted, it slid over the long log roller on the starboard gunwale and was swung inboard, just above the deck.

The big pouch was actually a net within a net. The outer bag was made of three-inch rope mesh, while the innermost was a fine mesh barely large enough for a finger to pass through.

One crewman stepped up and pulled a line. An avalanche of fish, squid, rays, pieces of broken coral and shells crashed onto the deck in a writhing mass.

Pap the cook hurried forward and pushed through the pile, grabbing fish and squid and flopping them into a wooden bucket. He disappeared down the forward hatch with it.

The big net was rigged again for trawling and went back over the side. Once more the engine throbbed into renewed action, the

Esperanza strained, and Captain Quintana went back to pumping his palms on the greased cables.

The cargo hatch cover was shoved aside. A crewman jumped down into the ice compartment and passed up wooden crates. As the *Esperanza* creaked and groaned her way through the heaving seas, the crew sat around the pile of fish and sorted the catch into the crates. All the *calamares* or squids went in with their heads one way, their legs the other. Small rays went in one box; large ones in another. The *rafallas*, because of their box-like bodies, went head to tail, as did the small sharks. The hake or *merluza* went in rows, and being slender fish they packed quickly and well. Small, brightly colored rock fish, the kind used for fish soup, went in a catch-all box, while a bulbous-headed fish the Mallorcains held up to us and pointed to the fishing-pole projection on its brow, went into a crate of its own. Their name for this angler of the deep, was *"rapa."*

"Very good to eat," the crewman named Ramon told us in Mallorcain. He was a large moon-faced man with no obvious neck. Like the others, his hands were huge.

It was light enough to snap some photographs now. I moved around the group taking shots from different angles. Then I went to the stern and photographed the captain. He was a stocky man, probably in his forties. Dark, swarthy face as if he had been in sun from the day he was born. He made a point of not grinning at the camera, or posing while I took the pictures. I appreciated that.

The wind was loud enough that I had to climb up alongside him to talk. I asked why he kept his hands on the cables all the time. With a combination of a few English words, gestures and slowly repeated Mallorcain words, he told me that he pumped the cables because he could feel for snags, the rocks that often caught the net. If the big pouch snagged, he had to stop the boat and back down on it to unsnag it, otherwise it would be ripped open and they would lose their catch.

Also, he said he felt for the dolphins. When I asked what he meant by that, he said the dolphins were the trawlers' worse enemies. They often attacked the nets and ripped them open to get at the fish inside. Captain Quintana had no use for dolphins.

I pointed at his hands and asked to see them. He frowned at this peculiar request, but he lifted them off the greasy cables and turned them palm up.

The other fishermens' hands had been large, but Quintana's was the size of small hams. His palms were three or four times normal size. Years on the trawl cables had taken their toll.

"*Gracias,*" I said. He nodded and went back to pumping.

15

Sea Rations

Pap passed out breakfast as quickly as he finished cooking it over his small bucket of coals. It consisted of charcoal broiled squid atop thick slabs of heavy crusted bread with olive oil drizzled over it.

The fishermen were busy with their tasks but I noticed that they furtively watched us, grinning broadly to see how we would react to their half-cooked breakfast.

"I don't think I can do this," Harper murmured under his breath, holding his topless squid sandwich in a way that suggested he would like to pitch it overboard.

"I know what you mean, but I don't think we have much choice. They're watching us. They want to see if we're going to go belly up on them, or what."

"I think I'd rather do that than eat. My stomach isn't feeling too great anyway."

"Don't even think about it," I told him. We're Americans for God's sake. Don't let them see we can't take it."

I bit a chunk out of the bread and squid. It tasted surprisingly good. "It's not bad," I told Harper.

I took another bite and nodded at the watching crew. They nodded back, grinning.

Harper nibbled around his squid, finally sampling it. Somehow, he managed to gulp it down, but I noticed his face was redder than usual. It wasn't easy for him to do.

Pap appeared with seconds. We both politely turned them down. With his other hand he passed us a large long-necked glass *porrón* filled with white wine.

The grinning crew ceased their labors and stopped to watch this new development.

From having seen it done before, and having tried it with the wine skin *botas*, we knew you were not supposed to put your lips around the slender spout and drink. Instead, you held the thing overhead and tilted it toward you, sort of like holding a straight-spouted teapot overhead and pouring the libation in the direction of your mouth.

To the amusement of the entire crew, only half the wine hit our mouths. The rest splashed on our faces and ran down our necks.

The fishermen roared. They thought that was the funniest thing they had seen in a long time. They gathered around as each demonstrated the proper way to drink out of a *porrón*.

It was an art. The trick seemed to be to start close to the mouth and once you had a steady stream splashing on target, you could then pull the *porr6n* back to arm's length and keep the thin stream arcing into your half-closed mouth. If you didn't swallow quickly enough, you were in trouble. You either choked, got soaked, or both.

The way to shut off the stream was to bring the *porr6n* closer to the mouth again, then quickly tilt it upward, abruptly stopping the flow.

One of the fishermen was apparently more expert at handling the *porrón* than the others. He was the big moon-faced Ramon. They pushed him out in front and handed him the *porr6n* to demonstrate.

Grinning somewhat shyly, the big man took the delicate glass wine container with his large rough hand. Holding it a foot from his face, with an abrupt downward tilt he shot a thin stream of wine out that struck him squarely in the deep seam running from the side of his nose to the corner of his mouth.

By tilting his head and keeping the wine directly on the seam, he adroitly ran the swift-flowing stream into the corner of his mouth without spilling a drop. His Adam's apple danced as he swallowed at high speed.

Finishing his performance to the loud approval of the crew, he held the *porrón* out to me, grinning and pointing to the crease beside his nose.

"Thank you but no thank you," I said. "You, are…" I pointed at him. "Numero *Uno!*" Number one.

Everyone laughed, repeating what I said while slapping the broadly grinning Ramon on his back, then the good-natured crew went back to work. Once all the fish were boxed, they were stored in the hold. Crushed ice was shoveled into each container, and it was stacked.

As the men worked, I moved around them taking pictures. They were much more receptive to us now. The wine-drinking episode had helped. Harper stayed close by to translate if I needed help. Between the two of us, we did fine.

Once the fish were packed away the men were free to do whatever they wanted. Some disappeared back into the forecastle. Captain Quintana was replaced by Gustavo at the helm. The captain went below to sleep.

Sebastian the engineer was the only one who spoke a smattering of English, and wanted to practice it on us. He said he had once been a schoolteacher in Catalonia, one of the northeastern coastal provinces of Spain. After his wife died, he had no family so he went to sea. Mainly because it suited him better.

I asked if what we had caught was typical.

"Sad to say, yes." He stood in the companionway of his engine compartment. It was hot down there where the pistons and tappets beat out a rhythmical noise. Rivulets of sweat trickled past the deep crow's feet lines in the corners of his eyes. From time to time he wiped them with a handful of oil-stained cotton waste. He kept his beret low enough on his head that only his bony face and bushy brows were evident. The hands sticking out of his ragged sleeves were those of a man used to the hardest kind of manual labor.

I told Sebastian that we were surprised by the many different kinds of fish in the fish market. Did the *Esperanza* catch those kinds of fish?

"No," he said. "Those good fish come from far away. The tuna closer to Africa. He said the big trawlers did that kind of fishing. The *Esperanza* got the leavings. And that was pretty bad."

"Was it always that way around Mallorca?" asked Harper.

"No, no. Once even the tuna came here. Now they are scarce. And there were big sea bass, and lots of lobsters. But when one has only the sea to feed everyone, and can't go far from home to find fish, then pretty soon few fish remain. Some of the fishermen in long boats still row far out and try for tuna with hand-lines or nets, he said, but it is a hard life and the schools hardly ever come this way any longer. He said Julio the cook, Pap, was once one of the oar-boat fishermen, but they made him stop fishing with them.

"Why was that?" I asked.

Sebastian shrugged. "Said he was getting too old to pull his weight any more. Even his two sons said that. They are in the boats. They replaced Pap with a younger man"

"That's very hard work," said Harper

"Indeed. Pap's whole life was working those oar-boats." Sebastian laughed but his thin straight lips weren't smiling. "The old man is still trying to show those young fellows a thing or two," he said. "He figures if he can prove to the long-boaters that he's still '*mucho hombre*', they'll take him back on the oar-boats."

"But how can he prove it?" I asked.

Sebastian shrugged. "By being better than they are. By doing something they haven't been able to do."

"Such as?" Harper asked.

Sebastian shrugged. "By making a fool of himself."

Harper frowned. "How?" he asked.

Sebastian pulled out a pack of Ideales cigarettes, offered us one, then stuck one in the corner of his mouth and lit it. He exhaled a cloud of smoke before answering.

"Pap lives at San Agustin up the coast from Palma. Many of the oar-boats work out of there. It's a rugged coast. Always been good for the fishermen there. Generations grew up fishing that place. They keep trying to fish the old traditional way. But the big fish are not there any more. They swim far away. So the fishermen sail far from the coast with their fishing gear. Sometimes they get tuna, mostly they don't. But the coast they fished to death. Near San Agustin, there is one big fish everyone knows about but nobody can ever catch. They call him *El Señor*. When they retired Pap from the boats last year, he swore he would catch *El Señor* and show everyone that he was not as useless as they thought. What bravado!" grinned Sebastian shaking his head.

"So, what happened?"

"What always happens," the engineer told me. "*El Señor* keeps breaking his lines."

"That thing must be a monster!" said Harper. "What kind of fish is it?"

"Who knows?" Sebastian took a long drag on his Ideales. "Nobody has ever seen it. My guess is it's a big sea bass. Big ones used to live in caves around the island until they all finally got caught. But nobody was ever strong enough to catch this gentleman. That's why they call him *El Señor*. He stays in this one cave and gobbles up every bait they bring him. Breaks all the lines no matter how heavy they are. What he doesn't chew through he snaps in two. Nobody wastes their time trying anymore. Just Pap." The skinny man's eyebrows lifted as he touched his forehead with a bony grease-stained finger. "*Poco loco* in the *coco*," I think. Sebastian's thin lips stretched into a grin.

At midday the crew began coming out of the forecastle where Pap had been working over his charcoal bucket of coals. Everyone sat around the big cargo hatch until the cook emerged with the noon meal.

He served it in two large metal dishpans. One was a typical Mallorcain *paella*, saffron rice with shellfish, shrimp, crabs and squid in it. The other pan contained boiled fish. The hungry crew surrounded the pans and grabbed handsful of the sticky rice concoction, shoving it into their mouths.

"Hey!" yelled Pap. "We got guests!" He looked at Harper and me expectantly. "Eat," he said grinning and rubbing his stomach. "It keeps away the sea sickness."

"Oh, oh," said Harper under his breath. The rest of the crew had stopped momentarily and were passing the *porrón*.

"*Comé! Comé!*" eat, eat, insisted the old man.

I scooped up a handful of rice. It was hot, sticky and loaded with the pungent flavor of saffron. Harper did likewise, making a show of really liking what he was doing.

The fish was something else. The best had been boxed. They were too valuable to be eaten by the crew. Instead, they ate *rafallas*, a species with horned heads and partly shell-like bodies. It was a trash fish we call a sea robin. Only the tail portion is edible.

"Those things are whole!" whispered Harper as he watched me take one of the fish. "They're not even *cleaned*!"

The crew watched us intently. I took a bite out of the fish's tail and ate it. "Ummm, *bueno*!" I tried to look pleased. The half-cooked fish stuck in my throat. I gulped it down. "Not bad at all," I commented to Harper who was also watching me intently to see if I would choke.

"But what about the *guts?*"

"Just do like they do," I whispered. "Eat around them." Cooking had turned them into small firm packets easily avoided anyway.

Once the crew saw we were at least trying to eat their fare, they lost no time digging in themselves. The men went at the fish as if they were eating ears of corn. The bones and viscera went flying over the side. In between sticky hands full of *paella* and gulped down fish, the *porrón* made its rounds. In fact, it never stopped. The long-spouted wine bottle moved from man to man around the circle. By the time we finished the meal, everyone was feeling warm and friendly. Everyone but Harper.

I wished I could help him. I knew he was feeling the rolling of the vessel more than ever, but was putting up a brave front. Having to eat half boiled, uncleaned fish in front of an audience while your insides are turning flip-flops was beyond the call of duty.

"Fake it the best you can," I said. "Just don't get sick."

He groaned through clenched teeth. "I'm tired of waving the American flag...lot rather go puke."

Ramon passed me the *porrón*. I took a fast swallow and passed it on to Harper.

"Here. Maybe this will help."

He shot me a look. "You kidding?" Without sampling the wine he passed it on to an eagerly waiting Sebastian who swiftly gulped his share plus Harper's too.

After the crew ate, Captain Quintana came on deck yawning. He dropped down beside Harper and had no trouble putting away his share of the fish and rice.

Glancing over at me he said, "No good seas today. To much tramontana. How is your health?"

"I knew what he was asking. "Fine, very fine," I said.

Captain Quintana shot a glance at Harper, but all he could do was grin crookedly and nod.

16

The Storm

Our day began like the previous one. The net was put out and the crew slept for three hours before it was hauled again, and the fish put away in the belly of the trawler. Breakfast was roast squid and *rafallas*. Harper and I both did better this time, managing to demolish several of the fish the way the crew did. They especially enjoyed watching us trying to manage their *porrón*.

The fishermen now accepted us, no longer eyeing us with suspicion. They shared what they had good-naturedly, and took pleasure in being able to answer our questions or show us how they fished. They said it was the first time they had ever met Americans like us. They seemed pleased that we were interested enough in them to share their simple but hard way of life. Their best compliment was to shake their heads and say, *"Americanos, si, pero turistas, no!"* Americans, yes, but tourists, no. Then they added, "We are all fishermen here!"

Sometime shortly before noon, Pap climbed quickly out of the forecastle with the news that his cockroaches were running around the mast foot like crazy. He said we could expect bad weather ahead.

We hurried to look. The cook was right about the roaches. I never saw such a nervous crowd. Their antennas were twitching this way and that. They were in a state of what I could only describe as nervousness, darting this way and that, twitching their feelers at everything in sight.

The way they moved around on the mast foot you'd have thought it had suddenly grown red hot.

At Pap's announcement the whole crew disappeared down the hatch, leaving Captain Quintana to push on the cables. Even Gustavo, the quietest member of the crew who spent every free moment either reading cowboy books, or sleeping, joined the crowd below. From their eagerness I didn't think they were headed to bed, mainly because the *porrón* disappeared below with them.

Curious, we stuck our heads down the hatch to see what was going on. Pap was in charge. His bucket of coals had disappeared. He had chalked a large circle on the rough deck timbers below. Ramon had picked cockroaches off the mast foot and handed them to the others. The big bugs were marked on their backs with matches dipped in white paint that Pap produced from his unlimited resources behind the mast. Then, all the marked roaches were placed in a small cardboard box. At a given signal it was over-turned in the center of the circle and lifted. The roach races were on!

A bit stunned with all this, and perhaps a bit boozy from the paint fumes while in the box, the race roaches momentarily stood their ground in circle center and twitched their antennas. That's when the betting began, and the louder it got the more agitated became the roaches, darting first that way, then the other, twitching antennas and wondering perhaps what all the hoopla was going on around them.

Betting was fast and furious on which bug would cross the line first.

Actually, it wasn't really that simple but that's the way we perceived it. In truth I believe they were having *quinellas* and other complicated betting arrangements beyond our comprehension. In any case the *pesetas* went in and out of the circle with each match, the men whooped for their favorites, and the never empty *porrón* moved around the circle continuously without ever touching the deck. The roach race was a huge success.

Pap's warning that his nervous pet roaches forecast bad weather was absolutely accurate. Darkening skies and worsening sea conditions finally brought the bad news in the form of a series of line squalls. With the freshening winds and growing seas *Esperanza* bucked and shuddered on her cable tethers. As conditions worsened the trawl was hastily winched in and its meager catch quickly dispatched below.

The *Esperanza* continued to fight her way back toward Mallorca. Without the big net to drag behind us now, it was easier sailing. By noon the vessel lay at anchor off the southern coast of Mallorca, in the lee of the inlet at Cala Pi.

"Close in is where we fish when the weather gets too bad outside," Sebastian told us.

Pap's *paella* and *rafallas* were consumed in the relatively sheltered cove, then the trawler weighed anchor and we moved further out where the net went down again.

Three hours later it was brought in badly cut by rocks. There was no catch. The crew stared at the deflated mesh bag with stony faces. The wind changed and the bad weather gradually moved in, diminishing the narrow area that could be trawled.

As the trawler headed toward Palma, the late afternoon sky looked like something El Greco painted over Toledo: blue, gray and angry. Our comparative calm was quickly changing. Expanses of water leaped and boiled as though from a rip tide, or an explosion of fear-crazed bait fish. It was the wind gusting at ever increasing velocity. Then as it blew harder but more evenly, the *Esperanza's* strumming rigging suddenly jumped several octaves from its customary moan to settle on a nerve-jarring wail. On the darkening horizon a trawler came out of port heading southward toward Cabrera. It was a larger, far more seaworthy vessel than we were, explained Sebastian. He also said they wouldn't make it.

In the next half-hour, two more vessels followed the first, all three strung out at even intervals like pigeons on a telephone wire. The crew of the *Esperanza* watched the black shapes enviously. When the first, then the second, and finally the third buckled from the squall and turned back, they were jubilant.

"There goes the *Santa Maria*," yelled Ramon, braced against the wheelhouse, his bull neck swelled tight against the collar of his worn jacket. He shook his fist at the black trawlers. *"Que se vaya hombre!* Get the hell out of there, man!"

The whole crew jeered.

It grew dark, a purple black darkness that glowed dirty yellow from an obscured sun. To our right, off the starboard side of the trawler lay the jagged brown rocky crags of the island, surmounted here and there with the crumbling remains of Moorish towers. At the base of the cliff, the frothing sea threw an angry white choker around the broken rocks,

Humping into the oncoming black seas, the trawler hugged this coastline, seeking some measure of calm. But instead, the large waves crashed into her port bows, flooding the foredeck and boiling out scuppers on her starboard side. Captain Quintana stayed on the stern poop while Ramon, wedged into the telephone booth-sized wheelhouse, piloted the boat. Harper and I clung to the portside ratlines and stays as best we could, dodging the spray. Oddly enough, it had not yet begun to rain where we were, but you could see it tearing up the water offshore.

One of the three trawlers on the horizon changed its mind about going into port, and instead came wallowing toward us at high-speed down-wind. The captain and the stone-faced Ramon stayed above deck. Sebastian was deep in his engine house urging his diesel into prodigious feats of speed. Pap and Gustavo hunkered down in the forecastle passing the *porrón* and racing Pap's pets. Nobody seemed unduly concerned about the weather, but Harper and I stayed topside where we could keep an eye on developments. If something cataclysmic occurred, we wanted to be ready to jump overboard.

I looked gloomily at Harper. "How are you at swimming?" he asked.

Captain Quintana shouted over the wind. The on-rushing trawler was just off our port bow, aiming to shave us close. Suddenly the whole crew was there with us, lining the rail.

Quintana jumped forward, the whole crew leaned out over the side as the trawlers streaked pass each other, the captain of the other trawler in the waist, leaning out, hands cupping his mouth as he shouted into the shriek of the wind.

Whatever he shouted made the crew jump in all directions at once. Quintana shouted orders and the *Esperanza's* bow chewed into the onrushing seas as Ramon spun the wheel and swerved the boat sharply to port.

It appeared that we were on a collision course with something. But what?

We lined the opposite rail with the rest of the crew, straining to see in the inky storm-slashed waters.

We weren't disappointed,

It was hard to say who saw it first but the yell went up, everyone pointed, and there close to our starboard bow on a collision course was a large dark-colored spherical object.

The fishermen yelled, Quintana shouted over the wind, the *Esperanza* shook violently as her diesel whined and roared in reverse, chattering deck beams in an effort to stop our forward motion. Then, begrudgingly she tried to crawl slowly astern. The seas boiled forward from beneath her hull. The engine roared, the vessel shuddered. With every throb, every violent eddying swirl, the black object seemed only to be sucked closer to the wallowing trawler.

I glanced up at the mast, calculating which way it would probably topple if we went over. Harper was already hugging the port gunwale, clinging to the stays.

The *Esperanza* continued to wallow. There was no collision. Sweat suddenly grew cold on our brows. The engine changed pitch, the boat changed course and we headed out to sea, apparently out of danger. Harper, looking sheepish let go of the stays.

The crew crowded around us jabbering excitedly. The object we had seen was a buoy marking the maw of a giant tuna net. We had almost torn it to shreds.

Not long after dark, the *Esperanza* slid into the smoother waters of the bay. Harper and I never saw it. We were jammed down in the crew's quarters having a last *porrón* with the laughing fishermen. In those two days, over four gallons of wine were consumed from that faithful *porrón*.

When we again climbed back up on deck, the *Esperanza* was easing into her slip along the wharf. Long, colored streamers of light glazed the still black water of the harbor. The wind had slackened considerably but outside the seas still continued to roll. Across the harbor the white *Ciudad di Barcelona* loomed brightly beneath spotlights as she loaded passengers for the night trip to the mainland. High on the hill the cathedral's spires were illuminated. Silhouettes of palm trees in the foreground nodded in the diminished breezes. People would soon be walking the Borne.

As we were leaving Captain Quintana grinned and shook our hands. He said we were always welcome aboard the *Esperanza*. Sebastian said he was sorry he hadn't taken us down inside his engine room and introduced us to his shiny machinery. Pap, luxuriating with one of my Philip Morris cigarettes he had saved for a special occasion, shook our hands and said, "*Venga a San Agustín. I show you where El Señor lives!*"

I told him we would come, and shoved my pack of smokes into his jacket pocket. We all shook hands again. "Good luck. Good fishing. *Vaya con Dios, amigos.*"

Walking home that night, Harper said. "They didn't really know us, and we didn't really know them. But, you know," he said, "I really hated to leave them."

I grinned to myself. I knew the feeling. We all felt it. We may not have been able to speak each other's language too well, but for two days we had shared our lives together and had come to know and respect each other. "Tell you what, Harper. Let's stop for a last toast to the crew of the *Esperanza*. To Pap, to Quintana, to Sebastian, to every-one…a last *copita!*"

"Hey! I'll drink to that," grinned Harper.

And so we did.

17

House Hunting

The final decision to find a house of our own that we could heat, came the morning after it was so cold at the Hotel Montenegro that we went to bed in our overcoats.

Days earlier we had studied photographs of rental villas in the windows of various Palma real estate offices. The prices were stunning. We didn't want to buy, just rent. Then we were further stunned to realize the asking price *was* the rental fee. We were further stunned by several majestic villas in more distant parts of Majorca, or even on adjacent islands such as Ibiza, whose rental rates were astonishing reasonable. Moreover, they all overlooked the sea. In each instance, however, there was a small catch.

It all came down to logistics. You could be sure that if you found a marvelous, fully-furnished villa overlooking one of the most spectacular seaside views imaginable, at a rate so low you blushed, then logistics were involved.

For example, the villa on Ibiza. The photograph was beautiful. It looked like a bridal cake. Plenty of balconies and terraces, the kind of place Hollywood builds for its island movies. Always with an incredible view. But that was about it. Most of these outlying places had less basic amenities than a movie set. No electricity, no running water, and no nearby support base. On Ibiza the only road linking that villa to civilization, was a goat trail. Yet, what a marvelous hideaway villa where your privacy was assured, where you had an island paradise to yourself. All you had to do was hire a donkey cart to carry in your supplies with perhaps an extra donkey thrown in should you and your wife care to ride some miles back to town.

Ah, those logistics.

As for those large, sumptuous Majorcan villas being offered at rates we could pay outside Palma where the ocean view was "guaranteed to take your breath away," they too suffered from logistical problems. It got so that the questions and answers flowing between us and the real estate people, all began sounding alike:

"Do these villas have running water?"

"Yes, in a manner of speaking."

"In what manner of speaking?"

"Well, it runs down to your sink from pipes in the roof."

"*In the roof*! Isn't that rather novel?"

"Well, not for Majorca. Especially for these exclusive coastal villas."

"Would you please explain that in more detail?"

"Well, as I said, most of them have running water. It comes from rooftop catch-basins and runs down into your toilet and sinks from pipes in the roof."

"I see. Rainwater."

"That's correct."

"But it hasn't rained on Majorca for months. What then?"

"Then you buy bottled water in town."

"How many bottles worth is a bath? Or let's say one toilet flushing?"

"I'm sorry, I can't tell you that."

"I see. What about electricity?"

"Well, none of these have electricity"

"Hmmm, I guess we could do with oil lamps. Does no electricity mean no refrigerator?

"Yes, we're afraid so. But they all have cool, louvered pantries and here everyone shops almost daily for perishable food."

"How close is the nearest shopping center?"

"Usually only a few miles away."

"What kind of heat will the villas have?"

"There are often fireplaces."

"Is there some place near where one can chop firewood?"

"Well, no, wood is a fairly rare island commodity. But deliveries can be arranged. If you live where vehicles don't go, then donkey carts will bring you wood."

"Thanks," I usually said. "We'll think it over."

Unfortunately, we were getting desperate. So were our friends who were in the same situation. It was already unseasonably cold weather on Majorca and winter wasn't even officially there yet. What would it be like when it finally arrived? We were already wearing all the clothes we had to keep warm.

We weren't the only cold natured ones either. It got pretty bad when the only reason you had to go downtown was to sit on the sunny side of the street with everyone else in the neighborhood just to get warm. We all looked like a bunch of iguanas in overcoats and scarves, huddled on rocks facing the sun, basking in its warmth, soaking it up for when we had to go indoors.

Something major had to be done. It was decision time. We didn't want to live like iguanas. We even tentatively wondered if we could get along with a donkey. We knew, however, there were certain logistics to that we hadn't even considered. For example, matters having to do with keeping one of those animals in food and board, not to mention toilet facilities and the like. Still, we had to do something.

With that thought in mind, Julie and I climbed on the motor scooter and set off questing for a house or apartment for rent where no donkeys were needed but where we could build a fire and get warm. That was the most essential creature comfort we desired: warmth. After that, come what may, we would figure out how to cope with the other logistics.

We had decided we could make do with oil lamps and even bottled water bathes if it absolutely had to come to that. And the Lambretta could negotiate most any goat trail the island had to offer. Maybe Julie could balance the groceries on her lap. We could work out those details later. All we wanted was a place with a fireplace and something to burn in it. We were that desperate.

We set off along Calvo Sotelo, the coastal highway heading west from Palma. We had no idea what to look for. The further we went, the less we knew what to look for. There were no "For Rent" signs in any windows. Not in any language. In fact we were not sure what the Spanish words for that would be. The British used "To Let," signifying what we were looking for. But the only word our Spanish dictionary gave for "rent" was *"renta."* so it seemed appropriate to look for signs that said: *"Por Renta"*. Only later did with learn that the correct Majorcan words for "letting" or renting something was *"alcilar."* So if we had even seen a sign with that word on it, we would not have been any better off.

Unfortunately, all such houses that looked rentable were closed for the winter. They were villas for summer vacationers. Not for winter guests in need of creature comforts. The day was gray, the weather chilly and **by** the time we reached Cala Mayor, a bathing beach in a cove with a spectacular view of the sea, our spirits were dragging.

The beach was deserted, the seas pounded wild and mercilessly. The cold wind off the water cut like a knife. We felt as low as Don Quixote and Sancho Panza on their trusty steed Rosinante just after tilting with a windmill.

A small hotel sat by the side of the road. Its tiny veranda and small tables must have been a cheerfully inviting sight to thirsty summer guests. Now it looked cold and empty.

Still, it was better than staying on the windy highway. We parked in front, picked a table out of the wind and I called inside requesting two *copitas* of cognac.

A smiling young waiter in a pressed white jacket brought them out on a silver tray. In my best Mallorcain, I asked him if he knew of any villas for rent in the area.

He failed to understand me, even when I injected several foreign variations on the words "to rent."

"One moment," he said, "I bring my superior."

Shortly a black-haired gentleman in a neat black suit appeared and came to our table. He squinted at us myopically through thick-lensed glasses with a cracked left lens. In a deep, soft voice he introduced himself as the hotel manager. "May I be of service?"

I repeated my question in Mallorcain.

He gently held up his hand to stop me repeating it with variations. "Please, in English."

I asked if there were any villas for rent in the area.

"Oh, yes. There are many villas here." He waved toward the hills behind him. "But what do you wish of them?"

"We'd like to rent one."

"He paused. "Ahhh…" he paused again. "For what purpose, please?"

"Well," I said, "mostly for the purpose of living in it."

"But we have rooms here at the hotel," he smiled broadly.

"Do you have any heat."

"Not until winter times."

"That's why we want to rent a villa. To make a fire to keep warm. To live where we can make a fire in a fireplace," I repeated.

"Ah-HAH!" our friend beamed on us, his cracked lens quivering with excitement. "Now I understand. You wish to *let* a villa for fire."

"Well, yes. That's about right. Is there anything nearby?"

"Hmmm, let me think." The manager rested his chin on his fist and thought.

In a moment he said, "Yes, I do believe there might be something up the hill. I would have to check first. Could you come back tomorrow?"

Our spirits suddenly lifted. "Yes indeed, we certainly can. What is your name?"

"Miguel Castellano." He bowed slightly.

We introduced ourselves. "Could we buy you a brandy?"

"No, no, thank you very much." He politely held up his hand. "I leave you now and if you care to return tomorrow at the same time, I may have news."

"Thank you so much," we said.

Back in Palma that afternoon we were elated over the possibility that we might be able to rent a villa we could heat. Joining Harper and Binky we told them our good news and invited them to have coffee with us on the Borne during the *paseo*, the late afternoon promenade in which everyone walking the boulevard looks at everyone else who is doing the same thing. They eagerly agreed, so we met them at a local sidewalk cafe with a good view of what we were about to see.

The *paseo* is one of Spain's most popular pastimes. Everything about it is steeped in tradition. We saw similar events in Italy and France, but these flimsy imitations pale in comparison to the Spanish *paseo*.

As a participant, or an observer, the Spanish "promenade" is performed according to traditional rules. Anyone failing to follow them is either a foreigner or ignorant of cultural manners. For example, "Look but don't touch" is one of the cardinal rules of personal conduct. There are others. To avoid chaos and confusion, people observe the rule of two-way pedestrian traffic, one stream of walkers heading one way, the other one going in the opposite direction, both streams flowing side-by-side.

Entire families often participate in the *paseo*. When walking together, it makes no difference which stream of walkers they are in. But when it comes to non-family groups, then the walkers generally separate according to sexes—all the males in one column, all the females in the other. The reason, of course, is so that the opposite sexes can see each other better. The main object then is subtle flirtation. Anything more overt than a poetic comment is frowned upon.

Old maids, old gents, families, and tourists usually go early to the boulevard's sidewalk cafes to be assured of a good seat for the *paseo*. That way, for the small price of a coffee or a drink, one has a ringside seat for the entire two or three hour show. If you are lucky, your seat is in the sun. That way, for a few *pesetas* you can be entertained, refreshed, and stay warm all at the same time. No wonder this poor man's street circus is such a popular pastime in Spain.

Few cultures in the world have ever brought the fine art of flirtation to such a high degree of finesse as has the Spanish. Each province—like its cuisine—has its individual nuances of flavor on this subject. And it requires no critical eye to discern that the Mallorcain *paseo* ranks high up the ladder of quality performances. Young Mallorcains can say more with an up-lifted eye-brow, a swift flash of ebony black eyes, or a certain suggestive smile, than most people manage to convey subtly in a lifetime. Even the way one dresses sometimes speaks louder than words.

Not that all of these silent signals is necessarily pleasing to everyone, however. For example, two middle-aged Spanish ladies wearing beautifully knit black wool shawls over their shoulders at the next table were profoundly disturbed by one young girl's attire, and minced no words about it. Not only did they feel that the girl's heels were too high, her shiny black leather skirt too short and too tight, her vestal white blouse too snug and skimpy, but they were offended most by the large eye-catching gold crucifix the girl wore low on a gold chain over her especially spectacular décolletage.

"My God!" whispered one of them. "She has to wear an extra large crucifix to protect what she's showing!"

The sight may have offended some ladies, but you can be sure nothing about it offended the men. They were too busy ogling the young damsel's charms, caught by them just as surely as the wily street vendor caught his crowd by the old knife-in-the-arm-trick.

Some of the young lady's male audience even broke into spontaneous poetic compliments or *propios* each time she passed, though admittedly, not many were original. It's not easy being a sidewalk Shakespeare when your eyes are suddenly smitten by blinding beauty.

You can generally tell where the budding street poet's eyes are by the nature of his *propios*. If he likes everything he sees, he may be so tongue-tied that the only smart remark he can think to make on the spur of the moment is, *"Guapa!"*

This utterance, pronounced deep in the throat, brought up and snapped sharply off the lips means variously: cute, neat, spruce, bonny, beautiful, or if in the masculine gender with the word ending in an "o": handsome, gallant, beau, or bully. Take your pick.

Unfortunately, however, this one word compliment may not always be thought of by the recipient as being appropriate, flattering, or original, but rather the equivalent of a lascivious under-the-breath wolf whistle. An ordinary *"Guapa!"* growled at just any passing beauty might even draw instant retaliation. For example, if the speaker is within reach he could get slapped in the face, depending on the tone of the *guapa* and whether or not it is accompanied by a leering look.

Otherwise he might get nothing more than a reproachful glare. Where true beauty is concerned, one has to be careful with compliments.

The real *propio* artists are those who come up with truly evocative compliments, the kind that are purely poetic, and hopefully original. For example, if the beauty has especially dazzling, vivacious eyes, one might—after an adoring look—say such things as, "Ah, such beauty. Beside your eyes, *Señorita*, the stars grow pale!"

If the girl hasn't heard that one too often before, you can bet that it won't bring on a slap in the face. Rather, it might evoke a swift, hot glance, a naughtily up-tuned curve of the lips, or at very least, a rapid flutter of the eyelashes. Payment enough for something a bit more inspired than a simple *"guapa."*

Perhaps the admirer is caught by the especially delightful way a girl walks, with all parts of her anatomy oscillating in perfect harmony.

Then, the sidewalk poet might say such things as, "*Señorita,* when you walk, your feet make lace!"

Whoever thought up that *propio* was an artist. No telling how far it got him before it fell into public domain.

Other compliments with artistic flair focus more directly on the woman's visible assets. None are intended to be lascivious or crude, only colorful and flattering, even far-fetched. For instance, "If St. Peter saw those legs, he'd turn in his wings and leave heaven." or, "If those legs were telephone poles, I'd walk the telephone line all the way to Paris."

The more original the compliment, the more likely the author of it will be graced by a flash of an eye, or a hint of a smile. Reward enough for these sidewalk Lotharios.

18

Villa Josépha

Returning to the small hotel above Cala Mayor a couple days later we were overjoyed to learn that Miguel had indeed found us a house for rent up the hill behind the hotel. He said it was a small two-apartment villa that overlooked the area. The landlady was on the premises at that moment. If we cared to go see the house, Miguel would be pleased to go along as interpreter.

The road was unpaved across the highway from the hotel. It went up a steep rocky grade that passed several small villas built on stonewall terraced land.

The white stucco *Villa Joséfa* stood tall to the right of the meandering dirt road above the beach at Cala Mayor. Everything about it went up, you walked up two flights of stone steps to the top of the stone terrace before reaching the ground floor of the bottom apartment. Another flight of steps took you another story higher past open shuttered windows to a small fenced porch. The apartment door was at the end of that.

A smiling middle-aged Mallorcain landlady dressed in black greeted us. She was quite lively and talkative, speaking so rapidly we caught only a word or two of what she said. Miguel introduced us. Her name was *Señora* Bonacho. She held wide the door and welcomed us inside with short steps and swift movements while keeping up a steady patter directed at Miguel.

Miguel did not try to translate everything she said. He kept his hands folded on his chest like a friendly mortician and quietly gave us his version of what the landlady said. Primarily she pointed out all the apartment's good features, explaining that it was brand new and had never been lived in. If we liked it, we would be the first renters ever. It was a two-bedroom, one bath upstairs apartment. Or we could have the downstairs apartment.

We all trooped down the stairs to see that one. While it was about the same size, it was a more somber apartment, which seemed to lack the brightness of the penthouse upstairs. When I conveyed this feeling through Miguel, the landlady heartily agreed. So upstairs we went to get down to more specific details. The living room was white and bright with a small fireplace along one wall. We eyed that darling with ill-concealed delight. I knelt and inspected the grates and peered up the chimney. It looked as though it had never known a warm bed of embers. Not a speck of soot in sight either.

"*Si, si,*" said our landlady as she watched me sensuously examine the source of our hoped for warmth. "Makes very nice fire." She pointed to the windows, one looking into a bare orchard, the other across the street to another empty house. "Very nice view. With a sweep of her hand she included the balcony for viewing the sea. "All very nice." Then we paraded into the kitchen.

"Is there running water?" I asked.

"Yes, of course." Even before the landlady pointed to the roof, I knew the answer.

"Rainwater," murmured Julie under her breath.

We didn't want to bog down on that minor problem at this late a date.

"Does the apartment have electricity?"

"Certainly. Why not?"

"Ah, then there is a refrigerator."

"No. No refrigerator."

"What does one do then?"

Señora Bonacho shooed us into the tiny kitchen and opened the door of a small wooden icebox against the right wall. It would hold about a 25-pound block of ice. A marble shelf and cupboards were to the left of a door opening onto a small back porch and a terrace.

I didn't have to ask if the stove was electric, or gas. It was neither. A large wood burning cook stove with four openings covered with cast-iron lids dominated the left wall near a convenient corner sink. I hadn't seen one of those in a long time.

Señora Bonacho pointed at it and launched into a lengthy explanation to Miguel. I understood not a word she said.

When she stopped speaking and paused for breath, Miguel, in his best mortician manner quietly explained that if we wanted hot water we had to start the wood stove. It in turn generated the heat that heated the water pipes feeding the bathtub in the nearby bathroom. If we failed to start the stove and keep it burning for a reasonable period of time, then forget the warm bath water.

"Where is the wood for the fireplace?" I asked, hoping that somewhere out the back door there might be a huge pile of already cut firewood.

"One has to order that ahead of time. A man will bring firewood— usually olive wood—and ice. Be sure you insist on dry wood, or the stove will be difficult to light."

"How exactly does one go about lighting the wood stove?"

"*No problema,*" announced *Señora* Bonacho. "Stand back, I am an expert." That much I understood.

She quickly produced a handful of kindling and crumpled newspaper. These were thrust into the stove. A lighted match was applied, the stove door closed and we stood back to see the results.

All that happened was the stove belched out clouds of blue smoke.

Our landlady muttered a few words under her breath, clamped a pan over the largest source of smoke, rattled the grates, spun the chimney flue and adroitly flipped stove lids with a poker. All to no avail.

We onlookers swiftly vacated the kitchen while the landlady stayed to rattle, bang and curse it out. Then abruptly she too ran out of the kitchen. As we stood watching the clouds of smoke rolling out the doors and windows everyone decided that something somewhere was plugged up.

Señora Bonacho said she would quickly get someone to peer down the chimney to see if the trouble lay in that area. Wiping soot off our faces, we acted as though this was a trifling matter, one that could be quickly solved with the proper workman.

Since they were still doing a few final touch-ups to the new apartment—a touch of paint here, a touch there—it would all be ready within a couple days. The landlady suggested that we get together on the following afternoon and if everyone was agreeable, we could discuss the rental fee and sign papers.

We told the *Señora* that we were indeed pleased with almost everything we saw and that if those minor problems could be taken care of, and the price was not too bad, we would be glad to rent the place. I asked Miguel if he could be available to act as translator during this transaction. He assured us that he would be on hand at the appointed hour.

Meeting back at the Villa Joséfa the following day, we were there when the workers swept up their last pile of saw-dust, touched the last spot with a dab of paint, and bid everyone adieu.

We were there waiting. So was the landlady. Miguel, our friendly translator, failed to show.

We waited a reasonable time while our expert at fire-making-in-the stove once more displayed her prowess without the ensuing clouds of smoke, and proudly showed us how easy it was to start the stove. If I understood her correctly, a bird's nest in the stovepipe caused the blockage.

Giving up on Miguel, we went ahead and discussed the rental price, eventually settling on an amount that was agreeable to all parties. Our new landlady was all smiles as we paid her a month in advance.

Señora Bonacho was pleased, we were pleased and everyone was happy. We got the name and address of our wood and iceman, and were told we could move in whenever we wanted. It couldn't have been soon enough to suit us.

Our going away party at the Hotel Montenegro was a memorable occasion in which all our friends gathered in the dining room after supper and shared countless bottles of champagne and told countless tales of misadventures here, there and elsewhere.

Harper and Binky made us promise to have everyone out for a house warming as soon as we settled in.

"If you folks can get along without running water, and learn to cook over a wood stove, maybe we'll get brave enough to try it ourselves," said Binky.

Peter Dorset, the primitive artist, said, "Just because you're going native on Rope-Sole Beach, try not to forgot your more civilized friends living in town. Visit once in a while."

We assured him we would. After Harper made a short speech, everyone toasted us again with more champagne. Then Binky brought out a long, slender package wrapped in tissue paper crowned with a large red bow. A going away gift from everyone.

It was a jointed bamboo salt-water fishing pole with a large spinning reel attached. They had even filled the reel with monofilament fishing line.

"That's so you can fish for your supper if all else fails," laughed Binky.

"Providing they learn how to start their stove," added Harper.

It was a bittersweet parting with our friends of the Hotel Montenegro. We weren't at all sure how things would turn out. But at least it looked as though we would be able to take care of our heating problems for the winter.

Faithful Vicenti and his snorting old Citröen got the dubious chore of transferring our ever-expanding baggage to our new address above Cala Mayor.

My wife got to ride with the baggage, big wine jugs, camera gear and fishing rod, while I followed Vicenti's vapor trail on the Lambretta.

Julie directed our intrepid taxi driver to Cala Mayor and the turn up our street: *Camino Viejo son Bote,*

Vicenti was willing to go all the way to *Villa Joséfa.* Unfortunately, however, his Citröen bulked about going up the last dozen paces since the rocky road tried to go vertical, but failed, just enough to discourage the wheezing old Citröen.

So we unloaded and carried the things the rest of the way, Vicenti huffing and puffing with each one of our two large, bulging soft-sided suitcases.

Somehow, between the three of us, we got everything up the hill, then up the flights of stairs to our upper deck overlooking the rest of the world.

We piled everything in the middle of the living room floor, found four glasses, and popped the cork of a leftover party bottle of champagne we had saved for the occasion. It was time to celebrate the fact that we had finally made it! We had *moved*! We were totally *free*!

"*Saludos amigos!*" cried Señor Vicenti, caught up in our elation and holding his glass on high. We happily joined him in gulping the bubbly. Then, along with Mr. Vicenti we toasted the feat of getting everything upstairs in one piece. We then went outside and toasted the magnificent view from our balcony. Then we trooped inside, toasted our new fireplace, our magnificent wood stove, and above all, we toasted our very own new villa. In fact, before we finished all of the toasts, we had to liberate yet another bottle of champagne buried in one of the bags.

Señor Vicenti stuck with us through the entire little celebration. Then he apologetically excused himself to go back to work. He left with such bounding high spirits I was afraid he might actually bound right off our stairs before he got down to his taxi. Waving his beret, he saluted us all the way to the bottom.

With a final glass of champagne, we toasted our disappearing friend as his Citröen lurched off down the rocky road. Brakes squealing, rocks flying, blue exhaust vapors trailing, it slued around the corner headed back to Palma. We hoped he wouldn't fly off into orbit along the way.

19

Survival Course

Once the effects of the champagne wore off and we slowly came back to earth, we faced the cold reality of what we had actually done to ourselves.

Here we were, miles from town, overlooking a deserted closed-for-the-winter resort beach with no food, no water, no phone, no heat, and nothing to burn in the fireplace. I didn't mention these facts to my wife. Instead I said as cheerfully as possible, "Well, here we are!" I grinned.

"It's a beautiful place," she said. "I can't believe we're actually here."

"Me either," I said. How interesting what people do when they want it badly enough. Here we were without an inkling of how we were going to survive.

"We have to get organized," I said.

"Okay, but let's unpack first," Julie said.

"Right."

While we did I pondered what came next. First, we needed food and water, then some heat to keep us from freezing in the night. I also wondered where the closest gasoline station was. I hadn't seen a gas station beyond Palma. One more logistic we had overlooked. Was this why the real estate people talked so highly of travel by donkey? With no vehicle fuel a grass-eating donkey might not be too bad. Except that we hadn't seen much grass either.

First things first. I suggested that we ride the motor scooter back toward Palma scrutinizing every kilometer of the way for supplies.

"What will we carry them in?" asked Julie.

"Good question. What have we got?"

"Well, we got the jai-alai basket."

"Be serious."

"I am. That's about it."

"What does everyone else use around here?"

"Those newspaper things."

"What newspaper things?"

Julie made a swirl with her hands. "You know, we saw them at the fish market."

"Oh yes." Fruit, fish and grocery vendors used sheets of newspaper to make a paper cone. They did it with a swish of their hands—presto, a cone! Into it went whatever produce you bought, then they tucked in the top corners and you hurried home before the whole thing spilled, leaked, or fell apart in your arms. Timing was everything.

"How many of those things can you carry on the back seat of the scooter?"

"Let's not even think about it," said my wife.

"Well, we've got to think of something. What else do we have?"

"The suitcases are all. Them and the wine jugs."

"We certainly can't balance ten gallons or whatever it is of wine on the scooter and ever hope to get it anywhere unless we tie it where my feet go and walk the scooter home."

"What about a taxi?"

"Good idea, but no phone. And Palma's a long way off for one to come just to take us to a store."

"The only other things we have are those suitcases. Can we do anything with them?"

"Maybe," I said. "The only one that fits on the luggage rack is the little hard-sided one we brought across the rivieras with us. Maybe if things aren't too tall, they'll fit inside that."

"It's worth a try. Let's go before it gets any later."

The scooter still had ample fuel in its tank, so off we went down the steep rocky hill from Villa Joséfa, turned left onto the paved Calvo Sotelo and headed back toward Palma. Clamped onto the luggage rack was our small green cardboard suitcase. I thought if all else failed, we could at least fill it full of rice and live for Lord knows how long. Maybe even add a fish or two I could catch for a *paella*.

A few kilometers down the road we found what we were looking for not far from Porto Pi. (Pronounced "pee," our Majorcan guidebook warned readers to be careful how they used the word because it meant the same in Spanish as it did in most other languages.)

After coming up a long hill, on the left side of the road we found a small grocery store. It was so small that a dozen customers would have had trouble fitting inside at the same time.

The store turned out to be a family affair, run by the aproned owner/manager husband and wife, along with their daughter and son. The family name was Solari.

Rather than laughing when we came in to buy a suitcase full of food, they seemed genuinely anxious to help us. After picking out several low profile food items, including rice, we opened the suitcase on the counter to see what would fit.

The rice, eggs, coffee, sugar, steak, bananas, and even the grapefruit were okay, but the Mallorcain melon was going to be a problem.

When *Señora* Solari saw us trying to close the lid on that beauty she quickly solved our problem. She led us to her net bag display. All kinds of net bags.

Demonstrating, she took down one of the brightly colored bags and stretched it bigger than a snare drum. When she released it, the thing snapped back to its original size no larger than a woman's limp opera purse. Plenty of room for half the items in the store!

We promptly bought two of them.

Between the bags and the suitcase we put away enough food to keep us out of harm's way. It even included two bottles of wine—bottled and corked for us while we waited—out of a large barrel of local red wine. A marvelous assortment of olives marinating in heavy wooden tubs tempted us, but we dared not risk trying to get those home on the motor scooter.

I showed the proprietor the name and address of our wood supply man. He nodded that he knew where it was. On the back of an old bill he kindly drew a small map to the man's place of business. It was just a short distance away.

As we loaded everything aboard the Lambretta, the entire Solari family moved outdoors to watch the procedure and to make helpful suggestions. The bulging suitcase went on its luggage rack where shock cords lashed it in place. Each of the net bags was slung over the pillion seat hand-hold the way you would sling saddle-bags over a horse: one on each side. That left Julie's hands free to hold onto the firewood when and if we could find the source.

Everyone waved, smiled, and told us to "Go with God." From the lopsided way the scooter handled when we wavered off down the road, I welcomed any assistance we could get.

A few blocks away toward Terreno, we located the woodman's business. The man, his hound, his horse, cart, and a large wood pile were squeezed between two buildings with a roof overhead. Underneath, his wood was stacked a story high. When we interrupted him he was chopping some large pieces into smaller ones.

"*Buenas tardi*" I said approaching the rickety wood fence behind which he labored.

The dog let out a howl. The old man in a frazzled straw hat dropped his ax in surprise and turned to squint at us. He was dark-complected with rough features like a rusty bucket after flattening by a highway truck. The long wood-splinter he chewed traveled from one corner to the other corner of his mouth while he eyed us up and down before speaking. And then all he said was:

"*Si?*"

"You have wood, *Señor?*"

"*Si.*" The long-eared hound continued to howl as if baying a full moon. The old man paid him no heed.

When he made no effort but to agree with me, I told him that I was in need of wood.

The woodman squinted over my shoulder to my motor scooter on its stand with Julie sitting on her pillion seat with the groceries. Again the splinter made a fast trip from corner to corner. Then, he focused back on me.

"Which wood?" he asked.

"Which wood do you have?" I countered.

"Olive and almond."

Not wishing to show my ignorance, I asked to see samples.

He gestured to two nearby piles. Since he said nothing more, it was up to me to discern which was which.

I examined both piles with a critical eye. One kind of wood looked a little darker than the other. That was the only difference I saw.

Then I asked the only question I could think of after having been warned by our landlady: "Is the wood dry?"

The old man stared at me. He wore about four layers of clothes, including what looked like the top of his pajamas under all the layers.

"Dry." he said. "Dry as horse apples on the street in the heat of summer." I wondered if I translated that right.

"Very dry." I agreed.

"Like old horse shit." he said.

"Uhhh-*huh.*" I pondered the piles again, still wondering which was which and which was the best.

Finally I asked outright. "Which is the best?"

"Best for what?" asked the woodman, his voice suddenly much louder now that his hound had stopped howling and was peeing on my pant-leg. I swiftly leaped out of range.

"Best for…for heat." I picked up a piece of newspaper on the ground and tried to wipe off the dog's doings.

"Well, that depends," said the woodman. He frowned, deep in thought. The splinter in his mouth made two fast laps corner to corner.

"For cooking, almond. It's fast. For heat, olive. It's hotter longer. But it's a bitch to light."

"Good." I said. "I'll take two of each."

"Two what of each—wagon loads?"

"No…" I held up my hands measuring the log-sized piece. "Two almond and two olive."

The man looked at me strangely. "You must have a very small need," he said.

"For now, yes. But tomorrow I could use a wagon load."

At this news the woodman brightened considerably. "Permit me," he said. He held out his crusty hand. My name is Frumke," he said. "Manolo Frumke."

We shook hands. I told him who we were and where we lived.

"*Si, si*. I know Villa Josépha well. In my younger days I used to court the lady who owns it."

"*Señora* Bonacho?"

"That's her. Does she still dress in mourning?"

"All black."

Señor Frumke slowly shook his head. "Sad." The sliver went around his mouth a couple times. "Twenty years now. That's lots of mourning for a woman such as her."

"What happened?" I asked.

The woodman shrugged. "He went fishing and never came back. He tapped his chest. "*Malo curazon*. Bad heart."

"What a shame," I said. We paused an appropriate time.

"Sell me my four pieces of wood. Two olive, two almond and some kindling."

"At once, *Señor*" His sleeping hound got up, yawned and came over to me. As he started to lift his leg again, *Señor* Frumke's boot caught him in the rear end. With a throaty growl the dog changed his mind and slunk off.

"Damn peeingest dog, I ever saw," commented the woodman. "He wets the wood and my customers complain like hell."

"Make sure mine is dry," I said.

"Off the top of the pile. Like dried dung," he assured me.

We roped two of the logs to the side of the scooter. Julie carried one and the bag of kindling. I balanced the other log between my legs.

Frumke seemed quite taken with our Lambretta load. "You have everything a man needs." He laughingly directed his remark at my wife. "Your load of wood will be at Joséfa in the morning. Good luck."

Somehow we made it home without a mishap before dark. Going up the rocky grade to the villa the scooter whined and bucked on the loose gravel like a skittering colt. But she climbed the grade and we unloaded her with a sigh of relief.

Two hours later, we cooked steaks and roasted potatoes in our fireplace. Then, in the comfortably heated living room by the mellow glow of candlelight, we toasted each other and our good fortune with glasses of musky-flavored red wine. The survival crisis was over. We had finally found us a warm home on Majorca.

20

Settling in

The next morning, after a soft knock on the front door, someone said, "Excuse me, is anyone home?"

I opened the door to a broadly smiling Miguel Castellano, the hotel manager.

"Hi Miguel. Come on in. How about coffee?"

"No, No. Thank you. I just dropped by to see how things went with *Señora* Bonacho."

"Not too bad," I said. "We missed you."

"Yes, I know. That's why I'm here. I must apologize and explain."

"No problem," I said. "We worked everything out."

"But please." Miguel held up his hand.

Julie came in from the kitchen. "Hi Miguel!"

"Hello, Julie," Miguel said in his deep voice. "I came to apologize about the other day."

"For what?"

"Let me explain," he said. "You may wonder why I helped you. Well, a long time ago I visited England. I didn't know anything about where to go or what to do. Some English people were very kind to me, and showed me what to do. I never forgot their kindness. I told myself that if ever I had a chance to help someone in similar circumstances, I would do so."

"We couldn't have done it alone, Miguel. I can't tell you how much we appreciate it."

"I understand," he said solemnly. "But about not being here the other day, I did not want the *Señora* to misunderstand why I was helping."

"Why would she misunderstand?" asked Julie.

"Well, here in Mallorca there are people who do that, make arrangements for tourists to get rooms, or villas. For doing so, those who are letting the rooms always pay the person a percentage, a service tip, you might say. I stayed away because I did not want the *Señora* to feel she had to pay that tip. I helped you because I wanted to."

Miguel's explanation left us feeling warm and grateful for the kindness he had shown us.

"Please," said Julie, "won't you have a small glass of wine with us?"

Miguel paused, as if to refuse, then smiled and said he would be pleased to have one. "Very small, please."

While we sipped the wine, I asked Miguel if he had lived on the island a long time. He said he had been raised on the mainland in Spain. His family lived in Madrid where his brother and sister shared a large apartment with Miguel's Mother and Father. Miguel said he worked only a few days a week at the hotel because there was no business now. It was winter and very slow. Only when the summer came did the guests arrive. Then everyone made money and things were good again.

Miguel did not stay long. He said he had things to do at the hotel.

"Once we're settled, we'd love to have you for dinner sometime," said Julie.

"Yes. That would be very nice. I would like that." Miguel stood up to go. He wore the same perfectly pressed black suit he wore when we first met him. His shock of thick black hair, parted low on the left side, made him look quite handsome.

I wondered why he had not repaired the cracked left lens of his glasses.

As I walked him out the door onto the porch, I said. "Miguel, thanks for making all this possible for us."

"It's nothing," he said. "If you need anything at all, I will be glad to help you. Just come down to the hotel." He told me what days he worked, then with a wave, he went down the steps, the lens of his thick glasses moving gently on the bridge of his nose like the wings of a crystal butterfly.

True to his word, our trusty woodman, *Señor* Frumke and his load of wood showed up promptly that morning. He and the long-eared hound walked beside his two-wheeled wagon loaded with split fireplace-sized logs. It was a large load, and looked like more than his horse might be able to haul up our steep rocky street. But they had no trouble whatsoever.

The squinting Frumke, helped me carry the heavy logs up the stairs and stack them under our back porch. The hound lay under the cart watching us. I kept an eye on him, thinking he might be waiting for a chance to jump out and do his business on me, but he acted perfectly innocent.

After the job was done, Julie brought us both a couple glasses of red wine. Frumpke, thanked her, smacked his lips and downed his in a gulp.

"Thank you much," he said. "But excuse my haste. I have several loads to deliver. This cold weather has made good business. *Adios.*" He waved and was off with his team following him down the road.

Gradually we began bringing something of ourselves to the stark white-walled villa. We mounted the jai-alai basket on the wall in a more or less artistic manner. The wine jugs went on both sides of the fireplace. I found some old fishnet on the beach and wrapped the clear jug in it, finishing off by whipping some line around the neck. When a friendly Palma real estate agent overheard us admiring some of his Spanish travel posters, he quickly removed them from his display and gave them to us. We were both surprised and pleased with his unexpected kindness. His gift added colorfully pleasant scenes to our otherwise blank, white walls, especially the bright red, gold, and black bullfight posters with their large block-printed names of bullfighters who fought memorable *corridas* of the past. Other additions came from treasures we found on our walks.

Part way up the brown hillside above our street sat a sumptuous, ultra-modern long, low, domed villa said to belong to the Spanish artist Juan Miro. We never saw it occupied, but its large, arched glass windows across the front with its touches of bright red against brilliant white stucco made the villa a work of art in itself.

A small, lone windmill sat just below the crest of the hill behind us. I photographed it against a sunset, the surrounding palm trees and nearby villas in deep silhouette.

Almond trees grew on the terraced land behind us, along with a yellow-blossomed tree the locals called mimosa. How different these blooms were from the complex fuchsia and gold blooms of the Florida mimosa.

On our strolls through this area we made some interesting discoveries. One was a half buried mill stone about two and a half feet wide and three inches thick.

This, we carefully excavated and carried home. Cleaned up and placed atop a large flowerpot, it made a fine table in front of the fireplace where we did most of our cooking.

On a subsequent trip we found discarded broken ceramic tiles from a bygone era. The beauty and complexities of their designs suggested that these were not the usual run of the mill tiles. In no time we grouted them to the top of the millstone and gave our fireside table some artistic class.

In our wanderings over the neighborhood terraces, a certain kind of soft stone used as a building material in the area intrigued us. Large sedimentary deposits were common along the coast where stonecutters had sawed the rock into manageable building blocks. It did not appear to be a sandstone. More like a compact, fine-textured limestone cochina. The island seemed to have an unlimited supply of this easily shaped stone and many homes were built with its blocks.

Mostly to see how well the material could be worked, I easily carved a hand-sized piece into a rock-reclining lizard. Other small pieces were given African mask features. When we found a rough, head-sized sphere of this stone, we lugged it home. I carved ancient features on it, the kind seen in Mexican ebony today. Smoking gave it a respectable patina of age. As a mantle centerpiece holding up our growing library between wine bottles, it was impressive. When we left the island, I planned to bury the stone head in our backyard.

Periodically we rode the motor scooter into Palma to give our friends progress reports. Eventually we had *Señor* Vicenti and his taxi bring us out a more ample wine supply in one of the large rope-covered glass jugs, used for this purpose. It looked as though it might now contain enough red wine to last us the rest of the winter. At least with it, and several bottles of champagne and cognac, we began to build a substantial reserve stock so that we could safely have a housewarming party without having to go to Palma to replenish the bar.

Heavy rains filled our catch basin with water so we no longer had a shortage. But since wine was more easily available than water, which we always had to heat up and sterilize before using, wine became our beverage of choice.

Once we felt fortified to entertain, we invited our friends to a champagne hamburger party. Our fireplace served as our cooking area because we kept it going for warmth. However, on this occasion we also fired up the wood stove, taking advantage of this facility to heat water for our bathes.

We made a special effort to invite Miguel from the hotel. He assured us that he would be pleased to come. But he failed to appear. Twice this happened. We had no idea what was wrong. When we finally cornered him and asked if there was some problem, he told us he had not come because he had no way to reciprocate. That was Miguel. We would have to work on him harder next time.

Binky and Harper thought our place charming. They asked many questions, apparently working up their courage to move out of the hotel. I suggested they contact Miguel to see what might be available for rent in nearby villas closed for the winter. In a matter of days, thanks again to Miguel's assistance, they located a place down the hill from us that was larger and had a spacious sunny patio. When they moved in, we had another house-warming, this time at their place.

Shortly before Christmas, a couple rented our downstairs apartment. They were British. He had retired from military service in India, and she was an ex-nun. Our new neighbors were Colonel Edmond Gwynn-Cannon and his wife Edna. One more house-warming party. We were fast becoming a small colony of foreigners.

The beach below our villas probably gave the name to our street. Someone told us that at one time it was the old sound where fishing boats were drawn up to over-winter. But not now. It was strictly a delightful little cove with a small beachside bar and pavilion. The sunnier days of the winter always attracted sunbathers. Occasionally we saw a few heartier types braving the cold waters to swim. They always turned out to be Norwegians of Swedes, on winter vacations to what they considered a "balmy" island in the Mediterranean. Often, we stood bundled up in our overcoats braced against the chill winds watching these visitors from the north frolicking in the surf. All we could do was shudder at the thought of it.

A new high-rise hotel was being built just to the left of the beach. In the beginning it was mostly girders and beams, slowly climbing skyward with Majorcan construction workers moving around the structure busy as ants. The only time they weren't scattered all over the place was when a busload of Norwegians or Swedes arrived to go winter swimming.

Whenever this occurred, all work ceased and the laborers crowded over to the beach side of the structure for a better view of the blond beauties in the group who were about to turn themselves into a mass of goose-bumps. At times the entire work crew was hanging off one side of the high-rise girders in such numbers I hoped the thing was well anchored. We were concerned that the entire structure might someday topple over from the heavy duty ogling that was going on.

On days when no one used the beach, I climbed the steep rocks beside it, worked my way out to a particular promontory point over deeper water, and tried the fishing.

The water was incredibly clear and cold. It looked as if it should be working alive with fish of all kinds. But if it was, they were not apparent. Not even the small ones. I bombarded them with dough-balls the way I had seen the local fishermen do, then tossed out the hook baited with bacon fat. All to no avail. I wondered what was wrong.

"Maybe the fish only feed at night," said Julie. "Maybe you need to try it then."

This sounded logical. I put off going until a night when the wind had ceased its usual howling and the seas their usual tumultuous pounding. Then with all my gear including a good flashlight to see what I was doing, I set off for my promontory point.

It was a moonless night. The wind was blowing stronger there, but it was not cold enough to be too uncomfortable. Twenty feet below me, the seas crashed into the rocks, creating a swirling caldron of foam. I envisioned all kinds of fish lurking around that pool of disturbed water just waiting to be fed.

Using the hand-light to see to make dough-balls I left the bait pail in the protection of the peak and walked out on a stone balcony over the water. I turned the light down on the surface a couple times to see if I could spot fish, then turned it out. I threw in the dough-balls, waited briefly, then cast in amongst them.

Nothing happened. I repeated the procedure several times, losing bait and having to retreat back to my bait pail and flashlight to get fresh supplies.

I fished that way for about half an hour. Still no bite. I was once again about to back off my precipitous perch and get more dough-balls when something hard suddenly poked me in the small of my back.

Surprised, I turned abruptly. A shadowy figure stood behind me. I could barely make out his silhouette in the darkness. He wore the patent leather Napoleon hat of the *Guardia Civil* charged with guarding Spain's frontiers. The man grunted something.

"What?"

He repeated the words. His dialect was not Mallorcain.

"Sorry," I said in Mallorcain. "I don't understand."

I realized then that he had jabbed me with the muzzle of his carbine. When I said I didn't understand, all he did was rack the bolt back and lever a cartridge into the chamber.

"*Bueno, bueno,*" I said, holding up my free hand. "*Que queres?* What do you want?"

He motioned me toward him, and backed up as I eased over to where I had my tackle.

Again I asked him what was wrong. This time I understood the word he grunted at me.

"*Contrabandista.*" It meant "smuggler."

"Who me? No, no."

"*Si,*" the shadowy shape said emphatically. Cautiously reaching down with the barrel of his carbine, he knocked my flashlight sitting on the ledge.

Then I understood. He had seen me flashing my light and suspected it was a signal to offshore smugglers.

"Yes," I said. "I understand now. But I am only fishing." I held out my fishing pole as evidence.

The carbine made vigorous negative movements under my nose. The guard let me know clearly that lights were forbidden at night on the coast because of smuggling. If I didn't want to go to jail *pronto*, he suggested I take my light and get the hell out of there.

So much for night fishing. It wasn't important enough to catch a term in the local jail. Besides, the fish never did bite.

Nobody knows about freshwater fishing on Majorca because the island has no freshwater rivers. Any streams are temporary rain run-offs after a torrential downpour. On particularly cold winters when snow might layer higher elevations of the island's mountainous region such as Majorca's 5,154 foot Silla de Torrellas, this eventually melts and flows down the island's craggy ravines, but the streams never last long enough to support fish life. Nor do they reach the sea before they soak in and become part of the lowlands aquifer, pumped up for irrigation.

Apparently however, there is enough captured fresh-water on the island—if only in the rooftop open catch-basins—to support a reasonable mosquito population in the summer. But when we learned that our area was called "The Mosquito Coast" we could hardly imagine any Majorcan mosquito even approaching the size and viciousness of those that live in Florida.

As we moved into late December, the weather became increasingly cold. Daytimes in the sun on our patios were fine, but by night the temperatures nose-dived considerably. We had no problem heating our living room. But our bedrooms missed the effects of the fireplace. There, you simply heaped on the blankets and hoped for the best.

Julie was especially bothered by the cold. She drew herself into such a knot at night that she was bothered by painful knee cramps during the day. More blankets from the landlady failed to help. It was a reflex action done in her sleep. The only thing that finally did help was her tying a spare pair of pajamas around her legs below each knee. The bulk of the garment prevented her bending her knees so much during sleep that they cramped. But nothing lessened the constant night cold. These villas were not intended for winter use.

It's hard to believe that Majorca's first inhabitants ran around the island naked, but that's what historians tell us. At 1,405 square miles, Majorca is the largest of the three main islands comprising the

Mediterranean's Balearic Islands. The island of Minorca 25 miles to the northeast being the second largest, and Ibiza, 55 miles to the southeast being the smallest.

Geographically, Majorca's backbone is a ridge of mountains running northeast to southeast with its tallest peak almost a mile high. This mountainous region comprises about one fifth of the island. The rest of the country to the southeast gradually drops down to dry plains and hills. The central part of the island is mostly flat country where hundreds of colorful windmills pump up trapped freshwater from the subsoil for irrigation. Marshes occur in the northeast, and the southernmost tip of the island. More good mosquito breeding areas.

Above water the Balearics are the emergent parts of a large mountainous submarine plateau in the Mediterranean almost midway between Spain and Africa. Underwater the islands drop precipitously into the deep, especially off the southeast coast of Majorca where a few miles offshore the bottom falls to 600 feet, then a few miles further it descends swiftly to over 6,000 feet deep. Minorca overlooks the edge of the submarine deep at 8,000 feet.

Little is known about the wild and woolly naked tribes that first inhabited Majorca but historians agree that their savage nature was probably what kept them that way until long after civilization came to the other main islands in the group. Sea-going Phoenicians from Carthage colonized the adjoining islands of Minorca and Ibiza around 500 BC, establishing Mago (Port Mahon) and Jama (Ciudadela) on Minorca in the name of the conquerors. But apparently, no one cared to tangle with the savage Majorcans until around 300 BC when the Romans finally established themselves at Palma and Pollentia, where they introduced the cultivation of the olive.

As they did everywhere, the Romans extracted the best a country had to offer for their own use. Pine pitch and men skilled at using slingshots were what the Romans wanted from these islands. So adroit were the Balearic natives in handling the sling that the island group derives its name from that skill. You can see the similarity in the word "*Bala*" or ball. Their slings were the one-handed kind that David used to slew Goliath, but Roman scribes recount that two-handed slings were also used with such efficiency that they could knock over a horse and rider.

Today, over 2,000 years later, the best "ball-slingers" in the world of Jai-alai still come from just one place—the Balearic Island of Minorca!

After the Romans came legions of other sea-going Mediterranean conquerors of all nationalities. Over the following centuries ownership of Majorca flip-flopped back and forth between different factions every century or so. Pirates plaguing the coastal communities forced towns to move inland in most of Majorca's port areas except Palma, which was more capable of defending itself than were the smaller, outlying settlements. In AD 465 the Vandals took over. In AD 534 Belisarius for the Byzantine Empire was in charge. The Arabs came in AD 901, laying the groundwork for Christianity and introducing irrigation that enabled the island to blossom. Then in AD 1229, Jaime I (James I.) King of Aragon and Count of Barcelona conquered Majorca and ruled the island as an independent kingdom. Under him, the island soon grew to become one of the most prosperous crossroads of the Western Mediterranean. Trade flourished into the Golden Era in which Majorca's mercantile fleet grew to number 300 large and 600 small vessels. During that time, some 30,000 sailors were registered in Palma. This prosperity and religious tolerance lasted until the Columbus era.

Today, traces of all these prior influences can still be found on the island, in its striking architecture, its innovative agricultural practices, its flavorful cuisine, its many-faceted language, and most fascinating of all, in the faces and personalities of its friendly people.

As we learned more about the island's history and her colorful people, the more we felt privileged to be a part of this incredible tapestry.

21

The Road to Bazanzan

Christmas was almost upon us. Palmas's stores began to reflect the coming holidays with a wider display of gifts and decorations. For the first time for us there would be two celebrations—one on December 25, the other on January 6, when Europeans celebrate the event.

I knew the season was almost there when Julie announced we had to put up a Christmas tree.

Since no one sold Christmas trees in Palma, it was up to us to get one in the time-honored traditional manner—from the forest. So, with borrowed hatchet in hand we climbed aboard the motor scooter and set out in search of a tree.

We drove west along the coastal Calvo Sotelo, scanning the countryside for an appropriate-sized fir that we could handle on the motor scooter. Deviating to a wilder looking side road, we finally found one that was not on private property. It was nice and full, about four feet tall. We chopped it down and with some difficulty, got it aboard the scooter without knocking ourselves off.

We probably looked a little odd motoring down the highway with Julie buried in the boughs that were pushing me into the windscreen. Anyone seeing us might have thought the tree was in charge. At times it was.

We mounted the tree in a sand-filled flowerpot on the dining room table. Strings of tiny colored lights were strung through it. Julie cut out and pasted together colored paper decorations for the boughs. The flowerpot was covered with a white tablecloth. Candles, pinecones and boughs went on the fireplace mantle and windowsills. When Julie finished, our little apartment looked cheerfully like Christmas.

At an appropriate time before the holidays, we began getting strange little cards tucked under our front door. They were holiday greetings from those who had been serving us so faithfully and well throughout the year. Or at least so said the cards. Each wished us happy holidays, then named the sender. For instance, we had cards from the mailman, *Señor* Puesta of the Post; the garbageman, *Señor* Reino of the refuse; the iceman, *Señor* Llado of the 25-pound block; the woodman, *Señor* Frumke of the firewood; Señor Paradis, our meterman of the electric energy department; and the street-sweeper, *Señor* Salvador of the local road maintenance crew.

Miguel solved the mystery of the little cards when he explained it was traditional for Mallorcains to show their appreciation for these services with small holiday tips to the individuals who had left the cards.

That sounded reasonable to us. For each card we received, we made up special addressed envelopes containing small monetary gifts appropriate for those many faithful servants, some of whom we had never seen. But one and all had our number. We wished each of them the merriest of holidays and sincerest hope that they continue performing their services just as diligently and efficiently as they had in the past. Where appropriate, Julie even added a seasonal touch to such things as our garbage package topped by a small red bow for a few days at the height of the season. I'm sure our garbage collector was cheered by the sight of that.

One by one on different days and at different hours, our public servants appeared at our door, hat in hand, announcing their professional service and expecting their tribute. Each was invited in, offered the expected *copita* of brandy, and with handshakes and toasts we passed them our offering. We toasted each other, toasted Father Christmas, toasted the coming New Year, and then they were off to visit other clients in the neighborhood. After all that good cheer, we hoped they made it home all right.

Slowly but surely we began receiving Christmas cards from friends at home who discovered where we were and had kindly mailed greetings well before Christmas. We missed our family and friends tremendously. It was our first Christmas aboard and each card from home made us feel that much more melancholy. And then came the Christmas card from George.

George was a retired railroad brakeman who had worked in a Midwest railroad yard most of his life. Sixty-five years of breathing the emissions of nine railroads, the largest steelworks, tin-plate mills, rail mill, and cement works in the world, had finally taken its toll on his lungs.

So George moved South to breathe a little fresh air into his life and to build a little house on the Gulf of Mexico where he could spend the rest of his days enjoying saltwater fishing.

I helped him build his place, coming down to the coast whenever I could. The house never got entirely completed because George never had quite enough money to finish it. But what was done suited him just fine. He fished every day he could and he and I shared many an enjoyable time in that pursuit. Neither of us knew much about it then, but we learned together.

When George heard that Julie and I were to be married and planned to go to Europe, he asked us to do something for him. He asked us to go to a town in France named "Bazanzan" and to send him a postcard from there.

He said he was there in World War I. He and another soldier had gone AWOL to "Bazanzan" and to hear George tell it, it was the most interesting place he had seen in the whole war.

"You can't miss it," he said. "That's the place where the pheasants chopped off the head of Joan of Arc. You gotta see it."

"I thought the peasants burned her at the stake in Rouen."

"Nope," said George. "The pheasants chopped her head off. Right there in Bazanzan. They even showed us the chopping block."

"The history books must have it wrong, then," I said.

"Yep. Those books got it all wrong." George insisted. "We saw where it happened in Bazanzan."

Nothing we said would dissuade him. We told George he must mean "peasants" instead of "pheasants" but as far as he was concerned they were both one in the same and they did in Joan on the chopping block.

George had his own way of seeing things and that was that. "And another thing," he told me the last time we embraced and said our goodbyes: "Send me a coo-coo clock from Switzerland."

The tale about Joan of Arc was quickly forgotten. The only thing that stuck in the back of my mind was the funny sounding name of the town. Knowing George, I was sure he not only mixed up pheasants and peasants but he probably had the name of the town wrong too. But one thing we didn't forget was the coo-coo clock. It was one of the first things we bought in Switzerland and shipped home to George.

Etta, George's old maid sister who had moved in to keep him company wrote how pleased he was to get it. "He's got it right in the middle of the living room wall. He talks about that bird every time it goes off."

She didn't say it, but I bet Aunt Etta had a word or two for that noisy bird as well.

Some time after we were in Switzerland we rented a car to drive to Paris. We were on our way and I was running my finger along the route we were following when suddenly I spotted the name of a town that had a familiar sound to it: it was spelled, "Besançon."

"My gosh," I exclaimed, "there's George's 'Bazanzan!'"

"Where?" asked Julie.

"Right there!" I pointed to it on the road map. "Just thirty-eight kilometers off our route."

"Are you sure?" Julie said. "It's not spelled right."

"I know, but when you pronounce it, it sounds right. Have we got the time to check it out? I sure would like to see where those pheasants did in Joan. And we promised to send George a postcard if we ever found it."

Naturally there was no way that we were going to pass up that opportunity. Surely whatever George had seen there would be worth seeing, if only so that history books would forever after be set right.

We drove to the heart of downtown Besançon, parked the car, walked to a sidewalk cafe ordered coffees and asked questions of the proprietor:

"*Pardone moi,*" I began.

"*Oui, Monsieur.*"

"Do you know Joan d'Arc?" I asked in English.

"Personally? *No Monsieur.* "But I know *of* Joan d'Arc."

"Was she ever...'keeek'..." with the sound effect I drew my finger across my neck, then quickly added, "here in Besançon?"

The rotund little Frenchman stared at me as if I had lost my mind. But quietly he said:

No, Monsieur. She was...'keeek'..." he drew his finger across his throat as I had, and added, "at the stake in Rouen."

"*Jamais ici?*" Never here?

"No. No. Never here in Besançon."

"Perhaps some other famous person?"

He paused thoughtfully scratching his head. "I think not," he said. "Not here. Paris maybe, but not here."

I thanked him, bought a large postcard that said in bright script letters across the top of several scenes of the city: "*Souvenir de Besançon.*"

While we drank our coffees I wrote George the bad news. We mailed the postcard to him from Besançon.

Months later, his reply reached us in the form of a Christmas card to our address in Majorca. It was the kind of card that appeals to tourists visiting Florida for the Christmas holidays. Souvenir stands always stocked them. The front cover showed Santa Claus and his reindeer in their sleigh sliding across a white beach under palm trees. The beach part had lots of glitter glued on it. Scrolled across the top it read "Merry Christmas From Florida."

Inside, George had penned a message that he had not bothered to punctuate. It all ran together, one continuous sentence that began: "We left the road on top of the hill and went to the left and came down through the grape vineyard the grapes grow on the side of the hill the town they call it the second city to Paris it is in a big deep valley we stayed about two blocks from what you will be looking for on the N.W. side of town…" And it ended: "…We were there 5 days and had to dodge the M.P. all the time caught a freight out of there after midnight you know it was a real live town then if you didn't see the chopping block where they chopped off Joan of Arc's head, I don't think you got to Bazanzan. Try to find it. Signed, George."

His card brightened our day, as it always does whenever I read it. He's gone now and we will never know what George thought he saw in Besançon. But to his dying day he believed he had witnessed an important piece of history there that had to do with Joan of Arc and a chopping block for beheading. All done by pheasants, of course.

22

Christmas on Majorca

A few days before Christmas, Harper and I caught the crew of the fishing trawler *Esperanza* in port. We had bought a carton of cigarettes from the overcoat lady on the Borne and a couple bottles of brandy to be shared by the crew. Also, I wanted to give them some enlarged photographs I had made of them in action.

"Good day, young ones," Pap called cheerfully from the foredeck when he recognized us. "Come aboard! You ready to go fishing again?"

All the men were there, getting the boat ready to go out that night. When we came across the gangplank everyone stopped what they were doing and crowded around us, grinning and laughing.

"We come bringing you survival supplies for the cold night," said Harper. We handed them the cigarettes and the cognac. "The smokes are to keep away the mosquitoes and the cognac is to keep out the cold."

"Whoapa!" shouted Ramon. "We won't get much fishing done tonight!"

"No need waiting for tonight!" shouted Gustavo, the reader of cowboy books. "I got bitten by a mosquito just a minute ago!"

So the packages of cigarettes were swiftly distributed and everyone lit up. A bottle of Fundador lost its cork and between it and the magically appearing *porrón*, everyone was soon caught up in the spirit of things.

Captain Quintana who had stood a little back from the others in his usual quiet manner, smiled at the proceedings without chastising his crew for malingering with us. I moved around the men and shook hands with him, apologizing for disturbing their work.

"*No problema,*" he said. "You and your friend are always welcome here. We thank you for your kind remembrances."

"These too are for you and the men," I said, pulling the manila envelope out from inside my jacket and handing him the photograph I had made of him in his sheepskin vest and beret. In it he was standing high in the stern, his massive right hand hanging limp, his fingertips of the left hand resting lightly on one of the cables as he momentarily relaxed after standing their all night, his eyes closed now, face turned down toward the deck, each deep line of fatigue in his dark face mirroring a lifetime of these moments at sea.

Quintana took the photograph carefully as if he were afraid his big grimy hands would ruin it. He looked hard at the photograph, as though trying to identify the man he saw there. The other crewmembers fell silent. Quickly I handed each of them pictures I had made while they were hard at work.

Oddly, no one said anything for a while. Had they never seen themselves in an unposed picture? They stared at the thin rectangles of black and white, holding them ever so delicately in their callused hands, squinting at them intently.

"Look here," said bull-necked Ramon holding out the picture I had made of him leaning out of the wheelhouse and shouting into the storm. "Who said I ain't pretty?"

"You show me reading," said Gustavo, his voice almost in awe. "Look," he held out his picture, "he has me reading."

"Do I really look like that with the *porrón*?" asked Pap. I had made the picture from a low angle and he was arcing a long stream of wine into his mouth. "You know," he looked up at the others. "I'm really quite good!"

"Don't believe it, Uncle. It's how Roberto made the photo."

"I know," grinned Pap broadly showing his missing teeth, "but photographs speak only the truth, isn't that true?"

Sebastian the engineer studied his photograph quietly.

I had caught him standing in the companionway of his engine compartment, leaning slightly forward, his hands clasped on the edge of the

cabin coaming, the tip of one thumb touching his grizzled lean chin. He
was looking pensively into the sunrise.

"You made me look very thoughtful and intelligent," he said quietly.
"You made me…like a school teacher. Thank you, Roberto."

"More drinks all around for our *campadres!*" shouted Ramon, swiftly
uncorking the second bottle of cognac and passing it around. Everyone
again took swigs, followed by the passing around of the *porrón.*

Harper and I hadn't intended to upset their schedule with this much
celebration. As soon as it was appropriate we told our friends goodbye.
Everyone wished everyone a Merry Christmas and prosperous New Year.
Then we hurried ashore while the crew went good-naturedly back to work.

The last we heard as we went up the wharf were the fishermen's
cheerful calls wishing us good health and good luck. I hoped they would
have full nets that night.

Several days later Julie and I received notification that the customs
office in Palma was holding a package for us.

"Looks like our Christmas presents from home have arrived," I told
Julie. "We'll have to go down and claim them."

We hurried to town on the Lambretta. The customs office looked
about as cheerful as the one I had gone through with our luggage at
Port Bou. Right down to the carbine-toting *Guardia* standing quiet as a
statue in the background to keep the law and order.

When we handed the uniformed official the notice they had sent us,
he disappeared shortly and came back carrying a well wrapped cardboard box. I recognized my Mother-in-Laws' neatly penned handwrit-
ing on the label.

The official sat the box on the steel counter before us and said.
"Open it."

"Open it?" I wondered if I had heard correctly.

"*Si, Señor.*"

"But these are Christmas presents."

The official said nothing. He just sighed and stared at me.

"I think you better open it," said Julie.

Reluctantly I tore open the cardboard carton to reveal its contents: two identically wrapped smaller boxes in gaily-colored Christmas wrapping and ribbons.

I pulled them out of the carton and looked askance of the official. He tucked his lower lip under his upper lip and looked bored. His hand gesture and the glint of his eye under his hat brim were answer enough.

I tore off the Christmas wrappings. With a final slitting of the Scotch taped lid, I lifted off the cover to reveal a pair of light blue jersey garments.

At this point the customs official took over, lifting the item out of the box and holding it in front of him questioningly. Then came the lower half of the garment. What he had was the top and bottom of a warm-looking pair of knit-cuffed pajamas.

"God bless your folks," I said to Julie. "They sent us warm pajamas."

The second package lost its wrapping and was opened to reveal a pink pair of the same style of pajamas. Apparently, Julie's plea to her folks to send us some warmer nightclothes had not gone unnoticed. We almost drooled thinking how warm they were going to be.

The customs official conferred with another official, produced some official looking documents that had to be signed, dated, and stamped with an official looking stamp, then we were told how much we had to pay to keep the packages.

The price we were charged in *pesetas* made me winch. It was at least three times what the pajamas were worth at home. Possibly they thought we planned to sell them as contraband and that was the going rate.

When Julie saw me scowling at the document and about to dispute it with the official, she quickly said:

"Don't bother. They're not going to change their minds.

I looked at the customs agents. They stared back at us unblinking.

I paid the fee and collected our demolished Christmas gifts. "Merry Christmas," I said.

No one in the customs office responded.

We finally talked Miguel into coming to our place for an informal dinner, not that any of our dinners were formal, but he seemed shy when a number of us were together. So this particular evening we had him in for a simple affair. I cooked steaks over the fireplace with baked potatoes and a vegetable. We drank wine through the meal and ended up sitting outside on the porch watching the sunset while we shared several snifters of cognac together.

Slowly but surely, Miguel began to loosen up and drop some of the formality he wore as comfortably as his always immaculately pressed black suit. It seemed especially difficult for him to step out of the role of hotel manager and join the guests in their relaxed and informal roles. But he was learning.

We missed hearing music. With that thought in mind we rented a radio from Radio Borne in Palma. We liked their ad. It read "Westinghouse Electric Refrigerators, Marconi Radios, and Phonographs for Rent and Sale." The radio was one of those all-band affairs. We brought it home and soon were sitting in front of our warm fireplace listening to music from all over Europe and North Africa. What a feast for our ears!

Planning to have friends in on Christmas day for eggnog, we went in search of the proper ingredients. No problem locating the eggs and nog. What proved difficult was finding vanilla and nutmeg. The Solari family grocery at Porto Pi was closely scrutinized for these necessities. Since the always happy Solaris derived a lot of amusement out of our shopping ventures, they always stood close by, grinning, and ready to help. When we were absolutely unable to find any bottle of vanilla extract, or box of powdered nutmeg, we dug out our dictionary and threw ourselves at their mercy. Where, we asked, were these terribly important missing ingredients for making eggnog?

No need trying to explain the word "eggnog" to them, it wasn't in anyone's dictionary. We could ask for eggs, fried, boiled, beaten, poached or scrambled, but forget about nogged. So we started with the essentials and requested first, vanilla. That word wasn't in our pocket dictionary either. After many gestures and giggles from the Solaris, another customer who heard the commotion and spoke both English and Spanish, kindly came to our aid.

"Yes, yes!" shouted *Señora* Solari, as soon as she heard the Spanish word. "That we have."

She disappeared from behind the counter, rummaged in her shelves, and appeared triumphantly with our request. She handed me a long, skinny dried up brown bean. The only resemblance it had to what we were looking for was that it smelled vaguely of vanilla. But how one was supposed to get that bean into the form we used in eggnog remained a mystery.

Rather than upset the delicate balance of our nog with the bean, I insisted that what we wanted had to come in some other more usable form.

After much additional discussion, *Señora* Solari and the rest of the Solaris, agreed. They all went searching and in a few minutes, *Señor* Sollari let out a triumphant shout.

Proudly he passed me a small glass vial about two inches long. Some white crystals inside looked like sugar. But they too had the aroma of vanilla. To be on the safe side we purchased several vials.

Next came the question of the nutmeg. It too proved to be a word not worthy of inclusion in our dictionary.

We went through the whole procedure again. Mustering all the help we could get from the other patrons in the store, we finally got across the meaning of what we wanted.

At last the nutmeg came forth—a pecan-sized nut wrapped in cellophane. We'd worry about grating it later. Now we were in business. With that final mystery solved, we thanked everyone in sight and hurried home with our eggnog purchases. Our visits to the grocery store must have been quite entertaining to the Solaris. Every time they saw us coming their eyes lit up and they grinned.

Christmas Eve we spent in Palma, looking at all the delightful decorations in the shops. That evening we met all of our friends for a typical Christmas dinner at Latz's place. This popular little oasis on Calle Pellaiures a short block from the Borne was a bar, snack spot, restaurant, and a little piece of home away from home for every foreign visitor on the island. Not only was the cooking superb, but Latz made everyone feel as though they had stepped into one of their own restaurants at home. We ate our Thanksgiving dinner there: turkey and all the trimmings including the surprise of having fresh cranberry sauce, thanks to the kind contribution of an American Naval vessel that happened to be in port at the time.

Latz's specialties were German and American which meant being able to obtain such delights as large shrimp cocktails, juicy hamburgers, thick chicken sandwiches, real German beer with wurst, and freshly made crusty pumpernickel bread. Moreover, if you were up to it, Latz's 2-plate-blue-plate special consisted of a memorable shrimp bisque, followed by a large plate of roast beef. After that, your taste buds simply stood up and cheered.

So it was on the eve of this holiday all of our friends joined us at Latz's to share in his marvelous Christmas Eve turkey dinner and all that went with it. As customary in Spain, we ate quite late and took our time enjoying it. After the superb meal, and the good coffee, liquors and conversation that followed, everyone was primed for the highlight of the evening: the Midnight Mass at the magnificent Cathedral of Palma.

This historic island landmark was begun in 1229 with the arrival of Jaime I who had the mosque of Almudiana consecrated for use as a church. By the end of the century, the cathedral's construction was well under way, but for such a masterwork, it took time. By 1601, Mallorcans considered the basic structure complete. However, the cathedral's two spires were not added until the latter part of the 19th century.

Today, Palma's cathedral ranks as the second largest in Spain. Visitors are advised to see it at dusk, otherwise, going into it from out of the harsh Majorcan sunlight, then emerging back into the bright light will leave the impression of having just been inside a day-time movie.

At dusk the transition is far more appealing, as it was for us during the Midnight Mass. The cathedral's doors are works of art. The towering single-vaulted nave with its many columns reaching sky-ward provide some clues as to why this church took four hundred years to build.

On this particular evening, the church was packed with people. The size of the altar was as impressive to us as the fine choir music with its multitude of voices. At one time during the service, nine robed clergymen were involved in the alter ceremonies, helping to make this Midnight Mass a perfect prelude to the holidays.

That night, after mass, we came out of church surprised to find the streets filled with people wearing funny hats and blowing noisemakers. More New Year's Eve, than Christmas Eve.

Majorca's "Christmas Eve" celebration came twelve days later on the night of January 5. Cheering crowds lined the Borne to celebrate the coming of the Three Kings. Arrayed in flowing gold and silver capes and turbans, they arrived on Arabian horses. Lighted by flaming torches, the three moved up the boulevard side-by-side. Every child there looked forward to the marvelous gifts the Three Kings would bring them the next morning.

For us, however, Santa Claus came on Christmas Eve and the evidence was quite ample that he had managed to find his way to our villa sometime during the night. Not only were there colorful wrapped gifts under our little Christmas tree, but I detected slight traces of sooty footprints in front of our fireplace.

Eagerly we looked out our steamed windows hoping to see tracks in the snow but saw instead a couple of Scandinavians in overcoats and swimming suits heading down to the beach for a swim. No snow, but it surely was a chilling sight.

23

Sticking to Business

Our new downstairs neighbors were exceptionally quiet people. Not long after our house-warming party for them, they had us down for tea. Colonel Glenn-Cannon was a tall, distinguished retired British officer with short gray hair and a ruddy complexion. Trimly built, he carried himself with a certain military bearing that belied his former profession. He dressed nicely, wearing natty sport coats over neatly kept military apparel. No formal shirt and tie for him, he always wore his open-collared shirts with an ascot. Though he spoke fondly of his tour of duty in "Inja," his British accent was hardly noticeable. He smiled a lot and thought Americans were quite humorous in their peculiar sort of way. His only admitted vice was Madras curry that was shipped to him from Inja. He apparently ate lots of it because he got frequent shipments.

Quiet, always well-groomed Irma, his slender wife, was many years his junior. She wore her short black hair parted down the middle and pinned primly in tight waves close to her head. Looking as though she had never been in the sun, Irma was quite fair. She never wore make-up. Her features were long and linear, her lips always held in a tight, prim pucker, even when she smiled. She catered to the Colonel's every whim. I could never imagine Irma liking fiery Madras curry on her food, but then, knowing that she had once been a nun who left the order to marry, I could never imagine her even remotely involved with marital

intimacy either. Yet, it seemed that she and the Colonel adequately ful-
filled each other's needs without a problem.

Well, almost without a problem. The first time we realized one might
be occurring was when their frying pan appeared on their back porch
near our steps.

We saw it there shortly after they took up housekeeping. It looked as
though it had barely escaped total incineration. That was the first of
many times it appeared that way. After each episode, the Colonel would
either be out there scraping and scrubbing it with abrasives, or the pan
would be soaking for days on end. That suggested a small problem in
the cooking department. But no matter, the Glenn-Canons often
dressed formally and ate out a lot. Probably from necessity.

One morning, a knock on our back-porch door came from the
Colonel whose informal heavy red bathrobe, slippers and ascot, suggested that something more than a scorched frying pan was in harm's way.

"I say, Robert, have you got a moment. "Sure Colonel, what's up?"

"Well, we seem to have a small flood downstairs and I wondered if
you might take a look at it."

"Be glad to," I said.

He led me down the stairs and into their kitchen. The scorched frying pan soaking in the sink suggested that the cooking problem was
still ongoing.

This new problem, however, was of a more serious nature. It was in
the bathroom corner some distance from the sink. The Colonel had
placed a bath towel on the floor to soak up water seeping from under
the base-board. The towel was soaked.

"Are you having any flooding upstairs?" he asked.

"Not that I know of, Colonel. The water to both apartments come
from the catch-basin. That means the trouble is somewhere below our
apartment."

"I'm afraid you're right. I realize this bloody thing is a plumber's problem but with us into the holidays, there won't be a plumber to be had until next week sometime.

Meanwhile, all our water may run out right here."

That was a bad thought. The leak was probably somewhere behind the wall panel. "It may be leaking between the inner and outer walls of the house," I said.

"I see a pipe chase just to the right of the sink," he said.

"A pipe chase?"

"Yes. That tiny door. It's for servicing the plumbing. I couldn't even begin to get into the thing. It's too bloody small."

"Got a screw-driver and a flashlight?"

"Yes. One moment." The Colonel disappeared momentarily and came back with a small khaki bag of tools. "I wouldn't be without this handy kit." He passed me the tools.

Squatting down between the sink and the bathtub, I pried open the small door with the screw-driver and peered inside with the flashlight.

It was a crawl space about one and a half feet wide running behind the bathroom facilities. All the pipes and wiring were against the outer wall, which was built of the island's soft limestone blocks. Turning the flashlight left, I saw the problem. A large puddle had formed under the iron water pipe bringing water down from above. Since it was not near a joint, a seam may have broken. What bothered me more, however, was the bundle of electric wires I saw lying near the water there. Apparently, the workmen in their rush to complete the two apartments had left the wires lying loose along the floor. The puddle of water almost reached the electrical cables. It didn't take a plumber or an electrical wizard to see this was a potentially hazardous situation. Backing out of the small opening, I told the Colonel what I'd seen.

He blanched. "Somebody could get electrocuted! What can we do?"

"We could try to repair it ourselves," I made the mistake of saying.

"But how would we even begin?"

One thing had to be done right away. "I think it would be a good idea to shut off the electricity at the fuse box on the back porch first."

"Bloody right! What about the water?"

"The catch-basin was only a third full when I looked last week. Maybe we could bucket out some of it into containers and siphon the rest through our bathroom window into the tub. That would be the closest place."

"Good thinking, Robert. The landlady left a long water-hose under our front stoop. That would handle the siphon part."

First things first. We hurried out the back door and pulled the main switch on the electric box. The water pipe repair was something else. This could be a major plumbing operation, the kind that local plumbers could put off until after all the holidays. By then, the Glenn-Cannons would be flooded out of their apartment, or worse. It began to look like a solve-it-yourself emergency.

I considered the possibilities. A replacement pipe was out of the question for us. But what about a repair job? After all, this was a gravity feed water system. How much real pressure was there on that pipe? Certainly, there had to be a way to repair it. But with what, and how?

I could think of only one possibility. I told the Colonel about the tile shop next to our grocery at Porto Pi. It had such things as the grout I had gotten there for our tile table project. Maybe they had something that would work to patch the pipe leak. Like the grocer, *Señor* Salvador and his tile shop seemed to stay open for business most of the time.

"I'll get Julie to help you siphon water out of the basin. While you're doing that, I'll go to Porto Pi and see what I can find," I said.

"That's awfully good of you."

"Not at all. Where's Irma? Can she help?"

"Certainly. She's sewing. I'll knock her up for this water closet thing."

The Colonel had his own way of putting things.

I took the motor scooter two kilometers to the tile shop. *Señor* Salvador listened sympathetically to my plumbing problem. He was a small, wiry, leprechaun of a man in a leather apron with pockets along the bottom. His wire rim spectacles, long gray hair and full beard, made the rest of him look even more diminutive than he was. No matter when you saw the man, he looked as though he had just come from the back room of a bakery. But the best I could guess it wasn't flour that dusted him it was a fine layer of tile dust. Whatever he did in the back room of his shop created fine white dust that layered him like powdered sugar on French pastry.

"I'm no plumber, *Señor*, but I think you need a pipe patch."

"That is possible. Do you have such a thing?"

"Let me think." The little leprechaun pushed his hand through his beard thoughtfully and a small cloud of white descended down his apron front. Suddenly he looked up. I saw a glint of enlightenment behind his dusty glasses. He held up his hand, then disappeared into his back room.

When he returned he clutched two small unlabeled cans and a sheet of heavy woven white fabric. He told me that he had just received a large shipment of this miraculous new material from France and had poured some of it into cans for me to sample. He told me the two had to be mixed before it hardened,. Each by itself was as weak as water. But mixed together the combination welded everything hard as iron in thirty minutes. All you had to do was mix fifty drops of the small can with the contents of the big can and the magic went to work.

"A bull couldn't pull apart whatever you glue," the tile man assured me. "The fabric will become the pipe patch. Soaked in this stuff it will harden like the iron pipe itself."

What he offered me was fiberglass cloth and the epoxy resins that made it set up.

"Just what I need," I said. "Also, might you have a bracket? I have to hold up some wires."

"Done," said my leprechaun. He not only found me a metal bracket large enough to hold the wire bundle out of the water, but also a small block of wood it could be screwed onto. By gestures and words he described how both jobs could be done with his materials, even the wood-backed bracket glued to the rock wall.

"Strong," he grinned. "Like iron."

Thanking him for his help, I gratefully paid the tile-man the amount he asked for his magical concoction and hurried home to solve the Colonel's water closet problem.

By the time I got there, the catch-basin crew had emptied our water supply into a variety of containers including our bathtub. Everything was ready for my main assault on the leaky water pipe.

I screwed the bracket onto the one-by-four-inch wood block and cut a large enough piece of the white fiberglass fabric to cover it with a slot for the bracket to stick out while the patch held it to the wall. The idea was to soak the cloth in the goop, slip it over the bracket, then hold it against the wall until it set. This I planned to do with my right hand. Meanwhile, another piece of gooped fabric would be laid along the bottom-side of the pipe over the break and held in place until it too set. After that, *voila*, everything would hold forever.

The crawl space was about ten feet long and one-and-a-half-feet wide, too narrow for my arms at my sides. They had to be ahead of me, so I could work. Any other position and I risked a dislocated shoulder.

To prevent things going wrong in this tiny working area, every move had to be planned in advance. Since it was going to be hot in the narrow space, *that* part had already gone wrong.

Timing was everything. The whole operation had to be carried off smoothly without a hitch. To be absolutely sure it was I worked out every detail in advance with the precision of a military maneuver. The Colonel loved this part of it. Planning and preparing for the attack he positively glowed with enthusiasm. Watching us, Irma too seemed impressed, but her enthusiasm was as effusive as the wall I was about to cement.

All equipment was readied and standing by—a beat-up paintbrush, a pair of Irma's old rubber dishwashing gloves, a wide roll of adhesive tape and an eyedropper from the Colonel 's medical kit, a flashlight, a pile of newspapers to catch drips, rags, the the fiberglass patch, and lastly the mounted metal bracket.

According to the instructions *Señor* Salvador gave me, fifty drops of the stuff in the little can were to be well mixed with the contents of the big can. Once mixed the goop would set in thirty minutes. Anticipating that my arms might not last that long holding the bracket and the patch in place, I wrapped two separate twelve inch long pieces of the wide white adhesive tape loosely around my forearms, figuring that once the patch and bracket were gooped in place and ready to dry, the tape would hold them until things hardened.

With everything ready I carefully squeezed fifty drops of the little can's clear liquid into the syrupy clear stuff in the large can. Then, noting where the hand was on my wristwatch, I stirred the mixture vigorously for at least two minutes. The Colonel synchronized his watch with mine, and we prepared to do battle.

Donning the rubber gloves, I gathered all my materials in front of me and pushed them into the pipe chase opening. Then I wriggled after them arms first, shoving the materials along between the walls while keeping my flashlight on the pipe leak ahead of me. It was an extremely tight fit. Sawdust and small blocks of wood left by the workman littered the passageway. Between the cold iron pipe sliding along my right ear and the clammy rock wall pressing against my right side it was not too comfortable. Added to this were the hard electric cables that lay under my right groin. The whole place was already beginning to get warm and smelled of wet sawdust and pungent fiberglass resin.

When I reached the wet, but no longer dripping, water pipe, I shoved my pile of newspapers into the puddle to soak it up. With the rags I carefully wiped the pipe dry and made sure no loose dust layered the rock wall closest to the electrical wires where the supporting bracket would go. Arms overhead, there was just enough room to work.

At first, everything went well. With my rubber-gloved hand I dipped one of the fabric patches into the goop, soaking it good, then painted more of the stuff over the cracked pipe. This done, I slapped on the patch, managing to get the length of tape off my arm without tearing off too much hair but managed to get some on my left arm in the process. After the patch slithered off a couple times, I finally got it in place and taped. The edges gapped but I would worry about that later.

Next I turned my attention to the wall bracket. Using the paintbrush I liberally slathered the goop onto the wall, all over the wood block, dipped the fabric into the stuff until it too was saturated, then slipped it over the bracket and slapped it all onto the rock wall.

Carefully, I smoothed both sides of the cloth along the wall and held the bracket in place. No muss, no fuss. How easy it was. I complimented myself on a nice job done. In that confined space *Señor* Salvador's magic resin smelled like strong diesel fumes but breathing wasn't half bad if I kept my nose and mouth buried in the wadded up newspapers.

After what seemed like more than ample drying time I tried to read my watch in the gloom. Best I could judge it either said I had twenty minutes more to wait or I was ten minutes over the thirty-minute mark. My holding arm prickled with needles and pins. Tentatively I eased up on the bracket. It slipped.

Back I went with the pressure, sticking down the disturbed glass cloth with my well-gooped, rubber-gloved hand. Another long wait followed. The patch over the pipe not only had unstuck its edges but the whole thing had slithered free and was supported only by the tape. With my left hand I sat the flashlight on end and slapped the patch back in place, holding it tightly.

Shooting pains in my bracket-holding-arm reminded me that I had wound a second length of tape around my right arm to avoid this kind of hassle. Looking at my right arm now I realized the tape was not only firmly stuck to every hair there but the end was also stuck to the rock wall. To get it meant taking my hand off the bracket and breaking the bond. No hope of getting at it, I figured.

After many more minutes elapsed, I eased my aching grip on the bracket to test how well it was stuck.

The whole thing sloughed off in a sticky mass onto the sawdust of the crawl-space floor.

Hastily retrieving it, I plastered it back onto the wall and held it in place again. Soon, my arm was giving out; I needed something to support the bracket. Keeping pressure on it with my hand I tried to maneuver either the goop can or some blocks of wood to my assistance with my chin. Nothing worked. All I succeeded in doing was getting some of the goop on my chin where it started to sting. Once again the bracket slipped, the cloth flopped back and liberally doused my unprotected upper arm with goop.

At this point things were getting a little out of control. I ached from stem to stern, breathing was getting ridiculous, sweat trickled into my eyes, and I was close to swearing loud and clear. But instead, I quickly plopped the bracket back against the sticky wall and with sticky fingers smoothed the tacky cloth back over it. At least I hoped I had hit the bracket. By now my flashlight had rolled under the pipe and I was largely in the dark.

More time elapsed. Surely half an hour was up. I strained to see my wristwatch but the minute hand was a shadowy mystery. Holding the bracket with my right hand, and the pipe patch with my left, and gritting my teeth, I counted seconds.

Three minutes later I noticed a thick strand of goop running from the cloth patch to the goop can. Painfully, with my left rubber-gloved hand, I unstuck it, only to have it stick tight to the rubber glove. A spastic jerk of my hand to free it succeeded in jerking off the patch again!

More determined than ever now to tape up the whole works and forget it, I tore at the strip of adhesive around my right forearm. It finally came unstuck, taking plenty of hair with it. Clumsily I slapped the tape over the cloth and the bracket and tried putting the whole thing back onto the wall.

Things were setting up all right. Everything I touched stuck to me. Everything but the tape which stuck to itself. In disgust I finally ripped off the bracket, grabbed the whole affair and squirmed backward out of the crawl space avoiding touching anything with my gooped hands.

"Hello!" said a surprised Colonel as I wriggled out of the hole. "Went bloody well, eh?"

"Not really," I said. "The bloody stuff sticks to everything but where I want it."

I laid the mess aside to strip off a new length of tape. My watch told me that the effort had been going on for almost an hour. *An hour!* What the heck was holding up the hardening, I wondered.

Like tenacious spiderwebs, long strands of goop threads were strung from my hands to the bracket patch. Rather than get the Colonel caught in the mess, and lacking any other means, I leaned down and broke them with the side of my face.

Back I went into the hole, squirming along the crawl space with the bracket and patch held in front of me. I jammed the bracket, patch and tape into position. Fine, until retracting my rubber-gloved hand. Everything came away stuck to it! In desperation I looked around for something that was not sticky with goop, something to push with that wouldn't stick. The handle of the paintbrush protruded from the goop can. Goop might be on everything else in sight, but miraculously not on the very handle itself.

Holding the bracket with one gloved hand, I shook off the other glove and reached for the handle. The brush and the jar came as one unit, the brush frozen solidly in the hardened half inch of goop in the can! It boggled my mind to figure how that goop had hardened while the same stuff on the bracket was only sticky. I discarded the paintbrush idea and slid my left glove back on again.

By now, the tape had stuck to everything except the wall and was a hideous gooey mass adhering mostly to the wrist of my twitching right hand, still doggedly pinning the bracket to the wall. Also, by now the patches of goop that daubed my face when I broke the strings were now making their presence known. The only way I could ease the smarting was to press my face against the cool rock wall to my right, where it promptly stuck, until I jerked away and banged my head into the pipe.

Meanwhile, my numb fingers stubbornly played a game with the by now terribly tacky patch of goop cloth. They pushed it tight to the wall, then tried to get away without lifting the patch, which proved impossible to do. Finally, I fumbled the paintbrush handle and attached can into position and punched the bracket and patch down until they appeared reasonably well stuck. The pipe patch was half on and half off. To hell with it, I was determined that the bracket would stay stuck.

Then came another long wait. This had to be it. If I remained perfectly still, I told myself, the whole thing would set. Besides, by now I was too beat to really move much anyway. My face smarted so badly I didn't care if the wall did stick to it, at least it was nice and cool.

My hands and arms were now *hors de combat*. Numb. Everything was sticky, stuck, or getting that way fast. I envisioned the whole thing setting up hard as iron with me firmly caught like a gnat in amber in my own handiwork. Dimly I wondered if the Colonel or my wife would even hear my feeble calls for help from behind the wall. And if they did, how would they ever extricate me with that stuff setting up, as *Señor* Salvador said, hard as iron?

After a length of time sufficient to have hardened the patch twice, I slowly eased up on my holding pressure with the paintbrush can. The bracket and patch held for one breathless moment, then slowly, miserably, sloughed off onto the floor!

I stared at it with smarting, bloodshot eyes. The monster had defeated me.

Disgusted, I slithered backward along the crawl space, sliding easier now in a puddle of perspiration and sawdust, dragging the debris
with me.

"My word!" The Colonel exclaimed as I emerged from the hole. He
just stared.

Totally disgusted and gooped from head to arms, my only concern
now was to get that stuff off me before it hardened permanently. The
one thing that would do the job quickly was the can of lighter fluid I
had thoughtfully placed near our clean-up rags. After all the misery,
here, finally, was salvation. Grabbing the solvent can and rag I pushed
up the spout and poured.

The can was empty!

"Oh, I *say!*" murmured the Colonel. But he didn't know the half of it.

I sagged down on the bathroom floor and stared at my goop-daubed
wristwatch. Even as I watched the seconds tick away, it welded tightly to
my wrist. The guaranteed-to-harden-in-thirty-minutes fiberglassing
job had taken an incredible hour and thirteen minutes! The timing was
a little off, I reflected gloomily, but *Señor* Salvador was right about one
thing—the stuff eventually hardened like iron!

24

Hot on the Trail

My slipshod repair job on the Colonel's water pipe surprisingly did the job. Apparently enough goop hardened on the pipe to stop the leak. At least well enough for us to refill the roof-top water supply and get on with life. Fortunately, more lighter fluid was found to keep me from permanently sticking to myself with *Señor* Salvador's miraculous cement. But I swore off any more plumbing ventures.

Since both our cooking and our creature comforts depended on our ability to build fires, we quickly became proficient at it. Our daily fire-making chores, however, required different sized wood—especially the stove.

When we ran out of kindling, I walked down to the hotel to see if I could borrow an ax. Paco, the hotel cook, a young fellow with a full head of tightly curled hair, insisted on carrying the ax home for me.

Not only that, but he insisted on doing most of the work with it, swiftly reducing some of our almond and olive wood into neat stove-size kindling.

Moments later, Miguel arrived to explain why Paco was so friendly.

"He wants to talk with you."

"About what?" I asked.

Miguel shrugged. His glass wings fluttered. "Whatever you wish to talk about. He hopes to improve his English."

"Fine," I said. I looked at Paco. He nodded and grinned from ear to ear. As I wondered what subject would be appropriate for our improving talk, a distant gunshot rang out from the hills behind us.

Paco's eyebrows shot up, his grin broadened. He pointed at his ear. "You hear?"

"Yes," I said. What is it?"

Paco held out his hands as though holding a weapon. He said, "*pahhhng!*"

I said, "*En Inglés*: bang!"

Paco repeated it: "*Bahng!*"

"*Bueno.*" I said. "Close enough."

"What do they hunt?" I asked.

His answer had to pass through Miguel. "Maybe quail," he said.

"You like hunt?" asked Paco.

"Yes."

The curly-headed cook beamed. "You come with me and we hunt then."

That's how it began. I tried to talk Miguel into going with us but he declined. In fact the mere thought made him laugh more than I had ever seen him laugh before. He shook so hard his glasses literally flapped.

Paco, it seemed, knew more English than he cared to speak about. Apparently, that was the problem. He wanted to try it out on me so I could correct him if he was wrong. It was a good arrangement. I could learn more Mallorcain words at the same time.

So, at dawn the next morning, Paco and I set off to go hunting. I picked him up with the motor scooter at the hotel and we headed west on the coastal highway toward Santa Ponsa. Paco's family lived about eight miles along the coast in a small stone farm house.

As we pulled into the yard, a big dark brown, long-eared hound stood up in front of a shed and barked.

"My hunt dog," said Paco. The hound looked like the twin to *Señor* Frumpke's dog. I kept a wary eye on him while Paco went in the house to get our hunting equipment.

He came out bearing two ancient shotguns and two leather shoulder bags for game. He was now dressed for the occasion. A bandoleer of shotgun shells was slung over his too small cloth jacket. A too small Jungle Jim straw helmet perched atop his head, its strap under his chin. Paco's squashed-down nest of curly hair made more shade for his face than his hat did.

Our hunting weapons were old double-barreled shotguns capable of firing only after you cocked their twin hammers. Each had a leather shoulder sling. Both guns looked like something left over from the Spanish Civil War. When they went off, I hoped we wouldn't go with them.

"We hunt up there," said Paco, pointing to the steep brush-covered hills climbing sharply toward the sky across the road from his house. He handed me my armament and bag and we started out. With the double-barreled blunderbuss slung over my shoulder, and my black beret pulled low over my brow, Paco said I could easily pass for any bearded Mallorcain goat-herder on the lookout for wolves that might endanger his flock. I almost felt the part.

Paco's hunting hound sniffed the air and laid down. He had no desire to join our hunting expedition.

Paco reached into his game bag and brought out a small, hard roll. As we walked out of the yard, he periodically dropped a piece of bread behind him.

This sparked the hound's interest. He begrudgingly got up and began following us, pausing along the way to pick up the scraps of bread.

Everything was fine for awhile. Then Paco ran out of bread. The hound took two more sniffs of the air to make sure that what he thought happened, actually had, and then he turned and made his way slowly back down the hill to the house.

Paco called and waved another roll at the disappearing hound, but the dog paid no attention.

"One very bad dog," said Paco.

We followed the hound back to the house. When we got there he was fast asleep in front of the shed again. This time he didn't bother opening his eye or barking at our arrival.

Paco went into the shed and got a long, frayed rope. He knotted one end of it to the dog's collar. Then we went hunting again, Paco dragging the comatose hound behind us.

Gradually, as we climbed higher up through the rocks and the scrubby growth, the dog began to come to and look a bit more interested in our enterprise. He sniffed at first one thicket, then another, lifting his leg and marking each place he sniffed. I couldn't tell if he was hunting or merely being sociable with the other dogs in the neighborhood.

Whichever it was, we loaded our guns and drew back the hammers to their safety positions. Paco explained that if we sighted game and wished to shoot, the hammer had to be pulled back one more notch before you pulled the trigger and "*pahnnng!*"

Our hunting strategy was to keep climbing higher while moving cautiously from thicket to thicket. Each patch of cover was approached with the highest expectations. A frantic flutter of quail wings could be expected momentarily, warned Paco, especially if the cover was getting lots of intense sniffing from the hound,

If no game emerged from the thicket, then we kicked it.

In the next few hours we did a lot of thicket kicking and the hound was still lifting his leg at each one even though he had run out of markers a long time ago.

"He is a real crazy dog," commented Paco. I told him I believed it.

Soon, we were huffing up forty-five degree rock slopes. The island spread out below us like a green and brown patchwork quilt.

At noon, high up on the mountain where you could see the sea in three directions, we stopped for lunch. Paco tied the dog to a bush beneath which he promptly curled up and went to sleep.

From his game bag my guide produced two lengths of *chorizo*, two long hard chunks of bread, and a bottle of red wine.

After slicing the bread with my jack-knife, I started to cut up the sausage for sandwiches.

"Wait," said Paco. "I fix better." He shaved some kindling, touched a match to it, then skewered our *chorizo* on sharp green sticks for roasting.

"Like hot dogs," I said to Paco. But he never understood. How do you explain a hot dog in a foreign language to someone who hasn't the slightest inking what you are talking about? Paco repeated the words in Spanish but he thought it had something to do with his hound being in heat. I dropped the subject.

The *chorizo* sausage, mostly fat, hot spices, some meat and lots of paprika stuffed inside a tough pig's intestine and smoked—was more flammable that a marshmallow held too close to the flames. It caught fire instantly but it never seemed to char. Flaming fat poured out of it. When it looked scorched enough, you blew out the flames and folded it into a toasted piece of bread. It tasted delicious. Especially when followed by a couple long swallows of the tart red wine.

After resting awhile Paco and I practiced our pronunciations of various things we saw in our surroundings. Then we finally awakened the hound and hit the trail again.

This time we angled obliquely down hill, from one rocky thicket to another. The dog showed no more enthusiasm for the downhill hunt than he had for the uphill hunt. It was all the same to him. At least now he didn't go through the pretense of lifting his leg at each of the thickets.

Suddenly from under a pile of old brush, a rabbit leaped out. At the moment, we were slipping and sliding down a rocky grade trying to keep our balance.

The rabbit was a big one. It went up the rocky hill with the agility of a mountain goat. The hound and I just stared at it, but not Paco. Just as the game was about to bound over the ridge and disappear from view, my companion's blunderbuss went off in a cloud of black smoke. It kicked Paco backwards a couple feet but he proved to be as agile as the rabbit, swiftly regaining his composure and scrambling up the hill toward the spot where he last saw his target.

My ears were still ringing when Paco gleefully picked up the quarry and held it up for our inspection. The old rabbit looked as though it had spent a lot of years running around in those steep rocks looking for something to eat. I wished it had escaped. But Paco was elated. He wanted it recorded for prosperity so I took a picture of him proudly posed with the game, his Jungle Jim helmet at a jaunty angle on the back of his head.

Then we were hot on the trail again, eager to find more game now that we were obviously in the heart of game country. The only one of us who wasn't charged up by the sudden action was Paco's dog. I wondered if he knew something that we didn't.

The lone rabbit was the only game we saw the rest of the afternoon. Halfway down the hill the hound realized where we were headed. Swifter than he had moved all day, he finally got himself in gear and took off downhill at full gallop. When we finally got back down to Paco's house, his intrepid hunting hound was already curled up and well into his slumbers.

That evening, on our back porch, Paco held up the cleaned rabbit and insisted that we allow him to cook it for us.

What could you say to a hotel's premier chef? We gladly turned over our modest cooking facilities to him.

Once he fired up the woodstove to his liking, it was just a matter of time before he whisked out of its oven a huge platter of rabbit paella.

We enjoyed it enormously. Paco apologized that the dish was not as good as his usual paellas. He said our stove was not as hot as his at the hotel. He wanted us to hunt up another rabbit so he could prepare the dish properly on his stove at the hotel. But we assured him that was unnecessary. It may not have been up to his expectations but I noticed nothing was left when we finished. Admittedly, the rabbit was tough, but I figured any rabbit that had lived where he did deserved to be tough.

25

A Dangerous Game

We had gone so long without a calendar that all our letters home simply told what day it was written. Since this caused some confusion at home, we tried to do a better job. With the New Year we made sure we found a calendar and kept up more closely with dates. It was therefore on January 12, that we received a note from the American Express saying that we should contact them about a notification of a package being held for us.

We hurried to Palma and found someone who knew something about it. It seems that a notification from the Madrid American Express Company to the Palma American Express stated that a package had arrived for us and was being held at the Barcelona American Express and would we like it sent on to Majorca. We had earlier written the Barcelona American Express that they were to forward anything that arrived for us. But now we did it officially one more time. So our local office was to inform the Madrid office to tell the Barcelona office that yes, we would like our package forwarded. The people at the Palma American Express thought it would take about one week. That would more realistically translate into about two weeks. Then we would have the pleasure of seeing it through our friendly local customs office. With luck we might get our Christmas package by the first of February. It could be worse. Like lost forever.

All our news of the outside world reached us either through our rented radio and the clear reception we had of the British Broadcasting System, or through copies of the *Paris Herald Tribune* available at kiosks on the Borne. News always seemed to reach us long after events occurred. With one memorable exception. On New Year's Day it was cold and rainy. Hoping to fine-tune our radio for better pick-up, I took off the back that evening and tinkered with its insides. Late that night, to our surprise, we tuned in the Rose Bowl football game being broadcast from New York. It was so late and the game so one-sided, we couldn't stay awake to hear it end. We could hardly believe our luck in being able to get that station. Exceptional atmospherics must have favored the airwaves that night because it never happened again.

The long-delayed Christmas package from home that we expected to be forwarded from the Barcelona American Express finally reached our post office on January 25, a month after the fact. We had similar problems with our packages reaching home. They had not arrived there by the 29th of January. Harper and Binky's gifts sent a week before ours had just arrived. Julie's great-grand-mother had thoughtfully sent us a fruitcake long before Christmas. It never reached us. Possibly it was held up indefinitely at the customs. No hard feelings if it was. Even those public officials deserved some kind of extra treat at Christmas. They never sent us their "Season's Greetings From Your Local Customs People" card. Perhaps they lost the address label on the fruitcake, or maybe they just felt amply compensated. Who knows?

Palma's postal authorities could not have been more helpful. Often, they went out of their way to make things easier for us. For example, when we learned that Julie's sister was planning to get married, we bought a wedding gift and had it wrapped appropriately for the occasion.

When the package was weighed at the post office, the man in charge said it was 50 grams over a certain weight, putting it in a much more expensive category. Instead of coldly demanding the surcharge, the man apologized profusely for this fact. He said if we wanted him to do it, he would gladly re-wrap the package so that it would not weigh so much.

We told him to go ahead. As he removed all the pretty wrappings, he kept apologizing, saying how sorry he was to have to ruin the appearance of the beautiful package. Of course, we told him that it was quite all right, but he made us promise that we would come back the next day so he could buy us a cup of coffee! Julie apologized to her sister that the gift wasn't wrapped too professionally, but explained how we got a couple cups of coffee out of the deal, thanks to a compassionate postman.

To us, this generosity was typical of the people of Majorca. Our languages and customs were quite different and I'm sure that our differences often amused them, as theirs did us. But it was shared amusement. No one ever took offense. All the Mallorcains we met were exceptionally fine people. Indeed, crime on the island seemed nonexistent. It would have been hard for us to even imagine crime there. After all, it was an island where people seemed to go out of their way to help each other no matter who they were. They were especially kind to us. We never forgot that, nor them.

In Palma one morning I was picking up a copy of the *Paris Herald Tribune* from a kiosk on the Borne when a voice at my shoulder said:

"When do you come to play *pelota?*"

I turned to see a familiar face, but the name escaped me. The man with the goatee swiftly re-introduced himself with a handshake. He was *Señor* Maximilian, the manager of Fronton Balear who had seen us buying our Flea Market jai-alai scoop.

"How goes your *cesta?*" he asked smiling.

"Not bad. My wife has it on the wall with artificial flowers in it?

"Too bad," said the manager. "Are you long here?"

"Now?"

"Yes. In Palma. I go to the Fronton now for a practice. Perhaps you would care to accompany me?"

Julie was shopping with Binky and I wasn't planning to meet them at Latz for lunch for several hours. "Sure," I said, "I'd like to come. Maybe I can photograph the action."

No problem," said *Señor* Max. "I tell you all about *jai-alai* so you can write a story for your American magazines."

Max drove a small Italian Fiat with a roll-down top. I followed it on the scooter to the large concrete building with no windows, only a sign over the entrance proclaiming it the "Fronton Balear."

Max led me into the dimly lighted building. A damp chill gripped the place that even the hot summer sun probably never dispelled.

"First I show you the fronton, or court, then we have some coffee, " said Max. He led the way into a large theater-like audience area where rows of upholstered seats descended to a floor-to-ceiling wire fence separating the audience from the court.

Only the court was lighted. Several men with the long, curved wicker baskets or *cestas* worn on their right hand were clustered at one end of the long three-sided court. They took turns slinging a base-ball-sized ball with these baskets so that it bounced off the front wall of the court. The baskets on their hands flung the small leather projectile so swiftly I hardly saw it leave the server's basket. But you heard it hit the distant wall, all right. It cracked so hard, the report sounded like a rifle shot.

As the ball rebounded, the players adroitly caught it in their curved baskets and hurled it back to the wall again, sometimes getting there by firing it to the side wall so that it hit the front wall obliquely, the rebound returning at an unexpected angle. It was an extremely fast ball game.

"Come, let's have coffee and I will tell you about it," said Max.

Tables, chairs and a hot coffee urn occupied the largest part of a small one-room restaurant near the ball court. Max poured us mugs of steaming coffee and we sat down at one of the tables. I pulled out a notebook to take notes.

"We Spanish love this ballgame or *pelota*, especially the *Balearics* who are world famous for the game," said Max. "You know the Romans praised them because they were such good slingers?"

"Yes," I've heard that. Is this where the game began?"

"No, no. Not here." Max shook his finger over his steaming cup of coffee. "In Basque country. Far to the north of Spain. That's where it began in the 17th century. Today it's Spain's national game. It is called, 'Pelota vasca', or Basque ball game. The rest of the world knows it as *jai-alai*. In Basque that means '*jai*' or 'joyous' and '*alai*' meaning 'festival.' A very big game in Madrid, Barcelona, Manila, Buenos Aires, Havana, Miami." He looked at me closely. "You know Dania, Florida?"

"Yes, I've been there."

"*Jai-alai* is very big there."

Max went on to explain that the terrific pace of the game called for players with great speed, endurance, skill and dexterity. Eight balls almost the size of baseballs were used in the game. The balls were thrown with the wicker basket fastened to a glove worn by the player. The game was a combination of baseball, tennis, and Lacrosse.

"*Jai-alai* takes a heavy toll on players and equipment," said Max. "That's why you found the *cesta* in the market. We go through *cestas* quickly. We have one man whose steady job is just repairing the *cesta*. When it gets too bad, it is discarded."

"The balls too take punishment. The fronton court is…"he paused, "how do you say in feet? It is 180 feet long and thirty feet wide. The ball strikes that front wall going up to 120 miles an hour, so hard on the wall that it is made of graphite blocks to keep it from shattering."

"But the back wall is all pitted."

"Ah, you saw. Yes, that's what happens on the rebound, after the ball bounces off the front wall. Because graphite is very expensive, here we can only afford concrete for the back wall. You see how it shatters."

"It hits so hard it sounded like a rifle shot."

"*Pelota* players have been killed by the force of that ball," said Max. "If they are hit, players' bones often break. It is a very dangerous game."

Max told me that most of the world's best players come from the Basque country and Minorca, the sister island to Majorca.

"Do you know the name Manolete?" he asked.

"Wasn't he a famous bullfighter who was killed in the bullring?"

"Exactly. At Linares in forty-seven. One of our greatest. Well, the 'Manolete' of *jai-alai* was a Basque named Eusebio Erdoza." Max said that while most American boys were playing baseball for the fun of it, eight-year-old Erdoza was undergoing a rigid seven-year apprenticeship in the *jail-alai* courts of San Sebastian, Marquina, and Bilboa, developing his eye, his footwork, and most important of all, his right arm.

In just a few years he was playing professionally, relying on speed, power and uncanny reflexes no one had ever seen in the sport before. By the time he was seventeen, Erdoza had made history across six continents and was considered the world's greatest player.

"He grew to be a fine 180-pound athlete," said Max. Like Manolete, nobody was his match. He was the best. He played professionally to fifty-four-years of age. *Muy insolito.* Very usual," said Max, shaking his head. "Then, at the *Fronton Novedades* in Barcelona, during a very…how do you say…intense moment, before a thousand *aficionados*…he dropped dead of a heart attack. *Colapso corazon* for the man with the arm of gold, Eusebio Erdoza. Tragic." Max shook his head.

The manager went on to explain that wherever the game is played, professional *jai-alai* is more a business than a sport. Both players and spectators benefited financially. Behind the scenes, as in bullfighting, there were the managers, administrators, matchmakers, ticket sellers, score keepers, bookies, and many others making their living off the game.

"*Aqui en España*, two games are played." Max held up two fingers, touching each as he explained: "*Quinielas* and *Partidos*, the second being most popular." He then launched into an explanation of what occurred. In the *Quinielas* he said that it involved up to eight players with only two playing at a time. Each player played for himself, keeping the ball moving between the three walls of the court until one or the other player missed or fouled out. The winner of that match stayed in, taking on the next challenger. In a game with eight players, the winner had to score seven points.

Partitos were played with two teams of two players each; a red side and a blue, designated by colored sashes worn around the waist. The players defended forward and back areas of the court with action alternating as it did when playing doubles in tennis.

Then there were variations or handicap games in which a two-man side might play a three-man side because one of the players might be unusually gifted.

"Erdoza was often matched single-handed against three players," said Max, "And he could be counted on to win."

The betting system seemed the most complex of all to me. Max said it was an art. It went like lightning. Bets for or against a team were accepted by white-jacketed bookmakers in the crowds who shouted odds, issued vouchers and carried on a frantic sign language with bettors during the game.

"There are always bets for the little man as well as for the big man," said Max. "Win or lose, everyone has fun." With that he reached inside his coat pocket and gave me two complimentary tickets to the next game.

After our coffees, he led me out onto the court where the players kindly stopped ricocheting the ball around the walls long enough for Max to introduce us. They wore loose short-sleeve white shirts and pants, with narrow colored sashes for a belt. All of the players came from Minorca.

One, named Echave, smiled as he strapped my right hand into the narrow, crab-claw-shaped basket glove and showed me how I should turn backwards, bounce the ball once, then in one motion scoop it into the basket and sling it overhand at high speed toward the front wall.

When I tried, everyone wisely ducked.

The ball went obliquely into the fence. Repeated tries were equally unsuccessful. Finally, I began to get the hang of it and managed to hit the front wall once. I ducked.

Everyone else instantly dropped flat on the floor.

Having at least managed to get the ball to the front wall, I thanked my benefactor and relinquished the *cesta*. After that, I asked Max if they minded posing for some action shots.

"Not at all," said the manager. "Just show them where you want to make the pictures." He repeated the request to the players in a dialect totally alien to me. I wondered if Minorcan ball slingers had a language of their own.

Anyway they nodded agreement and stood by for my directions. Most of what I wanted I had to mimic for them first. They caught on immediately, then like the pros they were, they often elaborated.

First I flashed some scenes of the ball being scooped up and served. Then we got some close action in front of the graphite front wall. After that we got a jump catch at the back wall showing the pitted concrete.

After that things really got going. The players seemed inspired to show me some of their fancier tricks, such as climbing up the wire fence to intercept a high fly. They were truly agile athletes especially gifted in acrobatics, their muscular right arms almost over-developed from playing the game so long.

The more complicated my requests became, the more they liked posing for the shot. As they got into the swing of things, they suggested even more daring poses. Someone would serve a ball so that it came back toward the other player on a line drive. I positioned myself where I wanted to snap the picture. The ball and player were always there at the proper instant, the player throwing himself horizontally through the air as though making a flying tackle, the sickle-shaped *cesta* always just ahead of him to scoop up the ball and fire it back to the wall. Over and over they did it, so that the flying ball, player and wink of the camera flash all happened right where we planned it.

In the final scene that we set up, two players were back, another was rolling on the floor from the apparent effort of flinging the ball to the wall, and the fourth one catching the ball walked half way up the side wall to intercept it. It was a classic. After that scene I thanked everyone for their help and called it quits before they came up with an even more unbelievable set-up. I told them that I looked forward to seeing them in action the coming night. They all grinned and saluted me with their *cestas*. What a great bunch of pros they were.

The next night Julie and I took Harper and Binky to the Fronton Balear. The place was crowded. *Señor* Maximilian, his hair slicked down and shiny, wearing a gray pin-stripe business suit with a bright red silk handkerchief in its breast pocket took the big cigar out of his mouth and waved to us in the corridor as we went in. Gallantly he made his way to us, met our friends with a courtly little bow and flourish, then graciously led us down the aisle to our seats. Along the way people loudly greeted him or pounded him on his back. Laughing, the fronton maestro waved to them with his cigar. He sat us in choice front row mid-arena seats, then apologetically hurried off. Truly, as the French say, Max was a man in his *milieu*.

During the game that evening, we saw all the acrobatics the players had set up for me that afternoon. Now, however, they were used at high speed during the actual course of the competition between sides. The falls, the lunging dives to catch a rebound, the scramble up the fence for a high angled ricochet toward the spectators' section, the side-wall walking, and the high speed serves, everything moved at fast-forward with only the resounding crack...crack...crack of the ball marking the sharp, swift metronome pace of the game.

Around us the crowd yelled, jeered, cheered, whistled and bet on their chosen players while white-jacketed bookmakers milled back and forth in the aisles shouting odds, taking bets, scribbling vouchers on tiny pieces of paper, putting them inside a slotted tennis ball and tossing them to the bettors, who removed the vouchers and tossed back the ball.

What was going on at high-speed on the court, was matched by the high-speed betting on the sidelines. No wonder the game was so popular. We became instant *aficionados*. At least as spectators.

Fired with enthusiasm, once we I got home I decided to polish up my game. The side of the house would make a great one-wall court. I bought a small, hard rubber ball, removed our basket wall decoration, and practiced my serves against the side of the house.

All went well until I began getting sharp looks from my wife and the downstairs neighbors. That ended my practice. The basket went back up on the wall as a decoration.

I never told Max about my short-lived career in *jai-alai*. He might not have thought much of my dedication to the game.

To help defray our living costs, whenever possible I tried to turn our experiences into marketable magazine features. In the States I had majored in journalism, been an editor of a Florida sport fishing magazine, written and photographed free-lance features for years on whatever activity interested editors enough to pay hard cash for them. Now that we were abroad, I was doing the same thing, but in a much more relaxed, not so high-pressured manner.

Rainy winter days on Majorca with cold, blustery winds making it highly disagreeable outside was my kind of perfect writing weather. While Julie worked her magic in the kitchen, putting her all into a thick Italian minestrone, or a wine-flavored French bouillabaisse served with thick, buttered slabs of crusty fresh-baked Mallorcain bread, I tried stirring the literary pot of our new experiences for possibly salable features.

My office was a thick pillow in front of the crackling hot fireplace. My desk was the broken-tile-decorated millstone sitting atop the big overturned flowerpot. It would have nicely supported a laptop computer but I chose instead a super-thin manual Swiss Hermes portable typewriter that required nothing more than an occasional ribbon. At just the right height, both "desk" and typewriter fitted nicely between my outstretched legs. Near at hand, on such cold, miserable days, was usually a large amber snifter of *Cento Tres* [meaning "103"] a mildly caramel-flavored Spanish cognac for both inspiration and comfort. Eventually, this combination never failed to bring forth the muse in one form or another.

Features I wrote for stateside consumption, such as our motor scooter trip across the rivieras, were mailed to my New York literary agent for sale to appropriate publications. Long after the fact, the checks gradually filtered back to us on Majorca. Features of a more European nature were sold directly to magazines interested in these subjects. For example, while we were in Neuchâtel, Switzerland, I learned that a scientific study was being made on the trout population in the lake there and a beneficial fish culture program was producing unusual results for Swiss anglers. My interviews and photographs formed a feature that sold to England's *Trout and Salmon* Journal for Game Fishermen in London. In Madrid, Spain's hunting and fishing magazine, *Caza y Pesca* accepted by tales about Florida sport fishing, translating them into Spanish for their readers. An American weekly magazine, published in Madrid as *Guidepost*, seemed pleased with the story and photographs about the "Hottest Game in the World," *jai-alai*. This magazine soon became a good market for other features. Our cozy little villa overlooking Cala Mayor was a fine place to write.

Toward the end of January the days suddenly grew warmer. We guessed that the African trade winds were finally working their magic on Majorca. A distinct, spring-like aroma filled the air. Just seeing the sun more often, helped. One day, when we looked out our back window behind the terraced rock walls to the brown grass hillside, we were astonished to see color that had not been there before. The almond trees had burst into bloom with an explosion of muted amber colors, their limbs covered with compact blossoms. If this wasn't a sign of coming spring, we didn't know what was! We hurried outdoors and climbed up through the field, reveling in the sunshine, the newly open blossoms and the fresh, tangy smell of salt air. At that moment—whether Mother Nature was deceiving us or not—we knew we had made it through the worst of the winter. Everything to come was anticipated as being pure pleasure for our winter-weary senses. We could hardly wait.

26

Springtime Majorca

With the warmer weather and the sun shining almost daily now, Julie and I spent more time on the Lambretta, traveling to some of the areas we had not yet seen. Usually we would fix salami and cheese sandwiches made with the small loaves of Mallorcan bread. With them we carried a bottle of good red wine, the everyday variety sold in bulk on the island. Everything went into our net bag and was shock-corded to our luggage rack.

One day, as we were about to take off on an exploratory trip, *Señor* Frumpke, who had just left us a load of wood, looked curiously at what we were taking along as a picnic lunch.

"*Porque no bota?*" he inquired He wanted to know why we did not have a *bota*, one of the goat-skin wine bags that are typically Spanish. He held his hand over his head and to one side, with his lips pursed as if catching the stream of wine squirting out of an imaginary *bota*.

"You are right," I said. "More typically *Españole.*"

"Yes. But also, more likely not to break. You know about *botas*?"

I shook my head. Frumpke looped his horse's reins over a corner post of his wood cart and I knew we were in for a small discussion on the subject.

"There are all kinds of *botas*," our woodman said. "Forget about those they sell the tourists."

"But the tourists buy them all," I said.

"Ah, yes," Frumke squinted at me with a devious smile. "*but* there is a difference. The tourists may not know it, but there is." He winked.

I waited for him to tell me the difference but he was waiting for me to ask. So I did.

"The difference is that the *bota* of the turista is PLAHS-tee-ka!" He spat the word out with obvious distaste.

I told him I had never heard of a plastic *bota*.

"They hide it," grinned Frumpke. "It's inside. You have to unscrew the top to see it."

"And that's bad?" I asked.

"Oooooo," he held his nose. "*Muy malo.*" Very bad. Then he hastened to add, "Unless you like plastic flavored wine."

"That would be a crime," I said. My woodman agreed. It seemed that most tourists would not even know that they were victims of such a crime because Frumpke felt they had no taste for wine anyway.

"But you both need to be careful," he warned us. "Purchase only the *autentico bota Españole.*"

When I asked how we should recognize the genuine article without having to look inside, Frumpke said the leather bag of the real *bota* would be flat and hard as a log of olive-wood. He knocked a piece with his knuckles to demonstrate its hardness.

"You must make it soft," he said.

Again, he waited expectantly for me to inquire about that process. When I asked, he immediately described how we were to toast the newly acquired leather *bota* in front of a warm fire, turning it from side to side, careful not to scorch the leather bag. Slowly, because the inside of the bag was coated with resin, we were to heat it and work it with our hands until the bag became limber. Then, and only then, were we to fill the bag with red wine.

"But do not drink it," he warned sternly. "It is very bad tasting." Instead, we were to throw that wine out, refill the bag, and let it set for a day. After that, we were not to drink that wine either. It was to be discarded. We would refill and empty the bag for five days, and then we might refill it and sample the wine. It should be just right, said Frumpke. Maybe a bit smoky flavored. "But that is the taste of *vino* from the *autentico bota Españole.*"

I thanked our woodman for that important information and assured him we would follow his directions to the letter.

"And remember," he added, "never let your *autentico bota* be without wine." If it stayed empty, he warned, the wine bag would go back to being hard as an olive branch and we would have to start the process all over again.

Frumpke spoke the truth. On our next trip to Palma we looked into purchasing an *autentico bota*. Most looked alike on the outside, with the possible exception of those made for tourists. They were usually more gaudily decorated. Some had leather outside, but many were plastic imitations. One even had sponge rubber. The real Majorcan *botas* hung from their cords stiff as boards, their leather dark brown, their caps and narrow tops made of shaped horn, rather that the slicker looking plastic of the tourist models. Understandably, they not only looked like poor cousins to the flashier and always pliant tourist wine bag, but they smelled different. The smell alone would have driven a tourist toward the less *autentico* model. Who could blame them for not wanting to purchase something that felt like wood, looked like wood and smelled like hot tar.

We found an authentic *bota* to our liking and promptly took it home for its fireplace seasoning. I slowly heated it, getting it to finally bend. I worked it into a pliable shape and got its sides unstuck from each other. Then began the seasoning with wine.

Five days later after five consecutive bagsful of wine were added and subsequently discarded, we gave it its last fill and sampled the results.

The wine tasted vaguely of creosote. It was a resin flavor we took a long time getting used to. But eventually, we grew to tolerate it, figuring that if we were going to use a *bota* at all, the only two choices we had was wine with a creosote flavor, or wine with a plastic flavor. We opted for what all Majorcans seemed to enjoy. At least we were *authentic*. It was a lot like learning to drink Scotch. It took time to educate the palate.

One of the things that fascinated us about Spain, was the amount of antiquity still present. Castles in Spain are cliches, but they exist, almost as grandly as the day they were built. One of the first palaces we explored was the Castle of Belver that has been sitting on a high hill outside of Palma called Puig de la Mezquita for the last 650 years. "Puig" means mountain despite being roughly pronounced "pooch" in Majorcan. And "Mezquita" has nothing to do with the island's mosquito population, it means "mosque." From its battlements you get the best view of the island. But what amazed us about the castle was the beauty of its architecture. Looking down on it from its highest turret you become aware of the circles, whirls, and radials that formed its perfectly symmetrical construction. It is a photographer's dream.

As we motored along the hills outside Palma, we were often stopped by roadways filled with woolly sheep with vivid red dye markings on their back; the sheepherders identification marks. All such herds were accompanied by smiling sheepherders and their dogs tending the flocks. Rather than try to motor through these slow-moving creatures we found the encounters pleasant excuses to park the scooter and ramble off on foot across the tall golden grasses of the meadows through recently blossomed almond trees. Then it was just a matter of finding a quiet place to sit under a tree on a hill with a view, soaking up the pastoral beauty of the place while occasionally savoring the rich, resin-flavored wine of our *bota*.

The almond orchards were a delight, and while we had not yet seen any of the ancient olive groves, we had read that the harvesting of both almonds and olives were much alike. But what enormous differences between trees. The almond is a frail, lovely looking tree, delicate of leaf, while the olive in all its large gnarled and contorted forms would make the ugliest gargoyle look graceful. But what wonderful fruit these two trees possess!

Almonds are Majorca's major export. The Majorcan farmer is a firm believer in letting Mother Nature take her course with no unnecessary interference from him. As far as he is concerned, the almond tree is his friend. Once the farmer plants the almond tree, it goes on growing forever. Once a year, when its fruit is ripe, the farmer goes out and beats his trees with a long pole to knock off the almonds. The almonds are picked up and taken home. This is almond farming.

Same thing happens with the olive trees. Those Romans planted on Majorca hundreds of years ago still bear olives. Once a year, when the fruit is ready for harvesting, the farmer goes to his olive trees with a long pole and beats the branches, knocking off the green olives. These are picked up and taken home. This is olive farming.

Majorcans feed their horses and mules a long green bean called algarrobas. These beans grow on trees. Need I tell you how the Majorcans harvest them? Right. Just like almonds and olives. Once a year they go out with long poles and beat the algarrobas trees. These beans are picked up and taken home to become feed for the animals. Apparently they like their menu because Majorcan horses and mules are a contented lot. Understandably, so are the Majorcan farmers. You might say they have reduced their farming chores not so much to a science, but to the basics. Apparently, the secret to being a successful Majorcan farmer is to never interfere with what a tree intends doing naturally. All it requires once in a while is a good beating. This is Majorcan farming.

Our exploratory trips along the coast were sightseeing photographic ventures. We recorded what we saw not so much because it might have some salable quality to it, but because the scenes were in some way uniquely beautiful, typifying this unusual island in the Mediterranean. Our machina fotographica missed nothing. The cathedral spires rising up out of an early morning fog, the quiet coves too beautiful to disturb, the sheep herds grazing under blooming almond trees against a back-

drop of dark blue skies too tranquil for words. And we also photographed the people, the huddled fishermen repairing nets along the
wharf, the lined, weary faces of black-shawled women selling old bottles, the fresh faces of children playing in the narrow streets, the droll
little switch-carrying donkey cart drivers, the tall, lean, sure-footed
waiters balancing trays of baking goods atop their heads over the
crowds as they traverse serpentine walkways, the full-skirted, black pig-
tailed young peasant girls dancing traditional folk dances in the mountain villages, the occasional, colorful Gypsies, the boisterous lottery
vendors, the gossiping women washing clothes in village fountains, the
quiet, peaceful look of an entire village of red-tiled roofs, as seen from
a high hill near the town of Soller.

Surprises seemed to await us around every corner. Heading west out
of Palma one day we followed the road to Lluchmayor, then to Campos,
on to Santanyi and Ses Salines. What made this route so astonishing was
the abundance of windmills. They were everywhere, filling the sky with
their four-bladed sails, the countryside green as an Irish meadow thanks
to the fresh water pumped up by all these wind mills. What a restful
sight for eyes numbed by the steady diet of arid brown or reddish rocks
common to the surrounding hills.

On one of our trips inland to the town of Inca, we were amazed to
see land-owners with greyhounds as house pets. When we inquired
about this, we learned that the dogs were brought to the island by the
Romans, who used the animals as fleet hunting hounds. Nobody knew
what they hunted, but hopefully it was game more fleet of foot that the
rabbit we disturbed on the high mountain peak. The offspring of these
greyhounds remain on the island today, especially in the back country
where these long-legged fast animals have plenty of room to do what
they do best: run.

The reason I wanted to visit Inca was two fold. First, the name
intrigued me. What was an "Inca" doing that far from Peru? The other
reason was to see an unusual kind of carving. Someone had told us that

there lived a wood-carver in the village of Inca, whose wood-carvings in the iron-hard ancient olive wood, were rustic works of art. So we headed northeast out of Palma, paralleling a railroad track, on a road that carried us through the dry hills and plains skirting the windmill country to our southeast, past the towns of Marratxi, Santa Maria, and Consell, to Inca, a distance of twenty-nine kilometers or about eighteen miles.

Not knowing where to begin our search for the wood-carver of Inca, we started by having coffee at a local cafe on the square. No need to go further. Sitting on a shelf along the upper wall of the café were old wine barrels and dusty olive-wood figures. The pieces looked much like miniatures of the giant Easter Island statues. One in particular caught my eye. It had been roughly cut out of a branch of olive-wood the thickness of a man's arm. What impressed me most about this particular work was that it looked so much like the *Esperanza's* engineer, Sebastian. Same long lean face, deep set eyes, and pursed, schoolteacher lips. Only difference was that the carving suggested a beard. Sebastian wore no beard but if he had, this was his look-alike in Roman day olive-wood.

The dark, stained, purposely aged carving could not have pleased me more. Though only about twelve inches tall, it was heavy. This olivewood likeness of Sebastian was the only Incan artifact we acquired. We never learned where the town's name came from.

27

Seeking *El Señor*

As the days warmed, we spent more of the daylight hours away from our villa. Julie and Binky often shopped the Palma market for fresh produce and fish. For some reason the island's chickens always turned out to be tough birds, so we usually passed them up for the always available fresh seafood at the fish market. Through our visits there and the chance meetings with Vicente, we learned that the *Esperanza* crew always made the Saturday morning market, then usually stayed in port until Sunday night when they went fishing again.

This reminded me of our promise to look in on Pap at nearby San Agustín to see how he was getting along with his mystery fish, *El Señor*. So, late one Saturday morning with the women doing their usual shopping, Harper and I decided to ride out to San Agustín and see what Pap was doing.

The fishing village was the next large cove up the coast from Cala Mayor, just west of us. The tram stop beside a kiosk and a row of tan-colored buildings on a small square was all the casual visitor saw of San Agustín. Beyond the buildings, however, lay a protected cove for fishing boats. In some places the brown rock reached out toward the water in long, low, perfectly flat steps, as though cut that way. Long wood oar boats were hauled onto these flat areas for patching and painting. They were the boats Pap once rowed with the long, heavy oars that roped to thole pins along both sides.

A rambling group of tile-roofed stone houses stood high above the water near the boats. Beneath a straw-roofed shelter, several workmen painted a boat. When we asked where we might find Julio Domingo, they said he had just walked up the street to a nearby ship chandler's store. We found him inside, purchasing fishing tackle.

"*Hola, pescadores!*" he greeted us with a broad grin and a warm embrace. "What brings you out here?"

We told him we came to see what luck he was having with *El Señor.*"

"Mostly bad." said Pap. "I only get to try for him on weekends now. But you are in luck. This moment I am purchasing line so strong he will be unable to break it."

I looked around the shop. It sold everything a fisherman would ever need. Nailed prominently on the wall behind the counter was a large, yellowing bullfight poster whose edges were curling. It was a painting of a tall, thin sad-faced matador, unmistakably Manolete, looking away from the bull that was charging past his mid-section. A sombrero and a bouquet of flowers lay on the ground to one side. It was a poster of his last fight in Linares. Someone had painstakingly pasted small sequins on Manolete's sun-faded "suit of lights."

The portly, bespectacled chandler in brown apron and black rubber boots appeared from behind stacks of boxes with a large spool of dark-colored fishing line.

"You must be after a whale with this heavy stuff," he said, setting the spool on the counter.

"Big fish, big line," Pap winked at me.

"What fish?" asked the merchant.

"The usual. *El Señor.*"

"Ah, *claro.*" Of course. The shopkeeper glanced at us, smiling. "Pap and *El Señor* make good business for me. They are both too stubborn to quit. I'll be *un viejo,* an old one before he ever catches that devil." The man turned and took a large chrome sportfishing reel off a top shelf where it sat with several others.

"Now this is what you need for *El Señor*," he said. He laid the fishing reel on the counter in front of Pap. It was the size of a soccer ball. It's chrome shined as though oiled. The deep-sea fishing reel was loaded with flexible wire line.

"There is no other shop on the island with an import like that," said the merchant proudly. "I rent it to foreigners who pay to go deep-sea fishing."

"Whew! I bet it would make short work of big tuna," said Pap.

"Phoof!" The stocky merchant jerked his head and looked over the top of his spectacles to indicate what sort of work it would make of them. "Man, a machine like that should be against the law it is so deadly for big fish." He sighed. "But nobody ever buys, they just rent." The merchant shrugged indifferently. "It pays for itself. I keep it clean."

Pap gave the handle a spin, cocking his head, listening to the music of the smooth, even, precisely clicking mechanism. You could tell the way he smiled what he thought of it.

"Maybe one trip with this reel and he would be yours," said Harper.

Pap cradled the large reel in his hands, not saying anything. Then he carefully laid it back on the counter and wiped his fingerprints off the chrome. "Yes," he said, "it would probably do the job swiftly. But then who would they say caught the fish?" He looked up at us. "Me, or this *machina?*"

The merchant nodded, scooped the reel off the counter, polished it quickly with his apron and returned it to its shelf. "You are right, *Tío*. These things should be illegal. The *exstranjeros* can have them." He turned back to the counter. "Now, how much hand-line?"

"Forty meters," said Pap.

The merchant swiftly peeled off the line, measuring it against a meter mark painted along his edge of the counter.

As he coiled the heavy line and wrapped it in a sheet of newspaper. He asked what else Pap needed.

"That wire line on the reel. Do you also stock that?"

"Certainly, *Tío*, for the big reel. But it is very expensive."

"How much just for a leader?"

"How long?" asked the merchant.

"Four meters," said Pap.

The merchant shrugged. "You have always been a good customer, *Tío*. I make you a good price. If you need more, know that I always have it at a good price."

"*Bueno*," said Pap.

The merchant cut the wire leader and wrapped it too in newspaper. He asked if Pap needed hooks and leads.

"No," said Pap, "I have a supply of both. Ignacio the blacksmith made me some fine big strong hooks, and I have the swivels."

Pap paid the shopkeeper and picked up his purchases. "*Venga*," he said grinning at us. "Come. Let's go see if *El Señor* is home."

We walked back down to the cove where the sprawl of red tile-roofed white stucco stone houses sat on the high ground behind the beached fishing boats. Several dogs prowled around the area. As soon as we approached, one of them made a beeline for Pap. It was one of the strangest dogs Harper or I had ever seen. It was one of those grey-hound-type hunting breeds common to the island. But this dog had a peculiar color pattern more like a tortoise-shell cat. Mixed patches of yellow, brown, black and white marked its body, all the way up to its large, rounded up-standing ears, as if its greyhound fore-bearer had somehow got crossed with an African hyena.

"*Hola, Fugly!*" Pap yelled and threw wide his arms.

A fast sprint plus two bounds and the skinny spotted greyhound kangarooed into Pap's arms so violently it knocked him backwards almost off his feet.

Recovering, he hugged the greyhound. The dog grinned widely and licked Pap's face with a long slobbery tongue. "Meet my baby," laughed Pap. "He's my best friend. *Mi amigo*, Fugly."

"His name is what?" asked Harper.

"Fugly," repeated Pap.

"That doesn't sound like a Majorcan name."

"No," said the old man, spilling the limber-legged hound out of his arms. "It's a foreign name. An *Inglés*, I believe. A British *marinero* gave him to me in Palma when he got too big to keep. I got the name with the dog." Pap grinned. "He swims like a fish."

Fugly bounced over and sniffed us. Apparently we passed inspection because he did a series of fast bounding circles around us, obviously ready for any adventure we might have in mind. Those weird spots made Pap's pet almost the ugliest dog I ever saw. But at least he was loaded with energy. And he seemed cheerful. From the expression on his face, he laughed at everything. Probably our guess at Fugly's lineage wasn't too far off. The Brit who named him wasn't far off either.

Pap led us to his house to get the rest of his fishing gear. He introduced us to his two sons who were outside, hammering caulking into the seams of an over-turned boat. Both were muscular men in their early thirties, thick, jet black hair, black eyes, finely shaped features, working barefoot in their undershirts and the heavy canvas trousers common to these fishermen. One was named José, the other, Ramos. They had powerful handshakes, warm, friendly smiles.

"You like fish with Julio on *Esparanza*?" asked Ramos.

We both smiled and nodded.

"How you like his cook?" grinned José, speaking English. "He good cook?"

"Numero uno," Harper said. "Not much sea sickness." He rubbed his stomach and smiled.

"Number one is right," laughed Ramos. "No Julio, no eat. Better he be good number one."

We all laughed.

A colored bead curtain rattled behind us. We looked around as a strikingly attractive woman with long black hair in a long black skirt with a black shawl over her shoulders came out bearing a small brass tray and two small glasses.

"*Buenas dias,*" she smiled. "May I offer you a small Palo? *Soy Maria,* Julio's *esposa.*"

"*Gracias, Señora* . Very kind of you," I said to Julio's wife. Pap ducked around her and went in their house, leaving us to deal with the amenities.

She filled the *copitas* from an uncapped bottle in her right hand. "Julio tells me he is taking you to meet, *El Señor.*"

"We hope so," I said, taking one of the glasses and making a slight motion in her direction as I sipped the strong drink. Palo is a traditional Majorcan liquor made of walnut shells. Taken straight it feels as though it is eating the enamel off your teeth.

We spoke of the fine weather and Pap's wife said how happy she was to see the *tramontana* finally stop blowing.

"When it is with us it is always so difficult for the fishermen." She extended the bottle of Palo. "*Encore?*"

"No, no, a thousand thanks," said Harper. "We need a clear head for *El Señor.*"

"But of course," smiled *Señora* Domingo. She shook her head. "That fish. It's all he thinks about when he's home. It'll be the death of him yet."

"Not today," said Pap, coming out through the clattering beaded curtain with his fishing paraphernalia. "We do business with *El Señor* today." The line and leader were neatly coiled and tied together to avoid tangling. A sharp hook almost the size of my hand was embedded in a large cork float. Pap slipped the coils over his shoulder and said, "Let's go." The spotted Fugly, lying lean and patiently quiet in the shade of the fishing boat bounded up and loped off ahead of us, his tongue lolling out the side of his mouth. He was grinning like crazy.

"Thank you for your kindness, *Señora* ." I sat my glass on the brass tray. Harper did the same.

"Not at all," she smiled. Then called after her husband, "Be careful, you hear?"

Without turning he called back. "I hear."

"*Suerte!* Luck," called his two sons. Still not looking back, Pap raised his hand and shuffled on over the rocks in his rope-soled shoes, a man on a mission.

We stopped only once, beside a fishing boat with large oil lamps on its stern that had just been pushed up to the beach. Pap spoke to one of the men who reached into a box and pulled out something. Wrapping it in newspaper, he handed it to Pap. Julio gave him a cigarette from his prized pack of Philip Morris I had slipped into his pocket earlier and we were on our way again. Fugly stood waiting well ahead of us, his tongue lolling out of his grinning mouth, his expression seeming to admonish us for our delay.

We climbed up onto the rocks on the other side of the cove, and made our way over them a short distance to another cove, this one quite a bit smaller with no beach below us whatsoever. Only at the far right, near less steep rocks did the cove funnel into a narrow gravel beach about wide enough for two people to sit. We stopped on a rock platform about twelve feet over the water. A narrow path led down to the water's edge below. Pap beckoned us to his side.

"Look over there." He pointed across the small cove to the opposite sheer rock wall. Below the clear blue water line could be seen the black entrance of a cave. The way the water turned deep blue with this black backdrop suggested a very deep hole indeed.

"That's where he lives *muchachos*. Let's hope he's hungry."

Pap carefully lay out his coils of line. He tied one end of the line in a slipknot around his wrist. The rest of the line was loosely dropped coil after coil atop one another on the ground. Finally, nothing remained but the long flexible wire leader attached to the big heavy steel hook.

With his foot, Pap unrolled the newspaper-wrapped packet the fisherman had given him. Inside, in all its pinkish purple glory squirmed a large, bulbous-headed octopus about twelve inches across from arm-tip to writhing arm-tip. It was nice and lively.

"*Viva el pulpo,*" said Pap, picking up the huge bait. Using a short length of line, he tied the large octopus securely to the shank of the hook. "I hope *El Señor* likes you." Fugly sat nearby watching intently, ears alert, lean body quivering. His narrowed eyes all but crackled sparks.

Once everything was ready, Pap held the line just above the leader swivel and began whirling the bait around and around over his head, gradually lengthening the line he held. Suddenly, he let go and arced the heavy bait out across the cove. The loose line on the ground followed it swiftly.

Once the bait reached bottom in front of the cave entrance, Pap did not move it for several minutes. After awhile he slowly took up slack in the line, letting it fall into a pile at his feet. From time to time he paused, then continued inching in the line.

"Look what I do," he said to us. "*Señor Pulpo* has just been to *El Señor's* front door. But The Mister makes believe he is not at home. He is an old and wise fish. He knows *Señor Pulpo* is there, but he knows too he cannot act the young fool by rushing out and gulping him down. That is how he got to be so old."

"But you pull the octopus away."

"Yes. Into my ground," said Pap. "That is my only chance. I am lost if *El Señor* grabs the bait and gets back into his cave. He wedges himself in like a rock and that is that."

"But you have no lead on your line. Won't the octopus hide under a rock?" I asked.

"Not where I put him," explained Pap. "The bottom is sand in this cove. There is no place to hide. With a lead on the line I would have no feel to it."

Pap's efforts looked flimsy to me. I saw no way a man of his light stature was going to handle a fish that might out-weigh him tremendously. Pap didn't even have gloves with him. I could just see that line with a big fish on it going wherever it wanted to go. But then, I had overlooked the fact that Pap was no novice with this fish. He and *El Señor* had encountered each other before.

We waited on the rock for a good half-hour. Nothing happened. The octopus seemed satisfied to stay where he was, probably weighed down to some extent by the big hook. I imagined the live bait flattened on the bottom, turning the same color as the sand for camouflage, watchfully keeping a low profile.

Fugly hadn't relaxed a muscle since we started fishing. He moved into the shade of a rock outcrop, but he remained sitting on his haunches, watching every movement anyone made. I had the eerie feeling that the greyhound was doing just what nature had taught his breed to do so well. If he were stalking a brace of gazelle on the Serengeti Plain, he would have done the same thing, patiently wait in cover, watching for the proper moment to strike.

"Uh-huh!" Pap sat up, his thumb and forefinger held the snug line delicately.

"What's happening?" asked Harper.

"*El Pulpo* just woke up," murmured Pap. "He feels nervous." Our eyes riveted on where the line entered the water.

Slowly it began moving on an angle away from the cave. Pap let the line slide slowly through his fingertips. "Uh-huh," he said again. "I think something is coming."

Careful not to upset the gentle tension on the line, he got to his feet. So did Fugly, his eyes never leaving Pap or the taut line angling down into the water.

Switching the slowly sliding line to his left hand, Pap reached behind him into his hip pocket and withdrew an olive wood thole pin, the kind we had seen on the oar boats that served to hold an oar. Then he switched the line back to his right hand so it slid gently over the wooden pin.

"*Venga*…." Pap whispered to the invisible participants underwater. "Come along now…you know it is only a big, juicy *pulpo. Venga, hombre*…"

The line began moving faster now. Pap made no move to hold it. All he said was, "*Si, Señor…Si, si…*take it all…good and deep…."

The line changed angle, still taut but moving back now toward the opposite side of the cove.

Pap braced himself. Reaching back for some slack he wrapped one turn of the line around the wood thole pin. When the slack tightened, he leaned forward with the pin in front of him, let the line grow snug, then suddenly snatched the wrapped pin back toward him, not once, but three times hard.

The line twanged taut, then surged forward with such violence Pap was dragged, sliding to the very edge of the cliff. But he grabbed the line with his other arm and between the thole pin's tight hold, and the wrap he got around his left arm, he managed to haul it back toward him enough to get the line over his back. Then, leaning back he bodily dragged it toward him.

In the water the line thrashed wildly back and forth in tight, short zigzags whipping the surface to a froth as though the fish were shaking its head violently from side-to-side.

We wanted to help but didn't know how. When Harper moved to touch the line and give Pap a hand, the old man shouted sharply for him to get back.

The tug of war between the man and the fish went back and forth, Pap gaining ground with the tight black line cutting deep welts into his back and shoulders. Then suddenly he had to let line go back, begrudgingly letting it slide back into the water. It dragged him to the very lip of the cliff where he simply could not hold on any longer without going over.

Suddenly, the movement ceased. The full weight was still upon it, but there was no surface movement back and forth. I looked to where it entered the water. It was closer to the other side now, pointing toward the black hole of the cave. I glanced at Pap. His face was still pinched up from the effort. Sweat flowed down his cheeks into his bristly white stubble. I suspect that he knew what had happened, but wasn't yet ready to admit it.

Keeping pressure on the line over his shoulder he reached out with his left hand and thrummed the line. *"Dica mi!* Tell me something fish!"

He thrummed the line again. Suddenly it surged forward a couple feet, then abruptly released.

Pap went over backwards. The greatest disappointment I've ever seen on a face was deeply set into the wrinkled creases of his weathered face as he slowly got up, dusted himself off and silently hauled in the line.

The end was frayed. He stared at the broken end sullenly.

"My God!" said Harper. "He broke it!"

Pap looked up sharply. "No. The rocks in the cave cut it." Pap slowly coiled the heavy line and slid it over his shoulder. He looked at us, but he wasn't smiling. *"El Señor* liked his lunch, but he didn't think much of my flimsy fishing line." Pap shook his head. "I'm going to have to do better next time."

We walked back to San Agustín with him, but no one felt much like talking. Fugly loped on ahead of us, as full of energy as ever. It was nothing new to him. He had been on this hunt before.

We didn't go back to see Pap make another try for *El Señor*. It all seemed a little sad. This old man trying to do the impossible with a wary old fish nobody over the years had ever bested. It was hopeless. I had pretty much decided the only thing that would best that monster would be a diver with a bang-stick, an explosive device on the head of a spear some divers use to hunt large sharks and 300-pound jewfish.

How wrong I was!

A little over a week later, it was in all the Spanish newspapers. Pap made the headlines! He had actually *caught* and landed *El Señor* on hook and line but almost lost his life doing it!

An out-of-breath Harper had rushed up our two flights of steps clutching the newspaper. Pap's picture was on the front page. So was that of his dog, Fugly. I couldn't believe it. There they were, both grinning at each other together.

In Spanish the headline blared, "GIANT FISH CAUGHT BY MALLORCAIN FISHERMAN!" The news article told how Pap had long been trying to catch the legendary fish, and last weekend he finally succeeded. He had used the sportfisherman's wire line, wrapping it around his body to hold the big fish. The struggle between man and fish had "endured for over a tortuous hour," said the paper. In the end, the great fish surged violently and pulled the fisherman off the rocks to "his certain death by drowning." Except for the angler's "valiant dog, Fugly." The greyhound "leaped with great canine courage," into the sea after his master, and succeeded in towing him to shore. There, Pap continued the "wild, ferocious battle" with the great fish and eventually subdued it. It was a giant conger eel measuring ten feet long and weighing 300 pounds, the largest anyone had ever seen! The picture of the catch with Pap and Fugly and a half dozen other people standing behind it looked like some kind of huge sea monster. Its eyes and gaping mouth were awesome.

Harper and I hurried to San Agustín to congratulate Pap. The place was alive with photographers. Pap was on top of the world. He told us jubilantly that the oarsmen in his longboat had restored him to his former position, "as long as I want it!" Pap laughed and shook his fist triumphantly in the air. He had waited years for this recognition, and now by gosh he got it!

The large eel was given to some scientists from Barcelona who wanted to study it. Manufacturers of big deep-sea fishing reels wanted to sign Pap up for advertising pictures of him holding their equipment. Even *TIME* did a column-length feature on Pap, showing his picture and stating that the ten-foot-long 300-pound conger eel was the largest ever caught in the Mediterranean.

As for Pap and Fugly, they just grinned from ear-to-ear at all the attention. Some dog food manufacturer even promised to give Fugly a lifetime supply of its dog food in exchange for an endorsement. I'm sure the offer made Fugly grin all the more.

They are quite a pair, those two!

28

Of *Bombas, Tapas,* and Snails

The first realization that all was not quite right with our plumbing came the day our water stopped.

A quick inspection revealed that our rooftop catch basin was bone dry. Not a drop remained. Two apartments of four people were suddenly as destitute for water as though we were marooned in the middle of the Sahara Desert.

I knew we had had no rain for a long time, but did that mean we now had to commission some one to start carrying water to us? A kind of Gunga-Din water-bearer with huge bulging goat-skin *botas* of water slung over his sway-backed donkey trudging up the long rocky road from Palma to bring us the essential essence of life. I even imagined him looking like *Señor* Frumpke, leading a horse-drawn wagon of firewood on one side and a water-bagged donkey on his other side. Or would he use a water buffalo?

My imagination went rampant. But then I hadn't had a glass of good cool water in…I couldn't remember when! Was I already dehydrated?

Julie was equally alarmed. But not quite to the point where she could envision serious problems, such as I did. An immediate problem that flashed before my eyes was: how do we now flush the toilet?

Just the thought made me want to go!

But I didn't bring it up then because Julie was saying how we still had lots of wine and champagne and we could somehow get through this crisis with those.

As she solved our immediate thirst problem, I visualized gallons of wine going down our toilet. How long could we stand that?

Downstairs, the Colonel and his wife were just inches away from pushing the panic button. They too were aware of how critical the situation was, especially concerning the toilet. I saw panic in Irma's eyes and knew that she knew but was too proper to put words to her panic. The Colonel, on the other hand, kept a stiff upper lip about it all. He said he still had an ample supply of soda water for his Scotch, and for his other personal necessities. It must have been some supply.

Our first move was to consult our friend Miguel who was gifted in solving emergencies of this kind. Surely, he had faced water shortages of this magnitude before.

I found him in the rear of the hotel, supervising the kitchen staff.

"Miguel, we're in trouble again. We haven't had rain now for almost a month."

The near-sighted hotel manager peered closely at me through his thick-lensed glasses. "Have you planted a vegetable garden?" he asked in his quiet, unassuming voice.

"No, man. We're out of water! There's none on the roof. Not enough rain for even one glassful!"

Still he stared at me without seeming to grasp the seriousness of the situation. Finally he said, "But…why do you drink rainwater?"

"That's all we have! That's where it comes from! Off our roof!" I was getting a bit short-tempered. Certainly, he of all people could understand our predicament.

But he couldn't. As he repeated the word "rainwater" he began his quiet laughter. It always began somewhere deep down inside him, first a chuckle that started those glass wings of his quivering, then it grew, even though Miguel never changed his expression much. As the chuckle came up, the wings began flapping, then you saw his eyes watering. Miguel's mirth was not so much an outburst of emotion as it was a suppression of it. He was good at suppressing such outbursts.

When he could finally talk without choking, he asked me again about drinking rainwater and I went over the whole thing with him, even to taking him out on the back patio and pointing to the catch-basin on our roof. That seemed to sober him. Now he seemed to understand what I was talking about.

"Ah, no indeed. That shouldn't be empty. There must be something wrong with your...how do you say it?" He made an up-and-down motion with his fist. "Your...BOHM-bah."

"My bomb?"

"Yes...but no bomba with a BOOM! Bomba with a PAM, PAM, PAM for *agua*."

"A water bomb?"

"Yes, yes, that's right," said Miguel, his eyes brightening.

"But I knew it wasn't. Something was wrong somewhere.

I bought out my trusty little *Collins Gem Dictionary Spanish-English: English-Spanish*, and looked it up.

For some really bizarre reason the word "bomba" in Spanish means "bomb" in English, as well as "pump." Miguel had been talking about a "water pump," not a "water bomb!"

"You say there is a water pump that brings us water?"

"Oh yes, certainly," said Miguel. "It is piped out from Palma, then all of these villas have their water pumps that pump the water up into that basin on top. Yours must have blown up."

A quaint way to put it. No wonder they call it a bomb.

"I telephone your landlady and explain the problem," said Miguel. "She will call the *bomba* men."

I thanked Miguel, relieved that our crisis would soon be in the hands of experts. He too was pleased that he had been able to help, beaming and rubbing his hands together in front of his perfectly pressed coat and buttoned black vest, his glasses fluttering. He would have made a great undertaker.

When I explained the situation at home, everyone breathed a sigh of relief. We all then rounded up pots and pans and went to see our neighbors. Binky and Harper's water supply worked perfectly. In no time we had enough water on hand to handle any emergencies.

The bomb squad arrived shortly after midday. They drove up in a miniature white truck. In large green letters on the side was announced: *"Palumbo e Hijo—FONTANEROS."*

If there was ever a father and son team that looked less like plumbers, this was it. Both wore funny little black hats that almost resembled small bowlers. One man, the father, was short and rotund with a tiny Hitler mustache under his little nose. The other was tall and skinny, with a long sad face, sleepy eyes and spiky black hair. They looked exactly like Stan Laurel and Oliver Hardy dressed as plumbers. Each carried a toolbox. Monkey wrenches stuck out of their overall hip pockets. A row of pencils and pens were clipped to their bibs.

"Buenas tardes, Señor…e Señora!" smilingly announced the round one, introducing himself and his son. "I am Pablo Palumbo, and this is my son, Saldo. We have come to inspect your *bomba.*"

I said I hoped they knew more about where that particular piece of equipment was hiding than we did.

It turned out that they did indeed. They had been on a similar mission here before, when the *bomba* was installed. They should be able to correct the situation momentarily. *No problema.* With that, the two trooped off to do their business.

I cornered Colonel for some serious plumbing talk.

"Tell me how we managed to empty that catch-basin when I did that pipe repair if we had water being pumped into it?"

"Maybe it wasn't working then either."

"It had to be. The idea of the thing, I think, is to pump water into the basin when it gets low. It should have filled up by itself when we emptied it, if that were the case."

"You're right. It would seem so. I really am in the dark about these things, ol' boy. I haven't the foggiest notion about matters of this nature."

"Wait a minute," I said. "I remember corking what I thought was an overflow pipe because it was feeding back water into the tank. I'll bet that was the pipe from the water pump. That's why water was coming out of it."

"Certainly makes sense," said the Colonel. "But then so does the idea that the affair on the roof is also a catch-basin for rain. I've seen the things in Morocco."

"Right. Same with our villa on Capri. That's all we had for water. Mosquitoes came out the tap but we got pretty good at filtering them through our teeth."

The Colonel nodded. "Does seem that if those basins were not intended to catch rain, they would have lids."

So it would seem. Apparently, to augment the lack of rainwater during times of little downfall, the pump kicked in with water from Palma. In either case it was nice to know we were not as bad off for water as it first seemed.

Some time later, Palumbo and son reported back that our *bomba* had blown a gasket or something and parts were needed from Palma. It would be another day or so before they would have us back in water again.

For the next two days we lived on borrowed supplies. It was not too bad. We relied on our friendly neighbors for our bathes. Naturally, these were all tub bathes. Nobody in our neighborhood possessed a shower. I wondered how fast one of those would deplete our water supply. Probably stress out the system to the extent of blowing the *bomba* again.

True to their word, in a couple days, our Stan and Ollie look-alikes worked their magic somewhere down the hill below our house, the pump was fixed, and we were once again with water. No lid went on our catch basin, so rain or drought we always had life's basic necessity. If nothing broke.

We shortly discovered that one of Majorca's most intriguing pastimes is browsing through her antique shops. What especially intrigued me were some of the things that turned up from out of the sea. The most common items were large Roman amphorae, the pointed bottom wine and food-stuff ceramic containers that traveled the Mediterranean nested on Roman ships. Some of these vessels apparently came to a bad end on Majorca's underwater rocks.

We saw so many of these amphorae for sale at such spectacularly high prices that I finally asked one of the antique dealers if many Roman ships had perished in the Balearics.

"Oh, I'm sure many have," he assured me. "Our amphora here is at least 2,000 years old."

"Ummm. That's a lot of lost amphorae."

"Yes, indeed. Divers find some," said the merchant, and fishermen catch them in their nets. They hate them because they often tear the nets. So they curse them, break them, and throw them back into the sea."

Even with some broken, I wondered how big a treasure trove of complete 2,000-year-old amphorae must still litter the bottom around the island just waiting for some scuba diving entrepreneur to bring up.

At another high class antique shop, when the merchant saw me examining one of the amphorae he had mounted in a specially made wrought iron stand so it sat up, I learned another interesting fact:

"I doubt that many of these jars came from shipwrecks," he said. "I suspect they were thrown into the sea on purpose."

"On purpose?"

"*Si, Señor*. To make happy the Gods of the Sea," my learned informer said. "Roman *marineros* believed that if they gave their sea gods enough wine to drink, they would keep the seas calm for passages. So they tossed over these jugs of *vino* to assure safe journey."

Made sense. Especially after I learned that some old Balearic sailors still toss a glass of wine overboard when the weather looked bad. When asked why they did it, they said, "for luck." Whatever the reason, it occurred to me that there might be plenty of Roman amphorae *still filled* with 2,000 year old wine just waiting to be found and picked up if one buckled on a scuba tank and took a look at the bottom. Especially around the ports where Romans first set up operations on Majorca.

Then, a chance encounter with another antique dealer changed my mind. As I looked over his amphora offering, also mounted in a nice wrought iron stand, he said: "of course you know this is not *un amphora autentico.*"

"Not real?"

"*Un amphora, si. Autentico, no.*"

"But the marine encrustation. The little shells, the wormy-looking things stuck on, the barnacles…not real?"

"Ah. *Si, Señor.*" The merchant smiled. "Those are real. The *jar* is real. But neither one is *viejo*. Not old. Make believe old." He smiled again.

I looked at the amphora with renewed interest, the way you might look at your fifty dollar bill someone has just pointed out is counterfeit.

The counterfeit amphora looked just as *autentico* as I imagined any looked. "How do they do it?" I asked.

"I am told they have a jar made locally, then leave it in the sea for a year to take on a patina of authenticity." The antique dealer shrugged. "You hardly see an original any more. But plenty of these are on the market."

So much for reaping a fortune in the antique amphora business. If originals were numerous, why bother making counterfeits? The fake Roman wine bottle business seemed as lucrative as the fake wine bag business. You couldn't be too careful, even in fancy antique shops.

Each time we were in Palma close to the dining hours, we observed the local custom of visiting *tapa* bars. The word means "lid" or "cover," the kind of thing we needed on our rooftop catch-basin. In this case, however, it meant the little saucers of appetizers sold at most bars in Spain. Throughout Spain, people go to *tapa* bars the way Americans might go to local watering spas for liquid refreshments before going home from work.

These are social events. Socializing is the main reason Spaniards go to *tapa* bars. The next reason is to eat. Drinks are far less important than eating appetizers in preparation for the main event that will take place a couple hours later.

To demonstrate how little important the drinking is, tapa bars serve their customers watered wine. Everyone knows it is watered wine but nobody cares. Good conversation is far more important. After all, a small glass of watered wine costs almost nothing. *Tapa* bartenders make their money off the "lids" of appetizers customers consume in prodigious amounts.

There is nothing too fancy about *tapas*, but one has a wide selection. Small boiled shrimp are basic *tapas*. So too are olives. They get fancier and pricier by what is stuffed inside them. You might want to start out with a small saucer of plain green olives marinating in olive oil and vinegar. Follow those with ripe black olives doing the same thing. The next might be olives stuffed with pimentos. After that you can progress to a variety of stuffed olives, some you can't even identify either by taste or looks. Smoked, salty anchovies are popular stuffings for green olives. Certain mussels and other kinds of shellfish often end up stuffed into olives as well. The really fancy olive *tapas* may contain more than one item stuffed into an olive, such as an anchovy, a cooked mussel, and a caper all together.

Julie always checked out the vegetable *tapas*. They come in all varieties, usually pickled in an olive oil marinade. Some kind of potato salad is always popular, especially when it includes bits of shrimp.

Snails are big at *tapa* bars. They usually come cooked in their shells with garlic and parsley butter. We saw no olives stuffed with snails, but that doesn't mean they don't exist.

Sometimes *tapa* customers ordered a favorite dish that could serve several at one time. The components always arrived in a fireproof bowl with the olive oil spitting and crackling from just having been taken out of the oven. Each little item was about a half inch long, and snow white. You skewered them with toothpicks and popped them down. They were unborn eels.

Fried circlets of squid, whole fried squid, pickled squid and various parts of pickled octopuses, sardines, and a variety of other small marinated fish are equally popular snacks at most *tapa* bars. The one item which we never got up enough courage to try were the trays of plucked and roasted sparrow-sized birds, heads and all. They never did much for our appetites.

Getting use to the island's snails as a desirable food item was also unsuccessful. We had sampled them at the *tapa* bars and found them different from the flavor of French *escargots*, but we tried. One day shortly after a brief warm rain, I noticed that the terraces across the street from our villa were dotted with people looking around the hedges and shrubbery for something. They carried brown paper bags and were picking things off the ground.

"Hey, grab a couple bags and let's go pick some wild mushrooms!" I called to Julie.

With our sacks in our pockets, we headed for the terraces. Visions of sweet butter-sautéed morel mushrooms on toast passed before my eyes. An Epicurean feast was at hand for the picking!

When we reached the terraces, however, we found no mushrooms. In fact, at first we could not see what it was the people were collecting. Only after moving up beside some avid hunters did we learn what it was.

"*Los caracols!*" They announced happily. "Wild Majorcan snails!" Opening their bag, they showed us their find. They were small brownish-yellow shells with their inhabitants slithering clumsily over their companions.

"But what do you do with them?" asked Julie.

"*Comé*," was the response. "You eat them."

"I mean the cooking. How is that done?"

Quickly our new friends gave us a speed course on the preparation of wild Majorcan snails. First we were to look for the shelled fellows after a light rain, such as what we just had. Apparently the snails become active then and slither around the neighborhood terraces for what purpose no one knew. But, that was when snail-hunters found and collected them.

The snails were then taken home and put in a container and kept overnight. The idea here was that this allowed the little creatures to void the contents of their intestinal tracts. Presumably it made them sweeter to eat.

After that, they were unceremoniously dropped into a container of boiling water. After that they were extracted from their shells. The next step was to stuff them back into their shells with garlic butter and parsley. After that they were briefly broiled and served. The snail lover then tooth-picked them out of their shells and ate them.

Whenever Frenchmen discuss this phase they always close their eyes and kiss their fingertips. The bliss on their face is self-explanatory. We understood what they meant when they did this with French snails. But was it the same out-of-world experience with Spanish snails? Never having tackled them from scratch before, we only knew what the end product tasted like in a restaurant. But now we were game to start at the beginning of this business by hunting down the wild and elusive snail itself.

Thanking our friends for this information and grasping our brown paper bags with determination, we set off in search of snails. As snail hunters we were very good. Between us we found double handfuls of the little creatures.

At home we deposited our find in the kitchen sink where Julie scrupulously washed them. Then she covered the sink with a dishtowel and went shopping while nature took its course and the snails did their business.

When we came home a few hours later, we found snails all over our kitchen. They had crept up the inside of the sink and easily breached the dishtowel barrier.

Back they all went into confinement. This time in a more suitable container with no easy way out. Again we left them alone to let nature run its course.

The next day we washed our catch and proceeded with the other steps of preparation. Once they were properly cooked and stuffed, we served them.

Sadly, there was no closing of the eyes and kissing of our fingertips. Something must have been lost in the translation because our gourmet Majorcan snails tasted like small garlic-butter-and-parsley-roasted rubber erasers.

Nothing seemed to improve them much, not even when I boiled them in wine, chopped them up and added them to rice. We may have over-done something, or forgotten to do something. They still tasted like shredded rubber. We never tried again. We left the Majorcan snail population to the more successful connoisseurs of that delicacy.

"I say, have either of you chaps ever experienced any of the Majorcan barbers?" the Colonel inquired one day.

We both admitted that we had not had that pleasure.

"Well, I have," he said, turning around to let us inspect his haircut and shave. "I must say it was something. Those blokes give you your money's worth and then some"

"In what way, Colonel?"

"If you go in for a shave, they shave you twice. With a straight razor. There's not the slightest chance that they don't do a good job the first time. But they do it twice to be doubly sure. After they've shaved you almost raw, they lotion your face. Now this isn't just some watered down flowery smelling water. This is pure, crude alcohol. *Un-be-liev-ably painful*," said the Colonel with a frown. "In fact, Robert, if you ever go to have your beard shaved off I suggest you carry a small rubber ball with you to bite down on good and hard when they lotion you."

"I think I'll stick with the beard." I said.

"Of course. Now the haircut is something else," the Colonel continued. "You best show them exactly how much you want cut off, otherwise you're at their mercy. If you want a crew cut, then you tell them you want it *pelado*, pronounced *pay-LAH-doh*. It means 'peeled' and I mean they know how to do that.

"After that watch out for the grease," warned the Colonel." They love to grease hair. They do it automatically if you don't stop them before they get their hands on the stuff. The way you avoid that is to screech, *seco*, meaning 'dry' and pronounced '*SAY-koh*.'

"Next they grab a bottle of rose water or something and slather it around your neck and face. It has a fragrance that would make a flower wilt. Then they hit you with the talcum powder, a whole big can sprinkled on a large paintbrush-looking thing that they brush all over you until you're sitting in a pink cloud of the beastly stuff. The only way to stop them from those last two things is to shout loudly '*NO!*' and make a move to throw off the barber cloth they've wrapped you up in." Colonel shook his head. "Honestly, I think I'll just grow a beard and forget all that nonsense. If only Irma would go along with it."

Our trips to Palma were always a treat. There were favorite bookstores to check out. One in particular on the upper Borne carried a good collection of used pocket books. We gave them as much business as we could afford. Most of the books were published in Great Britain. With new purchases under our arms, we often walked down the Borne and turned off at the Tirol for lunch.

What a prize this place is! Rudi's *Rathskeller* offers beer-lovers some of the finest brews that ever passed parched lips. We usually ordered an especially creamy kind of German beer that left suds halfway up the inside of the colorful beer stein when you drank it. Big wooden beer barrels decorate this typical alpine bar, and the beer that flows from the

Tirol's taps come in two choices: light or dark. Both are winners. Rudi specializes in the finest German food and beer, the latter available in six different-sized glasses ranging up to a magnificent 212 liters. That one was an all-day variety, the kind tourists often walked off with.

Knackwurst, blutwurst, sauerkraut, frankfurters, powerful Bavarian mustards, and crusty heavy loaves of freshly baked German bread, always made a stop at Rudi's one of the highlights of a day in Palma.

Also, it gave us an opportunity to check out all the local characters. Whoever, they were, and wherever they came from, they all eventually found their way to the Borne sometime during the day. Indeed, some of the more serious ones worked the street for a living.

One was named Beaner Scofield. He told us he came from Missouri, that he was living on an inheritance, plus whatever else he could pick up along the way.

The place where Beaner usually picked up business was by standing just outside the door of the American Express Company. He always got there early each day just before the busy time with tourists. He said he always checked the mail first to see if some kind relative had sent him a letter and maybe slipped a dollar bill or two inside.

After that, he stood outside the door, ready to be of service to any tourist in need, always of course, with the hope of pocketing a small tip for his consideration.

In time we realized that Beaner was one of the truly great actors on the island. Not only was he a great liar, but he was a born improviser. None of his acts was ever the same, though it always ended up by Beaner benefiting monetarily. Spontaneously he could devise the most incredible scenarios designed to separate people from their money. Beaner said he was gifted. The Colonel said he was a born scoundrel. You had to stand on the sidelines and catch his act to properly appreciate his abilities. Hollywood probably would have made him a wealthy star for his natural acting ability. Here's how he handled one of his "customers."

Beaner was standing in his usual spot outside the American Express one day shortly after the tourist boat came in from Barcelona. People went in and out of the American Express. Beaner, neat and clean, but dressed as the British would say, "a bit shabbily" stood attentively beside the door when a large American blond woman in a bright red dress with yellow accessories exited the American Express.

The woman glanced up and down the street, saw Beaner and approached him.

"Excuse me, young man. Do you speak English?"

"Yes, Ma'm," said Beaner.

"Well…" the woman seemed a bit flustered. "I'm new to Majorca but I plan to be here long enough to see a bullfight. I wonder could you tell me if it's safe to wear a red dress to the bullfights? I've heard so much about the bulls, and of course we'll be sitting at ringside seats…" Her voice trailed off expectantly.

"Let me assure you, Ma'm," said Beaner, without cracking a smile. "You are perfectly safe. The bulls, as you may not have heard, are color blind."

"Oh goodness, no! I had no idea! Why, the poor beasts."

"It's quite true, Ma'm." Beaner nodded in sympathy. "It doesn't bother them a bit."

"My!" said the woman. "You speak our language beautifully. Are you English?"

"On the contrary, Ma'm, I'm American. Been living on Majorca now for eleven years."

"Eleven years!" The woman's eyes widened. "Then you must speak Spanish fluently."

"Like a native, Ma'm, and I have never in my life heard one single syllable." Beaner pointed to his lips. "I read lips, Ma'm. I am totally deaf."

"Oh *my*!" The woman stepped back a pace. "You mean you've never even *heard* Spanish?"

"Not one syllable, Ma'm."

"Well, I just think that's marvelous. And you are reading my lips now?"

"Perfectly," said Beaner.

"Oh, you poor, poor man. And an American like myself."

"Yes, Ma'm," agreed Beaner. "I remember my native tongue only from childhood," he said. "The traffic there in the street and all the other noises, I don't hear them. My only means of communication is through what I read on people's lips."

"Ooooh! That's really remarkable!" exclaimed the woman. Then, very slowly and distinctly, she said, "Is…there…any…way…I…can…help…you?"

Beaner, bringing his full talent to bear, half turned from the woman, swallowed to make his Adam's apple move dramatically and brushed his hand quickly past his eye as though wiping away a tear. Then, turning back, his lips mutely formed a word, stammered, and reformed it in an effort to get it out.

"Yes, yes!" The woman leaned forward. "How may I help you?"

"M-m-m-money," stammered Beaner, looking sad-eyed and numb after the ordeal.

"Of course," whispered the woman. She reached into her purse, snatched out two one thousand *peseta* bills, and thrust them into Beaner's hand.

"Bless you," said Beaner as the woman hurried off down the street. Quickly, the old pro pocketed his windfall, and went back to looking innocent again.

When he saw me slowly shaking my head in disbelief, he shrugged. "Survival, man. Meet me at Latz's. My treat."

The Borne has its share of scalawags. Mostly the imported variety. After a day in Palma it always felt good to get back to Cala Mayor where the air was clean and there were no Beaners.

29

Help! There's a Bird in My Bath!

About two weeks after our plumbing problem with the faulty pump, one evening, as Julie was taking her bath, I heard a short shriek. Then a thud, as she jumped out of the tub. Next came:

"HELP! There's a bird in my bath!"

I rushed into the bathroom to find her scrunched up in the corner with a towel wrapped around her. A finger stuck out, pointing accusingly at the bath. *"There!* There! Can't you SMELL it?"

I looked into her bath. A bunch of bird feathers floated around on top of the water. Worst yet there was a definite aroma of something dead.

I groaned at the thought. A bird must have gotten into our catchbasin on the roof, drowned, and was now lodged somewhere in our water pipes, getting ripe.

While Julie dressed hurriedly, I checked the kitchen tap for an outflow of feathers, or worse. Nothing showed but the water had a decided bird-like fragrance to it.

Opening both taps failed to dislodge the victim. A few more feathers showed up in the bath water. To make sure the bird wasn't still in the catch basin, I grabbed a flashlight, climbed up on the roof and looked inside. A few black bedraggled feathers floated there, but that was all.

"Oh boy," I told Julie. "It's back to drinking wine and calling the bomb squad."

First thing the next morning I alerted Miguel. Again he stared at me in his best myopic manner. He spoke very slowly and calmly. "You say...there is a bird in your bath?"

"That's right, we need those plumbers again."

"Did it fly in the window?" asked Miguel.

"No, no, no. It came down through the pipes from the roof."

"It flew down..."

I stopped him because I knew he was getting it all wrong.

Quickly I explained that the bird must have drowned and *then* gone down the pipe."

"And has he come out yet?"

"No. *Nada*. Nothing. Just wet feathers. I think the thing's stuck in the pipes somewhere. Telephone the...you know...the *bomba* squad."

"Yes. All right. Should I telephone your landlady too."

I sighed. "I guess you'll have to. Jeeze," I said, "I hope Laurel and Hardy won't have to tear up the whole wall to find that dead bird."

"Laurel and Hardy?" began Miguel.

"Nevermind, Miguel. Just call the plumbers."

That afternoon the familiar truck with its garish father and son sign painted on its side chugged up our hill.

"*Buenas dias*, everyone! We come about the bird in your *tubo*. *Fontenaros Palumbo* and Son at your service!"

There was no mistaking that pair.

We showed the father and son team the handful of feathers we had saved, and let them each put their nose down to our bath spigot and sample the essence of ripe bird when I turned on the faucet.

"Poooghh!" said the father, making a face. "Truly *una abomanacion!*"

Son withdrew his nose smirking, and stated that something was dead.

"Unhappily, but true." Our master plumber's eyes wandered up our bathroom wall. "The question is: where?"

I took the pair outside and showed them the catch basin. They both climbed up and peered inside. Son picked up a feather and offered it as a clue. Father sniffed our water supply and said it wasn't that bad as water went.

The two climbed down off the roof and held a conference. They went into the kitchen and looked at the pipes that ran along the ceiling from the water tank. Then they both sniffed the kitchen tap water and conferred again.

Finally they came to a conclusion. Papa Palumbo outlined their plan of attack. First they would try a plumber's helper, a plunger. If that didn't work, they would push a limber cable down through the tank outlet until they reached the obstruction. If they could push it through, they would. Otherwise, they would measure the cable and have to attack the problem from outside by opening the pipes. It might even necessitate going into the wall.

There was, of course, one other solution: We could go off on a vacation for a week or so until the problem corrected itself.

No thank you, I told them. We have to get that bird out of there now if it means tearing down the wall.

"*Si, si, Señor*. We are with you. Son, fetch the tools!"

Being lighter and more agile than his father, the young Palumbo, Saldo, got to wield the plumber's helper in the catch-basin on the roof. After vigorous manipulations of the plunger, the faucets were opened.

Two feathers. No bird.

While the faucets were open and water trickled out, more pressure was applied to the plunger.

Saldo went up and down like a piston, to no avail.

The faucets were again ordered closed.

Father Palumbo rummaged in their truck and came up with a plumber's snake, one of those long, coiled cable affairs with what looks like a large bore drill on its business end. He passed it up to Son and issued orders on its use.

Bending low into our catch basin, Son began feeding the snake into the outlet of the basin.

I went into the kitchen. It sounded like squirrels hiding hickory nuts in our wall. It continued for some time.

Suddenly Son shouted. The Laurel and Hardy team conferred briefly, then Ollie rushed into the kitchen to announce:

"*Señor e Señora*, we are this moment at the crux of the *problema!* Either we have reached the blockage, or we are stopped by an acute bend in the *tubo. ABIERTO LOS GRIFOS!*" Open all faucets!"

We scurried to open all faucets, then stood back.

From atop the roof, Son cranked up his snake with great vigor. The worse noise you can imagine clanged forth from the rooftop to the kitchen and into the bathroom. It sounded as if the walls themselves were about to be rattled down.

Suddenly the bathtub went "bloop!" and water gushed into the tub.

I yelled, Julie shrieked, Papa Palumbo rushed into the bathroom to peer into our tub, then he too yelled.

On the roof-top, Son Saldo stopped snaking. "*Sta buena?*" he called.

"*Sta buena,*" we all chorused. And it was good.

Son retracted his snake. Papa Palumbo gallantly recovered the featherless corpse from our bathtub without an unnecessary display of it, and the water was allowed free flow for quite a while.

In the end, the Palumbos poured disinfectant into our water system and let that flow through. After that, they guaranteed us that we were all set with fresh, clean, birdless water once again.

"Thank you a thousand times," we said, truly relieved to end the trouble so efficiently. Happily we paid our bill and shook hands, offering the plumbing duo a couple well-earned *copitas* of cognac.

"Our pleasure, *Señor!*" said Papa Palumbo as we all toasted each other. He presented me with his card. "Please feel free to telephone us night or day when the next *problema* arrives.

We said we would.

We had no way of knowing it then, but our next problem was already on its way.

30

Gone but Not Forgotten

Their names were Louise and Farnum Baker. They had crossed on the same ship we had taken from New York City to Le Havre, France, with a brief stop at Cobe, Ireland.

He was an American from Boston; she was British. Her parents lived near London. They planned to stay awhile at her parents' place outside of London, then "they might do a fast trip to the Continent."

"If you come anywhere near Majorca, look us up," we wrote them while they were in England.

A few weeks later from Le Havre we received word that they had purchased a Vespa motor scooter and were coming to see us. One morning, as we planned to meet friends in Majorca, a man with a telegram for us motored out from Palma to deliver it personally.

It was from the Bakers. They were in Barcelona departing on the night boat, and would be looking for us on the wharf at Palma that very morning.

The sudden anticipation of guests produced a small whirlwind of activity at our villa. Julie hastily prepared the guestroom. Since we grocery shopped almost on a day-to-day basis, we would now have to double up considerably. No more carrying home what we could on the scooter, this was taxi business. And how was our beverage supply? If we remembered correctly, the Bakers enjoyed their libations. All of which had to be taken care of as soon as possible since our guests were due to arrive in Palma in a couple hours.

It was decided that I would be the welcoming committee. Julie would spearhead the grocery shopping, rounding up enough food to put us ahead of the game for at least a few days until we could get better organized. Once essentials were out of the way, we would all rendezvous at a certain sidewalk cafe on the Borne, and take it from there.

The Bakers, their baggage and their Vespa were indeed aboard the ferry boat from Barcelona when it docked on schedule.

"So sorry we couldn't have given you more advance warning, but we were soooo anxious to get here. My goodness, isn't that sunshine simply *FAB-u-lous?*"

Louise Baker was a trim, dark-haired girl with overly large brown eyes and a porcelain doll face. She was head and shoulders shorter than her husband, Farnum, who among other things, said he had once been a professional football player. He was a large fellow, squared from one end to the other. Unruly light brown hair, a wide, boyish face that broke easily into smiles. They had not been married long. She called him Farn, and kept a hand attached to him almost continuously. He called her Loo, which she thought was cute, except when they were in England. There, she said she made him call her by her full name.

Over coffee at the café where we met Julie, they told us that they had fully intended to travel across France on their Vespa, making their way to Barcelona and the boat to Majorca. But once they looked more closely at the road maps and saw how far it was, they decided to load themselves and the Vesta aboard the first train they could find that would take them all the way to Barcelona.

"Damn the expense, full steam ahead," giggled Loo. "We just wanted to get here with you on this *MAH-vel-ous* island in the sun. England is so *beastly* this time of year, you know." Her porcelain nose wrinkled daintily.

Farnum yawned and sprawled back in his chair. His legs reached into the Borne, as if he were born to this scene and had been an existential part of it all his life. He was dressed American Casual, in a dark blue sweatshirt that spelled "NAVY" across its front in foot high gold letters. He wore bleached, battle-weary blue jeans, and large scuffed leather hiking boots with big brass eyelets, leather laces, and tire tread rubber soles as if they might have been made from old tractor tires.

"About time for a little chow, isn't it?" Farnum smiled broadly.

We found a cafe and watched Farnum do justice to a brace of Spanish omelets washed down with two bottles of Spanish beer. The rest of us had another coffee.

After that we took the Bakers on a walking tour of Palma. Before we knew it, the day was more than half gone and it was time to feed Farnum again. This time it was a thick beefsteak (rare), and a double order of *patatas fritas*, washed down with two more beers. The rest of us settled for a bowl of *gazpacho* with a shared carafe of white wine. Farn cast longing looks at our cold soup dish, probably wishing he had ordered some before his steak. We were going to have an interesting time keeping ahead of our guest's appetite.

The Bakers moved in with us bag and baggage and we began life together like any totally dysfunctional family. Julie and I usually got up no later than 8 o'clock in the morning. Farn and Loo felt they were doing good if they saw the light of day before noon.

Noon, of course, was when Farn required food, both his breakfast and lunch ensemble. After that, while we cleaned up the dishes, the sun was just at the right angle, Farn said, for them to hit the beach and catch a few rays. So off they went in their swimsuits, robes, towels and sunglasses, to absorb a few solar rays on the sands of Cala Mayor. We usually wouldn't see our guests again until it was…you guessed it…time to feed Farn again.

Before the evening feeding period, however, came the Happy Hour. Farn quickly zeroed in on the little pantry where we kept our liquid refreshments. Thereafter, between feeding periods, whenever the spirit moved them, he and Loo helped themselves to Happiness.

The champagne supplies went first, followed by the cognac. After that it was our twenty gallon wine supply. Our alcoholic beverages disappeared almost as fast as our new guests did whenever it was time to wash dishes, cook meals, or grocery shop. I was beginning to wonder if Loo's parents hadn't sent them off to see the continent for a reason less complex than for them to absorb a little European culture.

After three weeks of catering to our guests, it became apparent that if we didn't do something fast, they were going to put down roots and stay for good. They already had a pretty good head start. The only saving factor, however, was that the Bakers were beginning to get bored with all their inactivity.

"How do you ever get along without a telly?" Loo wanted to know.

"Well, when we absolutely can't stand it any longer," Julie told her, "we go to Palma, sit down at an outdoor café on the Borne, and watch the tourists go by."

Farn and Loo stared at her.

"Only trouble with that," I said, "we see the same things over and over. So then we come home and watch a sunset. Lots of variety and great colors too."

"Ooooo, you're putting us on," said Loo.

We took them to all the scenic and historic sites, watched them ogle jai-alai until their eyes developed involuntary twitches, spent hours trying to catch a fish, spent days on the beach catching solar rays, and frequently had "Happy Hours."

This period, usually an end-of-the-day social function, was always a relaxed way of finding out about people. Farn could get so relaxed that he would almost out-do himself. He had an incredible imagination. He said his father had been a military man, and he was a military brat. The family traveled all over the world. There were few places Farn hadn't been and even fewer things that he hadn't done. At least, according to Farn.

When the newspaper described an earthquake in Alaska, Farn recalled being in Fairbanks during an earlier earthquake. He said he had just walked into a sporting goods store when the earthquake hit. When he started to walk out, the store had dropped into a crack and the street was now a story above him.

Certainly made sense to us. "Have another drink, Farn."

When he saw me taking photographs, Farn said he too was a professional photographer, showing me a worn card from his wallet that stated the bearer had taken a photography course by mail order.

When I mentioned being a scuba diver, Farn said he too was a certified scuba diver. But he had difficulty remembering which organization had certified him, or where exactly his certification card was. Besides, Farn said he didn't really need a certification card because the U. S. Navy had trained him. He was in underwater demolitions. He also played football for the navy before he turned professional.

Who could say nay? He certainly ate like a pro.

When Farn noticed my sport coat lapel had a small gold parachute pin that had been given me by a skydiving group I once photographed in action for a magazine article, he announced that he too was a skydiver. The military had asked him to test a new underwater camera they were developing. Wearing scuba gear, Farn had parachuted into the ocean, then dived down and made underwater photographs with the camera. "It worked fine," he said. "The Navy gave me one of those gold parachute pins in appreciation."

There was no way to corner Farn. He always had an out. I don't think he knew the difference between fact and fiction, but with his imagination he would have made a heck of a writer. Of course when I told him that, Farn admitted that he had done a little professional writing on the side too.

I didn't ask him to expand on that.

The first time we saw Farn's Walter Mitty side in action was when we came over on the boat together. One evening we were all watching a televised event taking place in Washington D.C. As the program ended, the camera showed the Lincoln Memorial, then slowly panned down into the reflecting pool while credits rolled. No one was really paying any attention.

Suddenly, Farn said, "There I am!"

We looked at him in surprise. He pointed at the television. "I took that picture," he said.

"Which picture?"

"The shot of the Lincoln Memorial, then down into the reflecting pool. My name was on the credits they just rolled. Each time they show that shot, I get a royalty."

Who needed a telly when you had Farn for entertainment?

The days that followed, however, grew heavier and heavier as our guests slipped deeper into their slack routine and let Julie and I take care of their every need. It got so that the only time we saw them was at meals. The rest of the time our guests were always occupied elsewhere. Most often either asleep, or on the beach.

Finally, it became totally ridiculous. Nearing her wits end, Julie asked in a hoarse voice, "How in the world are we ever going to get rid of them?" Isn't there *something* you can do?"

"Let me think about it." I said.

Ideally I wished it would be their idea to move on, rather than ours. But I had worn out hints in that direction. I already told them that we didn't want to hold them up, and that if they wanted to continue their continental trip, please feel free to do so. The rest of Europe was so much more actively engaged in the pursuit of culture than we were. They really should not miss that.

Loo said that actually they had found all the culture they could handle right there on Majorca. "We really don't know what we would do with any more, DAH-ling." Farn uh-huhed, as he sipped his coffee mug of champagne, echoing her sentiments exactly.

A solution looked hopeless. It appeared they were there for the duration…the duration of our tolerance, which at that very moment was coming to an end.

That night when I went to bed, my mind mulled over every possibility, every possible solution short of an ugly physical eviction. I fell asleep with dire misgivings.

Suddenly, however, in the middle of the night I woke up. The perfect solution to our problem hit me like a cold shower. But would it seem as good in the cold gray reality of daylight?

Morning came. I reviewed my plan. It still sounded good. But I didn't breathe a word of it to Julie.

That afternoon I slipped away to go down to the hotel and ask Miguel to phone in a telegram for me.

The next day while Julie and I were fixing lunch and the guests were sipping aperitifs on the porch, I saw the truck from the Palma telegraph office pull up our hill and stop.

I hurried downstairs. The man handed me a telegram. I opened and read it as I climbed back upstairs.

"Anything for us?" Loo asked brightly.

I handed her the telegram. "Oh, *my!*" she said as she read it.

She handed it to Farn. He read it and said, "Uh-huuuh."

I didn't mention the telegram again. Neither did the Bakers. On Tuesday, however, they thanked us for our hospitality, explaining that they really should be off to see the rest of Europe. Then they left in a cloud of dust to catch the boat for Barcelona.

When we were certain they were gone, my wide-eyed wife turned to me and asked, "What in the world brought that on?

I handed her the telegram. She read it aloud:

"Mother, me, and the kids arriving Thursday on the boat from Barcelona. Hope the nursery is ready. Love, Sister."

A smile lit up her face. "You *devil!*" she said. "Now, I've got to phone home and tell Sister she's got just two days to get married and have kids because she's due here on Thursday!"

I shrugged. "Whatever works!"

31

Up in Chopin's Room

We decided to motor scooter up into the mountains to see the monastery at Valldemosa where George Sand and Frederic Chopin spent a winter together.

Sandwiches were made and packed into the string bag. With the *bota* filled and ready for emergencies, we took the coastal road into Palma, then headed north on the road to Valldemosa, ten miles away.

It was a refreshing scenic route, the highway gradually climbing into the mountains. The only traffic we passed was an occasional mule-drawn wagonload of firewood and a cheerful farmer, heading toward town. The air felt cool and sharp, fresh with the moist, verdant smell of spring. Along the way we stopped often to marvel at the beauty of the almond trees now in full bloom. We sipped the cool, tart red wine from the *bota*.

The road always climbed higher, then, in the steeper elevations where serious mountains appeared in the distant mists, we found the small town of Valldemosa.

The monastery was simple and basic. Stucco and stone in drab hues matching the rocky nature of the island. We were shown the rooms occupied by Frederick Chopin and the then avant-garde woman author, George Sand, whose proclivity for dressing in men's clothes caused a stir in her time.

Their quarters were incredibly austere, devoid of any comfortable furniture. The bedroom cells were windowless and tiny. In the largest room, against a wall under the window sat the Pleyel piano that Chopin used while he lived there. The garden outside in the summertime might have added a touch of cheer to this scene. But not in the winter when the stone walls of their quarters must have felt cold and clammy, while outside the wind howled. Rain and occasionally snow were common.

One wonders why the two gifted artists ever came to such a lonely place at such a hostile time of year. Or why indeed they left Paris, that glamorous capitol of the world to come to this primitive island, travel by crude horse drawn conveyance into these mountains to live in sin together in a bleak monastery. Certainly not for artistic inspiration. Were the monks more tolerant of this behavior than Parisians?

Much later I located an old manuscript written about this period by George Sand. From it and parts of letters written by both Sand and Chopin, I learned something about the true but sad story of their winter on Majorca. Here briefly is what happened:

On November 8, 1838, a small party consisting of Chopin, George Sand, her two children and a woman servant, disembarked at Palma from the steamer *El Mallorquin*. They were delighted with what they saw of the island and the almost spring-like weather. Unfortunately, however, they found it impossible to find a decent place to stay in Palma.

Since there were no hotels and no ancestral homes to rent in town, they were forced to take lodging at a rough, waterfront inn that immediately upset Chopin with its highly spiced food, garlic smell, and abundance of cockroaches.

Thanks to the help of the French consul, Sand found the villa Son-Vent (House of the Wind) outside of Palma and rented it for them. It was a substantial residence with tile roof and stucco walls but there was only the kitchen for heat and furnishings were extremely rustic. It was—as so many places there still are—designed more for summer guests. On top of that it had a mean-tempered landlord. But according to Sand, life was pleasant.

A month after their arrival, Chopin wrote to an old friend in Paris with unrestrained enthusiasm: "Am in Palma, among palms, cedars, cactuses, olives, oranges, lemons, aloes, figs, pomegranates, etc.—everything that the *Jardin des Plants* has in its hothouses. The sky is like turquoise, the sea like lapis lazuli, the mountains emerald, the air is heavenly. Sun all day. Everyone wears summer clothes, it is hot; at night guitars and singing for hours on end. Enormous balconies with grapevines overhead, Moorish walls. Everything turns its face toward Africa, as the whole town does. In a word a marvelous life…."

In Paris, only four of his closest friends knew that Chopin and George Sand had slipped off with her family for a vacation on Majorca. Sand had wanted to go to Italy, but friends convinced her that Majorca would be the best place where as one biographer said, "they might conceal from the world what George Sand wanted to keep exclusively for herself, and what Chopin wanted to keep a secret at all costs."

She was an experienced woman of thirty-four, he was a young man of twenty-eight. The two had recently become lovers. She was a worldly-wise woman already famous for her writings, he was a petted rising young romantic composer already widely admired, but frail of health. Sand brought her teenage son and younger daughter to the island in the hope that its sunny climate would be beneficial to their health. She had invited Chopin along thinking it would also benefit his frail health. Unfortunately, however, during one of their walking excursions they had to return in a driving downpour. Chopin grew ill with a respiratory infection. When he began spitting up blood, three doctors that examined him told the locals that he might be tubercular. This, at a time when people were terrified of any pulmonary illness, believing that such things were as catching and deadly as cholera.

Consequently, the local natives demanded that Chopin leave their neighborhood. Fearing to approach them, their landlord wrote them a letter that he wanted them to leave at once because the house would have to be decontaminated inside and out, the furniture burned and the entire cottage whitewashed again before it could be rented to future guests.

Meanwhile, George Sand had leased them three rooms, "and a gardenful of oranges and lemons," in the Carthusian Monastery at Valldemosa.

Looking more like a Gypsy caravan, the group left for the mountain monastery in two-wheeled carts, Chopin wearing plasters, the children looking forward to the new adventure, the chambermaid frightened by this abrupt change of plans, and George Sand reveling in her role as nurse, guardian, and expedition leader.

It was ten miles to the monastery up a torturous, always climbing rocky road through thickets and heavy vegetation. It was a difficult, unsafe journey in which even the native horses and mules felt unsafe as they tread paths through the brush beside steep rocky precipices.

Finally they arrived at the monastery. To the romantic eyes of the artists it looked like something unworldly suspended between heaven and earth, a haven away from the prying eyes of the civilized world they had just left. The monastery was surrounded by a wall and buttressed on a terrace above a precipice. They had visited the place before and were impressed with its immense size and the fact that it was virtually uninhabited. A government decree of 1836 had expelled the Carthusian monks. It was now government property and the cells were leased to occasional tourists. Only three people inhabited it, the former monastery pharmacist, a porter, and a cook who prepared meals for visitors.

On December 28, Chopin wrote this letter to his Paris friend…"Built between the rocks and the sea, it's an enormous Carthusian monastery where you may picture me, with no white gloves, and with my hair uncurled, as pale as always, in a cell with doors larger than Parisian gates. The cell is the shape of a tall coffin, the enormous vaulting is covered with dust, the window tiny; outside the window there are orange trees, palms, and cypresses. Opposite the window there is my bed on thongs, under a Moorish filigree rosette. Near the bed is a square, rickety writing desk that I can scarcely use; on it (this is a great luxury) a candle in a leaden candlestick, Bach, my scrawls, old papers (not mine)—silence. One could yell...still silence. In short, I write you from a strange place...."

Chopin had brought some of Bach's music with him. He had also earlier requested Pleyel in Paris to send him an upright piano.

This was where the group lived for almost the next two months. During that time Sand wrote to a friend: "We are coming closer to each other with ever greater cordiality and happiness. What can one complain about if one's heart is alive?"

Yet, they were two dissimilar people. First, there was the difference in their ages. He had never married. She was separated from her husband, Baron Dudevant. They were different nationalities. Sand's personality was open and frank; Chopin was secretive and withdrawn. He was a romantic; she a realist. She had simple tastes and could easily do without luxuries while he was refined and enjoyed luxury. In Paris she was disdained in the aristocratic salons while he was worshipped. He could not tolerate ugliness or eccentricities in any form, whether in clothes or personalities. She, however, was completely indifferent to these matters. Moreover, their work habits were entirely different. Chopin would spend years polishing a composition before it was ready for publication. Sand would teach the children their lessons for seven hours a day, administer to his medicinal needs, and write far into the night, sending her manuscript to her publisher in the morning. Meanwhile, Chopin worked endlessly at fine-tuning his Preludes.

The Pleyel piano arrived in Palma but was held up by the customs officials who demanded what Chopin felt was an exorbitant ransom before releasing the instrument. Again, he wrote his Paris friend: "Nature here is beneficent but the people are thieves, for they never see foreigners so they do not know how much to ask for anything. Oranges come gratis, but a trouser button costs a fabulous sum. Yet all this is but a grain of sand—with this sky, the poetry that breathes in everything here, the color of this marvelous place which human eyes have not yet rubbed off."

But then came winter to Majorca.

Intense heavy rains alternated with snowfalls that buried the monastery garden. Shrill bitter cold winds whistled through the monastery galleries. For warmth they sought open fires but the smoke further irritated Chopin's lungs. The whitewashed walls of their quarters dripped humidity. The sounds of distant thundering surf below them coupled with the cries of famished seabirds soaring just outside their tiny windows, combined with the sounds of rain-swollen torrents rushing around the monastery to create an eerie symphony. Chopin wrote that the fog was often so dense that seabirds lost their way and beat their wings against the monastery colonnades.

Even stranger things began happening at night. Some biographers claim that the pharmacist, a former monastery servant had the habit of prowling the empty corridors at night, knocking at doors with a shepherd's crook and calling out the names of long-gone monks. Often he pounded on the doors of Chopin's and Sand's chambers calling, "Nicolas! Nicholas!"

Chopin believed at times that he was seeing the ghosts of long dead monks prowling the corridors and the nearby cemetery. Even Sand believed this was true. But other biographers claim there are letters that reveal how Sand's daughter, eleven-year-old Sollange, was so jealous of Chopin and his involvement with her mother, that she took every opportunity to try to drive him away. When she found some old monk's habits in the monastery, devilish Solange became the "Phantom monk of the monastery." To an already superstitious Chopin, these childish pranks must have made his life miserable, a fact that some say is reflected in his Preludes.

While Sand and her children took walks around the area whenever the weather permitted, Chopin spent most of his days in their apartment, gradually growing to dread the monastery that had once fascinated him.

As the winter advanced, storms washed away what little roads there were between Valldemosa and Palma. The group was cut off from communication with both Palma and the continent. Food at the monastery was bad, the bread often stale and soggy from moisture. Everyone grew ill from eating spoiled food. They got no help from the locals. Sand and Chopin felt that the people of Majorca had turned against them not only because they were considered eccentric outsiders but also because they never attended church, which placed them among the damned.

Chopin's health rapidly gave way to fever. His illness sapped his strength. He began to feel he was caught in a trap from which he would never escape.

In mid-January the arrival of the Pleyel piano from out of the clutches of the Palma customs officers lifted his spirits considerably and he took more pleasure in his work. Biographers believe Chopin drew little inspiration for his compositions from his ordeal at Valldemosa, writing music that more accurately reflected his fierce feelings for Poland. Yet, a considerable body of work was completed during his stay in this lonely place.

In February as spring came to the mountains, Chopin wished more than ever that he were in Paris. Sand on the other hand said she would like to stay there for another two or three years.

When finally they learned that the steamship *El Mallorquin* had resumed its weekly trips to Barcelona, they decided to leave. Chopin's Pleyel piano was sold to a local banker in Palma. On their final day the only transportation that would take them to Palma was a two-wheel peasant cart. The three-hour trip jolted them violently. Upon arriving in Palma, Chopin hemorrhaged.

The steamship they were to take now carried a cargo of swine penned on the deck. Their stench and squealing nauseated Chopin. To add further indignities, he was forced to pay for the dirtiest, worse mattress that could be found aboard since it would have to be burned after use by the sick man.

When they finally reached Barcelona, Chopin was more dead than alive. George Sand quickly requested assistance from a French warship lying in harbor and the group was taken aboard. French physicians immediately helped Chopin. After 24 hours they managed to stop his hemorrhaging.

Chopin recuperated for a week in a hotel room. When he was stronger the group started back toward Paris. Sand wrote a friend on February 25, 1839, "One more month and both Chopin and I should have died, he of melancholy and I of anger and indignation."

One biographer said of their winter in Majorca: "[Chopin] had not been dying all his life, but it is reasonable to say that after the visit to Majorca, he died slowly for eleven years."

In those years, Chopin and George Sand went their separate ways. When he finally died of tuberculosis on October 17, 1849 at the age of 39, Sand was not with him. Sand's popularity as a writer was waning. She wrote her "History of My Life," which she began in 1847 and completed in 1855. Sand died at age 72, on June 7, 1876.

Today, over 80,000 visitors a year make the pilgrimage to Valldemosa to see where Chopin and Sand spent their winter of love together in a monastery as bleak today as it surely was then. As part of the tour, visitors see and enjoy the dances of local peasant girls dressed in their native Majorcan costumes. Also, nearby we saw our first ancient olive groves. It takes little imagination to see grimacing faces, tormented bodies, and glowering gargoyles in the massive contorted trunks of these ancient trees planted by the Moors centuries ago. I photographed them in awe, thankful that I didn't have to make my way through these trees in the middle of the night with the winter winds whipping the bent and tangled branches. One wonders at Mother Nature's ability to create such natural monstrosities with no help whatsoever from men or monsters whose tormented forms are most often depicted here. Such trees might have inspired blood-curdling short stories by Edgar Allen Poe, but not pensive nocturnes by Chopin. The grotesque shapes probably added to his desire to leave the place.

On a quiet, narrow cobblestone street we stopped for lunch at The Hotel of the Artists. Stepping into the quaint, rustic hotel was like taking a step back into the past. After lunch we shared quiet conversation and wine with a Spanish author who lived on a small pension and wrote there. It was a warm, pleasurable experience. As George Sand probably did, one could easily imagine that to be able to live there in this aura of a golden age where one was not driven by financial necessities and could create whatever one wished at leisure, would be the ultimate luxury. Our Spanish friend was doing that. As we toasted him, we wished him good health and happiness. Smiling, he thanked us and replied that he had found both of these things there in Valldemosa

From Valldemosa we swung over toward the northwest coast along a cliff-side road where the rock walls, heavy in moss and lichens, ran with cold water making the slabs black and shiny. In some places the run-off torrents flowed across the pavement and continued their rush down the rock faces to the sea far below.

Just as the highway reached the cliff overlooking the sea, it turned abruptly inland and climbed to the small town of Deya with its population of a few hundred. This tiny picturesque mountain village is home to Majorca's main artist colony. An 1898 description of Deya said that its chief attraction was "the collection of strange and eccentric foreigners." We occasionally saw a few wild-eyed bearded characters resembling budding Van Goghs, but this was understandable. The town itself is a work of art.

Deya has an attraction hard to overlook. Its Old World charm is infectious. We saw the town bathed in the golden glow of late afternoon. It was the ideal light for viewing Deya. It gave its winding cobbled streets and weathered stone houses instant chiaroscuro. Rembrandt would have loved the light at Deya. Wherever you looked, you could frame the scene for a work of art. Certainly one-time resident poet and author of renown, Robert Graves, did not overlook this aspect. He lived there in a small house some 200 yards past the village from 1932 until his death on December 7, 1985. The famous poet is buried there under a simple concrete marker that is inscribed: "Robert Graves, Poeta 1895–1985." We were even then reading his captivating, *I, Claudius*. His works are widely available in Majorca's bookstores.

Graves was one of the post-World War I poets who wrote poems that blasted the romantic assumption that war was the consecration of youth by fire. Poetry about birds and pale moons suddenly seemed less important when poets such as Graves described this world of "murderers."

As for George Sand's later severe name-calling criticism of Majorcan people, Graves said, "George's hatred for the Majorcan people was bound up with the memory of her defeat at the hands of the Church…Well, Majorca has been my home for twenty-five years. I can say that if there is a kinder, friendlier, cleaner, or more honest people in Europe than the Majorcans, I have not yet met them. And from all accounts they were no worse in 1838."

It was not easy leaving that pleasant mountain village where artists down through the ages seemed to find creative inspiration. But the road was all downhill on the way home.

That evening Julie and I sat on our front porch enjoying the fragrance of the almond blossoms while sipping cognac and looking out over Cala Mayor. As Deya's golden sun set in a purple sea against a colorfully spangled sky, it marked the end of a perfect day. It was easy for us to understand why poet Robert Graves had elected to spend most of his life on this delightful Mediterranean island, and why it had attracted George Sand and Chopin. Such islands are what poets and artists understand best.

32

A Matter of Taste

One afternoon, Harper and I decided to visit *Señor* Segovia and his old bodega we used to frequent when we lived at the Montenegro. The object of our visit was to purchase some of his tasty local cognac, the kind that we knew Segovia stocked by the barrelsful.

Hola, hombres! Qué tal?" came the greeting from the somber depths of his cave. Still wearing his soiled leather apron and stocking cap, Segovia looked exactly as he did each time we came to his store. As before, he now moved out of the enveloping blue haze of his trademark Gauloise cigarette smoke and shook hands with us. As usual, his tongue snapped his nub of a cigarette butt from one corner of his mouth to the other without his wide grin even breaking stride. "You come for more champagne, no?"

"Not this time," I said. "This time we want some of your best *cognac de casa.*"

"And why not?" said Segovia, coming out from behind his counter and gesturing grandly toward his cognac collection: seven small kegs sitting on their sides lined up atop keg holders on a counter. Below them sat an equal number of stoneware crocks containing marinating olives, some stuffed, some green, some black. Semi-serious cognac samplers were often given samples of both cognac and olives. We, however, were *serious* cognac samplers. No olives for us. We wanted clear palates.

Segovia scurried around and found us two small glasses swiftly dusted with a swipe of a rag he whipped out of his hip pocket.

The seven kegs all looked alike, extremely old and venerable. Each
had an almost illegible word chalked across its front, just above the tap.
Apparently this was the way Segovia classified his stock, glorious names
befitting the liquid treasure aging in each keg: *"Primero, Superior,
Supremo, Esplendido, Privativo, Especial* and *Heroico.* Each keg also had
a different number from one to seven. If you forgot the name you could
always refer to the number.

Harper had warned me about what we were getting into. To fortify
ourselves for the cognac tasting session with *Señor* Segovia, he suggested we each consume a teaspoon of olive oil in advance, which we did.
The theory behind this was that the oil coated the lining of the stomach
and made one less likely to feel the overwhelming effect of the alcohol.
After all, when one takes on such a serious task, one needs to be quite
clear-headed. Also, theoretically, with a clearer head and sharper taste
buds one would then be better able to select the cognac of choice.

"Do you know cognacs my friends?" asked Segovia.

We both had to admit that we had only a passing acquaintance
with them.

Segovia shrugged. That was all he wanted to hear. He rested his arm
across several of the kegs as though they were old friends. " These babies
have had good cognac in them for the last twenty years," he told us. "Not
just *any* cognac. *No, Señor. Cognacs Especiales,* from the Segovia family
of cognacs." We would see.

He snatched away our glasses and gave us a sample of keg *Numero
Uno.* I held my glass up to the dim light filtering through his small
storefront windows. The amber liquid glowed like honey.

Segovia drew himself a glass, held it on high and said, *"Salud!"*

We saluted with our glasses. The double jigger of honey scorched a
trail of fire down my throat.

Segovia waited expectantly. Harper and I nodded thoughtfully, savoring the essence as we fought back tears.

"Not bad, eh? *Fantastico* for sore throats."

I wondered if he meant for causing them or for curing them.

By the time we reached cognac number three, Segovia insisted that we try that one twice. The reason being that he forgot to point out that it had an especially poignant flavor that one had to savor on the back of the tongue after one swallowed. Only then could it be fully appreciated.

We both re-sampled Number 3, swallowed and tasted the back of our tongues. Yes, yes…we had to admit that it was truly poignant all right. We were drinking small wineglasses of these libations and each one added to the pool of glowing hot embers growing in the pit of my stomach. I was no longer sure that Harper's home remedy of olive oil was doing us any good. Maybe we should have consumed a glassful.

By the time we had worked our way through sample cognac keg number five, and had saluted each one at least twice, Segovia was beginning to really get into his spiel about cognac. Harper and I stood there taking it all in and sort of weaving back and forth. I had to admit that the higher the number on Segovia's kegs, the better the stuff began to taste. The better it tasted and the closer we got to the end of the cognac collection, the more emotional Segovia got about his brews.

For a moment he stood, head-bowed and silent as though in prayer. Then suddenly, he blurted out, "I want YOU to take my mother to Ah-MER-re-ca!"

"Huh?" said Harper.

"*Si, Señor*. "OO-ESAY-AH!" he spelled USA in Spanish. Tears filled his eyes as he beamed at us.

"Take your mother to the USA?" Harper murmured.

"*Por qué, NO?* Why not? She is three hundred years old! I *insist* you take her!"

Segovia must have been tippling before we came in. Harper looked at me for help. I took a deep swig of Number Five again. The fire in the pit of my stomach was spreading throughout my body. I felt it in a rather detached manner. Everything was warmly turning numb. Still, I was cheerful about it, even to the point of wondering if maybe we *could* take Segovia's mother back to America with us.

Before settling that, however, we began eagerly sampling *Cognac Especial Numero Seis*. I remember it had a delicious caramel flavor that lingered well after the fire went down the throat. I grinned and held out my glass for *encora una, por favor*. Hit me again.

"My pleasure, *Señor*," and Segovia flipped the spigot to splash a super generous slosh of more caramel-flavored nectar into my glass.

"I must get you a barrel for my mother," he continued. "I know a good expert. But we must be careful, no?" Segovia laid a long brown finger alongside his brown nose and winked. "We must not disturb her during the transfer into the barrel, *no, Señor!*"

The by now quite drunk wine-keeper hoisted his lavish helping of *Numero Seis Especial* and with hasty gulps and noisy lip-smacking all around, we happily moved on to Number Seven.

"When would you want her?" asked Segovia, poised with his glass halfway to his lips.

"Has your mother ever been to America before?" tentatively asked Harper. I noticed his eyes looked weird when he looked at me, as though he wasn't looking at me, but *through* me.

"*Nunca!*" shouted Segovia rather loudly. "She has NEVER been out of her barrel. No one has ever taken her to America, or anywhere else. She is a VIRGIN MOTHER!"

With that, we both stared at him.

"Segovia, just what the devil are you talking about?"

"For three hundred years, *Señor*, she has been in our family. What a barrel!" He kissed his fingers. Tears streamed down his cheeks. "I swear to you, we can pour pure wine into her top and draw pure golden honey of a cognac out her bottom. All because of her mother. It must be three inches thick!"

Through the soothing warmth of Segovia's seven marvelous cognacs, it slowly began to make a little sense, but not much. All I recalled was a vinegar mother. But Harper quickly enlightened me. Segovia wanted to share with us the three centuries old build-up of fermented yeast he called "mother," that coated the inside of his family barrel. If we took the sample to America we could start a cognac barrel of our own, *with his old mother!*

Once we understood, we were almost moved to tears by his generosity. Segovia said an expert in such matters would have to be called in who would very carefully scrape the walls of the fermentation with exceeding care because if the family barrel was disturbed in any way it could ruin the whole thing. But done properly by an expert there was no fear, he said. The scraping would then be transferred to a virgin barrel, filled with his family cognac and Segovia's Mallorcain family cognac would go to America with us. What a mind-boggling idea! For a moment it seemed to have merit. But as we sobered a bit, the logistics of the thing brought us back to reality.

As gently as we could we told Segovia how much we appreciated the honor of owning his mother, but since it would entail such a dangerous operation we thought it best to pass up the opportunity. Better to keep his mother on Majorca where she could continue producing fine cognacs for generations to come.

Segovia wanted to give us a keg of his wondrous family cognac but we demurred. Instead, we had him bottle up a basketful of our selections for which we tried to repay him doubly, but he refused. Finally, the two of us managed to stagger out of his place of business with the little brewer still saluting us one last time with a final cup of joy.

This should have finished us for the day except when we reached the Borne we ran into our British primitive art friend, Peter Dorset.

"I say, you chaps are just the ones I wanted to see," he said. "Come see my discovery, my *nouveau* Van Gogh."

He whisked the three of us away in a taxi. We in turn shared some of the fruits of Segovia's mother with him. By the time we got where we were going, Peter was feeling almost as good as we were.

Peter's friend lived in an upstairs garret apartment. He was a French artist who like Peter had a primitive streak. What was particularly interesting was that this fellow whose name was Charcrute, or Chargroot, looked exactly like Vincent Van Gogh. Or more precisely, exactly like Kirk Douglas playing the Dutch artist Vincent Van Gogh in the film *Lust for Life*. The resemblance was uncanny. So were his paintings.

His six-foot-tall by five-foot wide canvases leaned against all the walls of his large studio. Each work of art was done with a five-inch wide house-painting brush using black paint on white canvas. All the canvases were slashed with these sharp, straight, angular strokes of black paint. The slashes overlapped each other. crisscrossed and did diagonals. There was not a curved brush stroke in the lot.

Harper and I judged the works with long, keen, thoughtful looks of appraisal while intermittently murmuring a slow "Uh-*huhhh*," or a long, lingering "mmmmmmmmm."

At each painting, Chargroot explained the different kinds of emotional turmoil he experienced as he slapped black paint on his pristine white canvases. Peter ooohed and ahhhed at appropriate places, pausing at several works of art to point out the details of certain agonizing strokes that he had spotted, details that I'm afraid both Harper and I with our untrained eyes failed to see.

It was quite a cultural experience, one made much more poignant by Segovia's classic cognacs. If Van Gogh had seen what this modern day look-alike was passing off as art, he'd have sliced off his other ear.

33

The Best of the Best

The first bullfight of the season was to be held in Palma. We had never seen a bullfight before. Considering what was involved, we were not too prepared for what we were to see. Hemingway's book, *Death in the Afternoon,* made us especially wary of what might happen to the horses. But, we needn't have worried. The horses participating in bullfights today wear mattress-like pads on both sides and underneath. What the man on top does—the *picador*—has a lot to do with holding off the charging bull who is anxious to get his horn into something solid.

The size of Palma's Coliseo Balear bullring is modest compared to those in Spain's larger bullfighting cities. Yet, there is nothing modest about the top name bullfighters who perform there during the bullfighting season. This was a special occasion. Not only was it May Day, the first of May, but it was also the *Festividad de San José Artesano,* a Feast Day commemorating Saint Joséph. Since every third male in Spain seems to be named José, on this day all Josés along with the rest of his countrymen celebrate the occasion with gusto. All businesses close, all work ceases, and merriment is the order of the day. The splendid bullfight at the Coliseo Balear promised especially exciting entertainment.

As do all such events, this one was to start precisely at five o'clock in the afternoon. To start later than that exact hour is considered very bad luck.

According to the bright red hand-bill we had, "This *Grandiosa Corrida de Toros,* would feature—God willing, and if the weather did not impede it—6 beautiful bulls—with the dark blue and yellow badge of the prestigious Madrid bull-breeder, Señor Duque de Pinohermoso. All for *los famosos Matadores de Toros:* Antonio Chenel ANTONETE, Guillermo CARVAJAL, and Antonio Borrero CHAMACO, along with their corresponding groups of mounted bullfighters or *picadors*, and dart-placers or *banderilleros.*"

There followed a "Price of Seats List" (inclusive of all taxes). The cheapest ticket in the place was very inexpensive and the seat was in *Andenados*, the last, outermost row at the top of the arena. This was usually where the rowdier, more raucous fans sat. Probably a good choice by the seating authority since it was too far away to hit the ring with a thrown cushion.

Prices climbed as the rows of seats came down closer to the bullring. There were also three categories of seating. You could either sit in the sunny cheaper seats of *El Sol* and look into the sun all afternoon, or you might pay a bit more for a seat in the *Sol e Sombra*, sun and shade section, where you stared into the sun only half the time. Or, you did the tourist thing and splurged, sitting entirely in *Sombra*, the shady section where you hardly ever had to squint.

These sections were sub-divided into different priced rows and again, the closer one got to ringside or *Barreras*, the more expensive the ticket. A ringside seat in the shady section at Coliseo Balear was the most expensive, while the last rows in the house were the furthest away and least expensive. At least at ringside you had a better change of hitting a bad bullfighter with your rented cushion if you were so inclined.

Not wishing to be taken for tourists as Mr. Hemingway said might happen if we purchased seats in the shady section, we got them in the sunny section, eight rows up from the ring.

According to the hand-bill:

"The doors of the Plaza will open an hour before the event. A brilliant band of musicians will add pleasure to the spectacle by playing the choicest pieces of their varied repertoire. One will rigorously observe all the regulations dictated by the Authority for the rules of the bullfight. One will not fight more heads of cattle that those announced, and if any are unusable during the fight, there will be no replacement by another. No one will be given a pass to leave, and children that are not at the breast will need tickets."

All very clear. We were in our allocated seats in the sunny section eight rows up from the bullring slightly less than an hour before the performance. We didn't want to miss a thing.

From conversation around us we quickly learned that the two matadors to watch were the Spaniard named Chamaco, and the Mexican named Carvajal.

We knew nothing about the bullfighting reputations of these men but we had brought our friend Miguel with us to try to help with the explanations, despite the fact that he claimed he knew little if anything about bullfighting. It didn't take long for the local *aficionados* around us to realize this fact, and to educate us in these important matters, *pronto.*

"Wait until you see Chamaco," said a man in front of us. "He is *fantastico*. He will make the Mexican wish he had never come today!".

"I saw Chamaco fight at Ventas in Madrid" said another. "He was a dream. I swear he was so classic. Every move. *Maravilloso!* He was marvelous"

"Of course," said yet another man. "He does it correctly, like a Spaniard. "I have seen Chamaco work the bull so beautifully you think everything is being done in slow motion. "*Increible!*" Truly incredible.

I glanced over at Miguel to see if he was getting this interchange. The wings of his classes quivered slightly with amusement at the comments being made by the men around us. He leaned across Julie to say something to me.

"You hear what they say about this man, Chamaco?"

I nodded. "He must be a very fine bullfighter," I said.

Miguel shrugged. "I really don't know. I'm not that much an *aficionado*. But I believe he is very well thought of in Spain." He smiled.

"Just being Spanish is enough, you know. Especially when a Mexican is on the program." His glass wings quivered again.

"But why? " I asked. "They enjoy bullfights in both countries don't they?"

"Yes, I think so. But it's how they do it that makes them different," said Miguel. "Spanish bullfighters are supposed to fight...how do you say it?...*Muy serio*. Very serious and proper. *Muy clasico*. Very classical, no tricks."

"And the Mexicans?"

Miguel laughed. He shrugged. "Who knows? Sometimes they are not too *serio*. They are always very colorful, you know. Sometimes they do things that the Spaniards think are...show off. You understand?"

I nodded.

"You see," said Miguel, "being in Spain now all the people here are against Carvajal because they think he does not respect the way Spanish do the *corrida*. He will have a hard time. Not just because of Chamaco, but because of the crowd."

"What about the third bullfighter?"

Miguel grinned. "He doesn't even have to be here." His bushy eyebrows arched over his glasses.

As the stands filled with people, across the ring from us a small brass band, apparently the "brilliant band of musicians," began playing "one of their choicest pieces of their varied repertoire." It was a ragged *pasadoble*, with a few instruments quite a bit out of tune, but a rousing rendition guaranteed to get the spectators in the mood. The late afternoon sun felt good. Someone in the rows ahead began circulating a *bota*. The slender jet of red wine arched artfully into the men's mouths. Sporadic applause followed. The early arrivals were in a holiday mood.

Scattered throughout the crowd were just as many women as men. Many wore a finely made lace mantilla over their shoulders, a fresh rose pinned at the neck of their blouse. Their thick rich black hair gleamed in the sun. Many were matronly types accompanied by their husbands.

The unaccompanied single girls, usually two or three together, wearing high-heeled shoes, tight black skirts, white blouses with the rose, and a light sweater or *mantilla*, did not go unnoticed by the single men in the *Sol* section. As they climbed up through the rows, the short black skirts pulled skin-tight and the high-heels clicked provocatively. Each step they took in their high-heeled shoes was accented in staccato cadence by attentive male onlookers with a sharp and in unison, "Tat-tat-tat-tat-tat!"

Sometimes if the footwork was accompanied by a considerable amount of wiggle, these movements were appreciatively acknowledged with a sing-song "ta-dah, tah-dah, ta-dahhhh, ta-dah-di-dah-dah-dah-dahhh…" Or if the young lady was especially well endowed and was not shy about flaunting her better points, the male chauvinists in the crowd showed their enthusiasm with a staccato, "Oh-LAY, oh-LAY, oh-LAY!" In the event that the object of their attention acknowledged their salute with a wave or a smile in their direction, the whole section cheered. It was a wild crowd. Most of them looked as though they were probably named José.

At precisely five o'clock, kettledrums roll and the crowd silences. A trumpet blares, the band strikes up a vigorous throbbing brassy *pasadoble* called "*La Virgin de la Macarena,*" and with a roar of approval from the packed arena, the *corrida* begins.

Out into the hard-packed sand arena they come, into the harsh sun glare led by two black-garbed *alguaciles* or baliffs in white-ruffled collars and plumed hats, costumes from the Reign of Philip II, explained Hemingway. They would receive the key to the bull door from the president high in his lofty presidential box overlooking the arena.

Some distance behind them come the matadors, three abreast in their skintight glittering sequined suits of silver and gold, lilac and rose, green, pink, blue, crimson, orange, each sequin a separate sun.

They stride purposely out of step with each other, their left arms bent waist high, wrapped in intricately embroidered ceremonial capes the colors of the spectrum, their right arms swing loose. They face forward into the sun, their expressions grave beneath their squared black *monteras*.

Marching with pride but less swagger in files behind them are the bullfighters' helpers, his *cuadrilla*, in diminished splendor, their suits of lights less bright but blending together into one kaleidoscopic rainbow—the sword handlers, the *banderilleros* or dart-placers, and on mattress-padded horses casting squared shadows, the *picadors* in wide-brimmed beaver hats with brown cockades, sitting armor-heavy on their mounts.

Behind them trot the brace of mules in jangling harness and burnished collars hung with tiny bells and fluttering flags while whip-cracking, red-shirted muleteers clutch their reins, and trotting *manosabios* workmen bring up the rear of the procession like the flickering tail of a comet.

The procession moves across the smooth sand ring from sun into.shade, stopping before the planked, curved red wall of the *barrera* beneath the president's box. Thunderous combers of music and applause roll down on the participants of this ancient spectacle.

The black-garbed bailiffs on their black steeds, reminders of the days of kings when armed soldiers had to clear the squares before the fights began, are now symbolic keepers of the Gate of Fright.

The key is thrown down to them from the president's box. They carry it across the ring and deliver it. As the lock snaps in the *toril* gate, attendants hastily rake smooth the last marks of the parade from the sand. Near the gate, a man holding the dark blue and yellow bull-breeder's ribbons stands ready to pin them to the bull's back.

The trumpet sounds. The bolt slides. The red *toril* door swings open.

Out of the black rectangle rushes the black bull, head up, alert, its back carrying the well-placed colored ribbons. It rushes out into mid-ring and skids to a halt. The bull snorts, paws sand, and surveys the crowd.

Across the ring a large yellow and magenta-colored cape billows out over the wall of the ring. Seeing the movement, the bull charges over and slams himself into the rapidly retracted cape. He slams the wooden wall a couple more times with his horns, splintering boards, then withdraws and jauntily trots around the ring.

Another cape appears and the bull charges, then a man with the big cape is in the ring making wide, especially unskillful movements as the bull attempts to hook it with his horns.

Miguel leans over and explains that the bull is caped by members of the *cuadrilla* to see how he acts, how he hooks, what his qualities are. The matador must sum up the bull's characteristics in less than a minute so that he will know how to fight the animal.

A trumpet sounds. The man on the mattress-padded horse enters the ring. Miguel says the *picador* is the most disliked performer in this drama. His job is to test the bravery of the bull by inviting a charge. He holds the bull off from the horse with a long thick pole that resembles a blunt jousting stick used by knights of old. The bull charges the horse at about fifteen miles an hour, hurling his 1,000 pounds of fury at the padded horse and rider. The mounted man catches the raised back muscle on the tip of the *pic* while trying to hold the bull at bay.

The bull seems unaware of this small inconvenience, and continues to push the man and horse into the wall of the bullring. The crowd erupts in a cheer. They cheer for the bull because his repeated charging suggests that he fears neither man nor beast and that is what this special breed of bull has for centuries been bred to do.

A trumpet call retires the *picador* and brings on the placing of the three-foot-long paper-wrapped darts in the bull's thick neck muscle. Like the pic-ing, this maneuver is to tire the bull's huge tossing muscle so that in the final act, when the man reaches in over the horns with the slender, slightly curved sword, the bull is less likely to suddenly lift his horns and gore the man.

Watching a bandy-legged *banderillero* perform is like watching a ballet dancer pirouetting his way across a busy boulevard while barely avoiding being run over by a careening taxicab.

Done correctly, according to Miguel, the basic act is a graceful head-on collision between the man and the bull with only the colored darts making the connection. Everything happens at high speed with the darter and the bull running to meet each other.

At the precise moment of contact, the man who is running on a slight diagonal to the bull's line of charge, goes up on his toes, reaches over the horns and straight-arms the darts into their target, his momentum carrying him on past the bull. Timing is everything.

Another trumpet call and the final stages of the drama begin. The first bull is to be fought by Antonete. He looks good in his gold and silver suit of lights. He goes to work with his muleta, the small red fighting cape. The crowd periodically responds with loud simultaneous "*Olés!*" But it is apparent that there is nothing special about this performance. Antonete is not the one they came to see.

The matador steps to the barrara for his sword. He makes a few more passes, then goes in over the horns, thrusts downward and the deed is done. The rattling muleteers with cracking whips remove the bull and the *manosabios* smooth the sand.

"Now," said the man in front of us, "we'll see some real work!"

Chamaco is a lean, dark-complexioned man in a striking black-and-white sequin skin-tight suit. With the preliminaries out of the way, he capes his bull flat footed, seemingly indifferent to the animal's presence as it thunders past him, first on one side, then the other.

The crowd rewards him with explosive "*Olé's!*"

The passes grow more complex. Chamaco's feet seem rooted in one spot, the magenta cape floating in his skillful hands always guiding the charging bull past him, then around him the horns inches from his groin.

Chamaco switches to the small red fighting cape spread by two sticks clasped in his one hand. Again he roots himself to the ground and makes the incredible passes that leave the crowd screaming. He does it effortlessly, bravely. No bravado here, just pure classic bullfighting say his fans around us. And in the end, he dispatches the bull with one swift sword stroke.

The crowd roars its appreciation. Suddenly people everywhere are waving handkerchiefs. Miguel shouts that they are beseeching the president to specially reward this stunning performance.

He does, awarding the matador not one—which is generous enough—but both ears of the bull he has so skillfully and bravely fought. His helpers collect the trophies. Then, a grinning Chamaco makes his victorious walk around the ring while his admirers cheer and fling tributes to him—bouquets of flowers, hats, cigars.

"Cha-MAH-co!…Cha-MAH-co!" they chant. The smiling matador continues his circle holding high his two well-earned trophies while his helpers pick up the tributes from his fans, saving the flowers and cigars, skimming the hats back into the crowd.

"Let's see the Mexican beat that!" shouts the Chamaco fan in front of us, taking a healthy swig from his *bota* and graciously passing it around. He offers it to us but we smile and decline.

The trumpet sounds for the next bull. The crowd quiets. Suddenly, a tall, slender black-haired matador walks solemnly out toward the center of the ring, dragging the large magenta and yellow cape beside him. He wears a stunning lime-green and silver-sequin suit that glitters in the sunlight.

It's the Mexican, Carvajal. His whispered name travels swiftly through the stunned crowd. Like the other matadors, he is resplendent in his suit of lights.

The crowd is struck dumb by what the man does next. Very calmly, in the center of the ring, Carvajal spreads the big magenta cape out on the sand, then kneels down directly behind it, facing the red *toril* door.

As if they were one person, the entire crowd sucks in its breath. The trumpet blares, the bolt slides and the red door opens.

All eyes rivet on the rectangle of black. The crowd is silent. Suddenly hoofs clatter hollowly on planks and out into the sunlight as if shot out of a cannon, charges one very large snorting, skidding, black bull. If sparks were flying out of his nostrils I doubt if anyone would have been surprised. Sun glints on the huge rack of curved sharp horns atop the animal's head.

The bull looks at the crowd, looks at the man on his knees, then jerks his head to look back at the crowd again.

He paws the sand and snorts.

Carvajal shouts. "Huh, *toro. Aqui!* HUH!"

The bull swings his head back, seems to sight on the figure kneeling in mid-ring, paws twice, lowers his horns and charges straight for the man on his knees.

Once more the crowd as one suck in their breath and hold it. Some people half rise from their seats and point, too stunned to believe what they are seeing.

The bull never veers. It thunders across the sand like a locomotive. Nor does the man move for one long hair-raising three seconds, and then, just as the collision is inevitable, Carvajal lifts his arms.

The broad magenta cape sweeps up off the sand like a living thing as the matador keeps it floating up into the air and around over his head, a sweeping pass that catches the bull's attention and veers it to the left, wrapping the animal completely around the man.

"*My God!*" screams the Chamaco fan in front of me. "A *faro* pass!"

"Like a lighthouse," shouts Miguel to me. But by then everyone is on his feet. So is Carvajal, adroitly passing the bull back and forth past him with astonishing dexterity as he stands perfectly straight, pivoting in one place on the sand.

The crowd goes crazy.

Then abruptly, the man spins the bull around into a perplexed stall that stops it in its tracks. Carvajal indifferently drops the cape to his side just two feet from the bull, raises one finger high overhead as though to say "I alone can do this," then turns his back on the seemingly mesmerized bull and strides calmly back to the barrera, dragging his cape behind him.

The crowd applauds loudly. Even the Chamaco fan in front of me claps but not with enthusiasm. "That's not bullfighting," he crows. "That's just showing off!"

We sag down into our seats, emotionally zapped. All we can do is look at each other and shake our heads while the band plays and the drama moves into its next phase.

"What did you mean by lighthouse?" I hurriedly ask Miguel.

"The pass he did. *Faro* means lighthouse. The cape sweeps around like the light from a lighthouse."

The trumpet sounds. The mounted *picador* on his padded horse moves into the ring.

But suddenly Carvajal is out in the arena again, waving him away. He doesn't want the bull weakened in any way. Again the crowd is stunned. The *picador* and his mount withdraw.

The trumpet again, announcing the next act, the placing of the *banderillas*, the three-foot-long paper-covered slender wood darts designed to help weaken the bull's tossing muscle. As the man with the two *banderillas* moves out into the center ring to attract the bull's attention, Carvajal comes trotting out toward him.

"Now what?" says the Chamaco fan in front of me.

Carvajal takes the long darts from the man and sends him back to the *barrera*. He will place the darts himself.

The crowd applauds this decision. Seldom do the people see a full matador take this unnecessary risk. "More tricks," murmurs the man in front of me.

Carvajal does not go to the bull. He stays in the center of the arena holding his arms straight up over his head, holding the *banderillas* by their very ends, the sticks jutting forward in front of him. Then he calls the bull.

"*Ho toro!*" He stands on his toes, arches backward and claps the two wooden shafts together. "*Aquí, brava!* Here brave one! *Venga, toro!* Come on, bull!"

At the sharp sound of the sticks the bull looks at the man, snorts, paws the ground with his forefeet.

"*Sí!*" Carvajal does a slow pirouette. He snaps the two sticks together again sharply. "*Venga bonita!* Come on, beauty!"

The bull takes one more look at the glittery figure of the man moving in the center of the ring, then he lowers his head and charges. Sand spurts from his hooves as his bulk moves swiftly toward the man.

Carvajal turns and starts trotting ahead of the bull's horns, running in a serpentine path, arms still overhead with the darts pointing ahead of him.

The man and animal almost merge when suddenly the man takes an abrupt step sideways and stops, his back to the bull. The bull charges past, grazing the glittery green and silver figure as Carvajal brings his arms down.

For an instant the two are joined, then separated, the man standing stock still, the bull's momentum carrying him out into the arena, the pair of perfectly placed *banderillas* fluttering gaily from his humped neck muscle.

"Oh-LAY!" bursts from the crowd's lips.

And to prove it was not just a lucky move, Carvajal calls for another set of *banderillas,* and places them exactly the same way as the first pair.

By now the stands are in an uproar. Everyone is applauding.

But Carvajal isn't finished with them yet. He calls for a third set of *banderillas.* Again, he stands still in the center of the arena, calling-the bull. This time, almost in slow motion, he lowers the two barbed sticks together, breaks them over his knee, and holds the two darts overhead that are now only half as long as they were, doubling the danger of placing them.

"Sweet Jesus and Mary!" says the Chamaco fan in front of me. Everyone is on their feet. The crowd is silent, holding its breath.

Carvajal's voice is all that is heard as he does his slow green and sil-ver pirouette in *media arena*, holding the diminutive darts high over-head, the sun glittering on every sequin of his suit.

The bull charges him full tilt. Again the matador dances just ahead of the thrusting horn-tips, the man and animal rushing across the arena, and then again, as if by magic the man stops, spins sideways as his arms drop…the bull rushes past and another set of gaily fluttering colored flags mark the success of the encounter.

The crowd is ecstatic. People roar their approval. Nobody bothers to stop shouting until Carvajal takes his small red cape and puts on a dis-play of intricate cape-work with the bull that few aficionados in a life-time of bullfights, ever see.

The arena is as still as a tomb one moment, then thundering with *olés*, the next, each roar following each completed pass made by the man in the lime-green and silver sequin suit.

Miguel tells us later there are upwards of thirty-five specific passes in bullfighting, five or six basics; the rest variations. According to what the aficionados in the stands said, Carvajal worked from the easiest to the more difficult.

The bull finally rushs past so close it repeatedly bumps him. But Carvajal no longer watches. He stares up into the crowd.

Behind us a woman screams. " Look! The bull is on railroad tracks!"

And indeed it seemed the animal was. It charged straight and true each time, without swerving or erratically tossing its horns. It was the kind of bull matadors dream about, but seldom get.

And when the final moment came, Carvajal completed it just as per-fectly as he had his entire performance.

The crowd was delirious. Band music blared. People shouted. People cried. The whole place roared totally out of control for a long moment. Then the whole place turned white with a sea of handker-chiefs being waved.

In the uproar I looked at Miguel and shrugged. He yelled back, "They beseech the president to give him awards!"

The president in turn signaled his reply.

They awarded Carvajal two ears and the tail.

"*Tambien una pata!*" chorused the crowd. "Also a hoof!" To award a hoof as well may have been warranted, but it was not granted. Ultimate trophies such as that are awarded only to gods, said Miguel. Apparently in the president's mind Carvajal had not quite achieved that status.

When the broadly smiling man made his triumphant walk around the ring he was barraged with flowers, cigars, hats, and various pieces of intimate feminine underclothing.

As he drew opposite us, the man in front of me suddenly leaped to his feet and hurled his *bota* into the ring. With one hand, Carvajal scooped it up, unscrewed the cap and arching backward squirted a long thin stream of red wine into his clenched mouth. Then he hurled the *bota* back toward where it had come from.

"The former Chamaco fan waved both arms and shouted." You, *hombre* are *Numero Uno*, Number One! *Salud!*"

Bullfight fans can be fickle.

There were other bulls to be fought that afternoon but I don't remember them. All I remember is that one and what the man in the lime-green and silver suit of lights did with it and to us. Never before or since have we felt anything like this. It left us shaking with emotion. We had witnessed a rarity. A perfect fighting bull and a matador who knew what to do with him. During the years that we lived in Spain we saw many more bullfights, but none quite like this one. For our first *Fiesta Brava*, on that first day of May, in that small ring on Majorca, we had seen what aficionados call "The best of the best." It doesn't get much better than that.

34

Arrivaderci, au Revoir, Hasta la Vista

It was apparent that time was running out on us. Tourists were beginning to arrive in Majorca by the droves. Winter had gone, spring was going, and summer was just around the corner. It was the time when living things get restless. This was especially true now on Majorca.

Our greatest shock was to learn that our close friend, Miguel, was leaving the island. He came to see us to apologize.

"Miguel," I said, gripping his hand. "No apology is needed. We can't tell you how much we've appreciated your friendship and help."

His eyes glistened. He looked down. "Your friendship—you and Julie—has meant much to me also," he said. "But maybe our parting will only be for a short while. Then you too will be coming to Madrid and we can celebrate." His eyes brightened at the thought.

Miguel told us that he had found a job as the manager of a hotel in Madrid. Naturally he would take it because it meant a great deal more money that he was making in Majorca, even at the height of the summer season. It also meant that he would be with his family again, his mother and father, brother and sister.

We understood how important this move was for Miguel.

But it was like seeing part of ourselves leave...which of course we knew was not far off. Saying good-bye to loved ones or close friends, is never easy. We walked Miguel down to his waiting taxi and embraced him. We told him we would contact him in Madrid as soon as he was established.

Then he was off, waving to us from the small back window of the old taxi, his glass wings catching a last glint of light.

The Colonel and his wife were the next to leave. This too came as a surprise. We more or less thought they would be there forever, they seemed so permanent. But they were no different than the rest of us winter refugees. They were off to England to visit his family for the summer. They made sure we had their address and everyone promised to write. And then, bag and baggage, they too left in a taxi and a cloud of dust.

In the next two weeks it seemed we were telling so many friends in so many languages good-by. It made us realize how impermanent we all were, those of us who had come just for the winter.

No leave-taking is ever done at once. At least ours never seemed to be. It was a gradual thing that included getting rid of all the things we had collected that would not fit into our suitcases. Items too good to discard had to be given away, shipped ahead, or shipped home.

That included our conversation piece—the jai-alai scoop. Somehow we would have to learn to start a conversation without it. It was to be shipped home. I told Julie that there was no telling how many times we would need it for starting conversations in Florida. She made a face at me.

Our fairly large library was to get the same treatment. But we had to be selective. Nothing weighs more than books. We pruned everything down to the absolute "must keep" category. The jai-alai scoop, my flamenco guitar that could almost play *Green Sleeves* by itself, the Spanish bullfight posters, the iron-heavy olive-wood bust from Inca, our souvenir set of *banderillas*, our soft-woven Majorcan rope basket, my Majorcan rod and reel that had never caught a fish, and our fine pair of huge old flawed glass Majorcan wine jugs—all were to be shipped home. All these odd-shaped things would be taxied into town and dumped at the office of the expert Majorcan packers, boxers and ship-pers who made a tidy business of this sort of thing.

Señor Vicenti and his recalcitrant Citröen was our means of transporta-tion. He coaxed his big old vehicle up our hill and we crammed everything aboard. I squeezed in with Vicenti and we chugged off to Palma.

The commercial boxing people's eyes lit up when Vicenti and I began dragging in our collection by the armloads. They assured me there would be no problem in boxing all our treasures and sending them to America post haste.

Then I asked what it would cost.

For sentimental purposes, that was a mistake. But for practical pur-poses it had to be done. What my query revealed was that the two large ancient old flawed glass wine jugs—one clear or almost so, and the other a smoky green—both of which would have looked so good beside our stateside fireplace—would cost us a small fortune to ship home.

I asked if the price was based on what exactly they were—items sal-vaged from a flea market—or as antiquities?

The price they asked for the two jugs suggested that they considered them valuable antiquities. I bit my lip and in a moment of weakness, said they could keep them.

The rest of our irreplaceable items went home, though I admit we probably could have left the jai-alai scoop and the soft rope basket with the clay water jug behind. This parting with sentimental things is grim business. I paid my bill and turned my back on them.

In the next couple weeks we bade good-bye to our friends with a series of going away parties they had for us. The Preegs were the only set of old friends who were staying on Majorca. They planned to remain at least through the coming summer and would decide where to go after that.

Our going away party at our villa with Harper and Binky was a memorable affair. At least most of it was.

The occasion began with champagne long before dark so we could see what we were doing. First we toasted our venerable life-size stone head with its incised, candle-smoked Aztec features. It had helped hold up our books all winter. But now with the books gone the head looked lonely on our mantel. I took its picture and then we decided to give it a proper send off—the one I had planned ever since I made it. Sort of a Viking Funeral kind of thing without the fiery boat or the dog at the feet of the deceased. Just toasts and a quiet interment in our backyard to the future consternation and glory of whomever one day found it.

After our tributes and toasts Julie and Binky served up an incredible seafood supper. By then, Harper was already wearing his turban.

Some people wear lampshades when they get plastered. Harper wears a turban. Not one he always carries with him for party purposes, of course. Just one he improvises at some appropriate time during the festivities. All he has to do is disappear into the bathroom momentarily, and voila, the deed is done. He reappears with the bath towel atop his head, all neatly twisted into a large turban. On this occasion it happened to be a pink one. Since we'd all seen his turban thing before, we usually took no further notice of his headpiece. All it announced anyway was that Harper had reached a certain degree of inebriation in his celebrating.

Frankly I always thought he looked pretty good with the bath-towel atop his head. Harper had a kind of oriental look about his eyes anyway. The more he drank the more oriental he looked. The turban completed the picture. I think Binky liked it too.

Followed by a champagne-sipping informal procession of the others, I gently lifted the heavy stone head off the mantel and we went out our backdoor with it. I carefully stepped off so many paces in a certain direction from our back porch and placed the head carefully on the ground. A shovel was produced and I dug a two-foot-deep hole. A final toast and we buried the stone head. But what's a funeral without music, Binky asked? She was all for going home and getting her cello to play funereal passages more suitable to the solemnity of the occasion, but we talked her out of it.

I said I thought it best we all stayed clear-headed because there was still one more important *objet d'art*—our heavy mosaic millstone—and some remaining rare Segovia house cognac to be disposed of.

Everything went quite well. Of course it was well into the early morning hours as the Preegs were going home that we took up this awesome endeavor. Admittedly by then there was some spontaneous hilarity and teetering around when Harper in his turban, and I tried to carry the heavy tile-decorated millstone down the two stories of stairs by wobbling flashlight with the wives giggling and kibitzing every step of the way. Harper's turban slipped down over his eyes and for a moment I thought we might lose both him and the millstone we were gingerly manhandling on that narrow stairway between us.

Somehow without dropping it and shattering the masterpiece into a thousand fragments, we managed to get the thing safely down the two flights of narrow stairs, down to the road, then down the loose, treacherous rocks of the steep hill, and then up two flights of more stairs to the Preeg's place without any of us self-destructing along the way. Rather amazing.

Finally arriving huffing and puffing with it in the Preeg's living room, our wives used Harper's turban now to mop our fevered brows. We placed the heavy artifact back atop its inverted flowerpot where it was to now take up permanent honorary residence indefinitely I suspect.

After that I can't remember whether we either finished off Segovia's fine cognac, or found a final long-lost bottle of the Preeg's champagne. But no matter. Harper spent the night sleeping on the floor beside the millstone table with a smile on his face, the empty champagne bottle clutched tightly in his arms, and his faithful bath towel turban wrapped around his shoulders. What a great going-away party!

A week later we received Miguel's address in the mail. There was no longer any reason to delay. We loaded our Lambretta with our basic bags, waved and shouted good-bye to the wildly waving Preegs on their front porch, then we motored along the coastal road for the last time to Palma to catch our boat.

It was to be an overnight trip. We would stop briefly at Ibiza, then early the next morning we would arrive in Valencia, Spain, and start motoring to Madrid.

It had been love at first sight, our winter on Majorca. It had become everything we dreamed of—an enchanted semi-tropical island in the Mediterranean halfway to Africa. An island of warm, incredibly kind people. For a moment in time we had shared their lives, their customs, and their friendship, and hopefully left something memorable of ourselves with them. When we said our final good-byes to our Majorcan friends, they said that *"adios,"* was too final. Instead they said, "until we meet again." And we replied, "yes, of course, *hasta la vista!*" And we all smiled.

(The End)

9 780595 090587

Printed in Great Britain
by Amazon